The Compass
and the Radar

The Compass and the Radar

The art of building a rewarding career while remaining true to yourself

Paolo Gallo

BLOOMSBURY BUSINESS

LONDON · NEW YORK · OXFORD · NEW DELHI · SYDNEY

BLOOMSBURY BUSINESS
Bloomsbury Publishing Plc
50 Bedford Square, London, WC1B 3DP, UK
1385 Broadway, New York, NY 10018, USA

BLOOMSBURY, BLOOMSBURY BUSINESS and the Diana logo are
trademarks of Bloomsbury Publishing Plc

First published in Great Britain 2019

Cover design by Buro Blikgoed/buroblikgoed.nl

A catalogue record for this book is available from the British Library.

Library of Congress Cataloging-in-Publication Data
Names: Gallo, Paolo, author.
Title: The compass and the radar : the art of building a rewarding career
while remaining true to yourself / Paolo Gallo.
Other titles: Bussola del successo. English
Description: New York : Bloomsbury Publishing Plc, [2018] |
Includes bibliographical references and index.
Identifiers: LCCN 2018023346 (print) | LCCN 2018033579 (ebook) |
ISBN 9781472958808 (ePDF) | ISBN 9781472958815 (ePUB) |
ISBN 9781472958822 (eXML) | ISBN 9781472958792 (hardback)
Subjects: LCSH: Career changes. | Vocational guidance.
Classification: LCC HF5384 (ebook) | LCC HF5384. G356 2018 (print) |
DDC 650.14—dc23
LC record available at https://lccn.loc.gov/2018023346

ISBN: HB: 978-1-4729-5879-2
      ePDF: 978-1-4729-5880-8
      eBook: 978-1-4729-5881-5

Typeset by RefineCatch Limited, Bungay, Suffolk
Printed and bound in Great Britain

To find out more about our authors and books visit www.bloomsbury.com
and sign up for our newsletters.

To Lalia and Sadika.
Please tell me: how can I be so lucky?

Contents

Acknowledgements

I have to confess something: it wasn't me who wrote this book, it was written by you.

I've simply collected stories, tales, examples, teachings from different sources. I feel like a child who has finished a jigsaw puzzle with a million pieces or like a medieval storyteller who travels from town to town sharing stories which are increasingly richer and more fascinating after having learned new things at each stage of the journey. This is why I'm grateful to many people who, at different times and in various roles, have helped me not only with the book *The Compass and the Radar*, a journey that has lasted four years, but also as a person.

I wanted to listen and learn from well-known credible authors: Daniel Pink, Adam Grant, David Kantor, Viktor Frankl, whose books are mentioned several times; Rene Carayol, Peter Senge, Linda Hill, Dorie Clark, Vicky Culpin, Daniel Kahneman, Dan Ariely, Chris Argyris and Jeffrey Pfeffer. Ben Zander, a person who transforms your life with his music and positive energy, also gave me advice and encouragement. I can't fail to mention the people who have influenced not only the book but also the way I think, in addition to the people in my family. Professor Klaus Schwab, founder of the World Economic Forum, whose foreword I'm honoured to include; Ngozi-Okonjo-Iweala, a leader, an extraordinary woman whom I deeply admire.

I want to thank Bloomsbury who believed in my book, with particular thanks to Ian Hallsworth and Vafa Payman – their advice and teachings were fundamental; I add a special thank you to Emily Bedford.

Lucia Crenna, Luigi Porta, Giulio Petris, Pepe Pedullà, Thea Chiesa, Jean-Luc Vez, Clarence Clemons, Aretha Franklin: how could I not think about you?

I don't know how to give my thanks for a hundred different reasons to Mario Masarati, Yury Boshyk, Karin Parodi, Massimo Grandis, Gary McGillicuddy, Stefano Losi, Antoine Platon, Mel Rogers, Lee Howell, Aulikki Kuusela, Nina Nordgren, Roberto Amorosino, Massimo Magni, Stefano Olmeti, Adrian Monk, Stefano Trojani, Stefano Donati, Anja Kaspersen, Howard Donovan, Claire Hoang, Emilia Garito, Julien Hawari, Salvatore Pedulla, Franscesco Bogliari, Rosamaria Sarno, Matteo Achilli, Marianna Poletti, Roberto Tinniriello, Franco Furno, Valeria Vescina, Koku Warszewki, Roberto Bocca, Sara Giunta, Maria Latella, Rick Hendricks, Hermes Gazzola, Herve Maluassena, Alessandra Losito, Claudio Di Salvo, Valentina Revay, Gunnar George, Alessandro Lantieri, Peter Vanham, Fabiola Giannotti, Gianmario Todato da Ruos, Fabrizio Macri, Alberto Pravettoni, Guiilermo Miranda, Marta Pelizzi, Gladys Bresciani, Gabriele Gabrielli, Antonio Maturo, Mike Kuusela, Gib Bolloch, Serena Scarpello, Enrico Sasson, Francesca del Nero, Roger Campbell, Annika Mansson, John Stepper, Sergio Spinelli, Alois Zwinggi, Peter Hill, Jim Cookson, Omid Ashari, Oscar de Montagny, Leonardo Vecchi, Ghislaine Bagdhadi, Borge Brende, Laura Cavatorta, Michele Caracciolo, Andrea Piergentili, Matteo Paravicini, Emilio Cristobal Rubio, Massimo Sterpi, Massimo Scarcello, Massimo Marella, Tobia Degsell, Peter Cheese, Alessandra and Luigi Gnudi, Gianmario Verona, Saverino Salvemini, Mohammed Hawar Ismael, Bruno Szarf, Cynthia Hansen, Jean Bradier, Ken Avis, Huey Nhan-O'Reilly, Joseph O'Reilly, Sergio Castagna, Phillipe Jouvet, Geraldine Ragot, Chenye Guan, Mark Jones, Ramiro Zacarias, Richard Veneau, Giulia Lanza, Marco Albani, Enrico Cappelletti, Nerio Alessandri, Achille d'Antoni, Enrico Dandolo,

Alexander Caillet, Anthony McAlisdair, Jennifer Blanke, Frode Hvaring, Manuela Morelli, Elena Melchioni, Elena Antanacopoulou, Mary Connaughton, Filippo Sabatini, Carlos Scartascini, Marc Erzberger, Alain Couttolenc, Leonardo Quattrucci, Luca Ponzellini, Samantha Forusz, Francesca Baronio, Pier Giorgio Aliberti, Andrea Sylos Sabini, Debbie Perry, Brigid Holleran, Margaret Henderson, Bruce and Doreen Leighton, William D. Eggers, Elisa Prati, Guido Paolucci, Marcelo Guigale, Pierre Lebleau, Anne Thomas, Noreen Doyle, Gianfranco Minuto, Simone Puksic, Vincenzo Ganci, Peter Hill, Marta Pelizzi, Sabine Chouciar, Emily Deschaine, Ivan Scalfarotto, Natasha Alexandtrov, Giovanni Petris, Valeria and Carolina Gibertoni, 'my' Human Resources Teams in Washington, London and Geneva – 300 amazingly talented people – The Men's group in Virginia, the 'Mitica 3B' in Milan, the Georgetown University leadership coaching cohort 39, 'my' students at Bocconi University. Sorry if I've forgotten anyone.

There are people I haven't met and don't know personally, but who continue to inspire me with their example. The magistrates Falcone and Borsellino, General Dalla Chiesa, Mother Teresa, Rosa Parks, the journalists Federica Angeli and Roberto Salviano: these people have shown how the courage of their convictions doesn't have a price. They said no to the mafia, corruption, injustice, racism. They're my heroes along with thousands of other people who – simply – have also said to them 'No, I disagree'. The world progresses thanks to them. Thanks to all my heroes, the people I've mentioned at the end of the fifth chapter, the Lions. Thanks also to the 80 countries that I've visited, the hundreds of books and records that have inspired me, made me think, dream, to the despair of my wife, 100 heavy boxes that always go with us every time we move, to Bruce Springsteen, 68 concerts that I've enjoyed intensely over 35 years of militancy, passion, tears of joy and sweat.

By writing these pages and remembering these people I realize two things: first of all my luck in having met simply extraordinary people and what I've learned from each of them. I've understood that any person can offer you something precious and priceless and that the treasure is not hidden on a desert island but it's inside us, if we look hard for it.

The second element – a fundamental aspect – is how much gratitude, love and respect I have for Fatna and Sellam Semmoune and, of course, for my father Renzo, who has always been beside me ever since he passed away too soon, and also the six women in my family: for Anna-Maria, Francesca, Bianca and Dana, respectively mother, twin sister, niece and aunt who continue to fight, smile, get angry, hope and move forward, despite everything.

To Lalia, my companion and the true love of my life who keeps saving my life, practically every day. I asked her – or rather, I told her – to marry me the day after meeting her: since then we've spent 23 years together, waiting for the next 100. Finally to Sadika, my daughter, she came like a shining star into our life and everything changed, everything made sense. Her existence fills me with infinite love, unbridled joy and gives deep meaning to my life and that of all those who know her. Nothing gives me more joy than watching her grow, laugh and listening to her sing the songs she invents every day.

This book is dedicated to them, Lalia and Sadika. When I see them together, mother and daughter, I witness the miracle of Absolute Love: many years have passed and I still can't believe how lucky I am.

And yes, Dad, you were right: *nothing else matters.*

Paolo Gallo
Geneva, August 2018

Message from
Prof. Klaus Schwab

One of the characteristics of the fourth industrial revolution is that it not only changes what we are doing but it brings about profound changes in ourselves and our relationship with the world, changes made at a speed, magnitude and intensity different from anything humanity has ever seen before, and which will influence the very essence of our human experience. All industries will see their business models dramatically change: the jobs will be very different from those we currently do, today's children will do jobs that don't exist yet and the jobs we're doing will disappear. Fifty per cent of the world's population is under 27; we have both the highest number of unemployed people and the largest number of vacancies. How can we help them find a job? How can we contribute towards giving them a purpose, not just an income that is sufficient to live with dignity? We need to reflect on how the changes of the fourth industrial revolution will affect our work and us.

Ever since I became a Professor of Strategy at the University of Geneva and then Founder and Executive Chairman of the World Economic Forum, many students, colleagues and friends have asked me for advice on their career: should I work in banking? Consulting? Industry? University? I tell everyone that to have a successful career, you need two tools. First a compass, our talent, which helps us stay on the right course. Second, and what is the radar? a radar that will help us avoid obstacles, dangerous situations and dead ends. We need both tools for our professional and personal journey.

Albert Einstein said: 'If I had an hour to solve a problem and my life depended on the solution, I would spend the first fifty-five minutes determining the proper question to ask. For once I know the proper question, I could solve the problem in less than five minutes'.

Paolo Gallo, the author of this book, is Human Resources Officer at the World Economic Forum and also a transformational coach. Using a creative and engaging mix, he explains how to find our talent, our compass and how to find the job that fits perfectly with our values. He also helps us understand organizations, their cultures and their complexities, to build authentic trust and cooperation. Therefore by way of in-depth questions and reflections, the book offers practical tools to help find a job anchored to our moral compass, our system of values. Chapters like 'The pact with the devil. The price you pay for your career' provide practical tools to help make the right choices in difficult moments that each of us will experience during our careers. As Executive Chairman of the World Economic Forum, I have personally met all the world leaders: I can guarantee how important it is for leadership to be based on ethical values and how, like ethics, trust can only be restored if we're really able to learn to collaborate, instead of competing or, much worse, stacking the deck.

After reading Paolo Gallo's book, I believe that the concept of a successful career will be radically transformed into something very different from our current model, more profound and important for all of us, not just for a select few. This new concept of what a successful career *really* is and what matters is completely in line with the mission of the World Economic Forum that I created: how to improve the world starting with the way we relate to each other, as human beings. The book closes with questions that we cannot answer based on our ethics as responsible leaders.

We are at the beginning of the fourth industrial revolution, a historical era of radical transformation and profound changes: we need to anchor our being to our values. *The Compass and the Radar* helps us to reflect on what really matters and how to remain respectable people while doing what we care passionately about.

Klaus Schwab
Founder and Executive Chairman, World Economic Forum

Foreword

It's no secret that the future of work is in flux. Whether it's the rise of artificial intelligence and automation, the development of new and increasingly prominent fields like data analytics, or the rapid changes in how professional development is conceptualized and delivered, the shifts have been profound.

White collar knowledge workers are no longer immune to disruption. Moving forward, it's not just truck drivers and factory workers who will be displaced: the lawyers and the fashion buyers and the finance pros are almost certainly next.

Which makes Paolo Gallo's *The Compass and The Radar* not just an important book, but a necessary one.

In a world of unpredictable change, it would be foolish to hold your finger to the wind and pick your professional direction based solely on which industries are thought to be most lucrative or secure. Nothing is 'secure', and you rarely succeed in a field you have chosen only for instrumental purposes, or at a company where you're in a constant state of culture clash.

It's just as foolish, of course, to look only inside yourself. Solipsism is fine when it comes to choosing hobbies: we might watch sports or collect stamps for our own pleasure. But to make a life for ourselves, we must also be clear: how are we helping the world beyond ourselves in a meaningful way?

To build a successful career in the modern economy, we must have both ingredients: a keen sense of what we value and what lights us up inside, as well as an understanding of where we can make a contribution that will genuinely benefit others.

To do that, we must be brutally honest with ourselves. When tradeoffs must be made, what will we sacrifice? What do we cherish above all else? Where do our skills add unique value, and where are they merely average?

For nearly two decades, Paolo Gallo has been on the front lines of the future of work as a top talent leader at the World Economic Forum, the World Bank, and more.

A truly global leader, he has coached everyone from senior executives to fresh-faced new hires on how to dig deeper and answer the questions that will enable them to reach greatness.

As he describes, our starting point must be the compass: identifying our core values, skillsets, and passions. When we combine that with radar – a nuanced understanding of the world around us – we have the tools necessary to create a thriving work life.

In a rapidly changing workplace, there is no magic recipe for professional success. Instead, like a chef seasoning his or her creation to taste, it's about making small, smart adjustments along the way.

Paolo Gallo is an indispensable guide to building a meaningful career and life. By embracing your compass, you'll have the self-knowledge necessary to choose the right path for you, and by learning to monitor the radar, you'll be able to avoid the occasional (and inevitable) obstructions that arise. Good luck on your journey.

Dorie Clark
Adjunct Professor, Duke University Fuqua School of Business, and author of *Reinventing You*, *Stand Out* and *Entrepreneurial You*
July 2018
New York, NY

Introduction

The first day of school

My father made a difficult promise to me and my twin sister: he would be there for our first day of school. He worked for Olivetti in São Paulo, Brazil and came back to Italy only twice a year, in August and at Christmas. The big day finally arrived, but when we woke up our father was not at home. We felt hugely disappointed, but the blow was softened by the excitement of starting school. The first day went by quickly; when the school bell rang at the end, my father was waiting for us at the gates. Seeing him was a moment of overwhelming joy for me and, together with my sister, I jumped into his arms. On the way home, we inundated him with our stories: what we had done, the names of our new classmates, the teacher, the blackboard with all the coloured chalk, the map of Italy on the wall.

At home, while we all sat down for lunch, our stories continued. At the end of the meal my father wanted to first talk to my sister and then to me, so I followed him into the living room, where he asked me to sit down in front of him. He was silent for a few seconds, then he looked me in the eye and said: 'Paolo'; it was the first time he had called me by my name, everyone in the family always called me Paolino. 'Paolo, starting tomorrow, don't talk about what you did, but ask yourself if you love what you do, what you have learned and if you've managed to help others: nothing else matters'.[1] He put his hand on my shoulder, looked me in the eye again, as if I were an adult, and stood up. A few hours later, he took a plane back to Brazil: he had kept his promise.

Among the millions of words I have heard and read over time, *that sentence* spoken by my father, on 1 October 1969, is the one that has influenced my life the most. What did I learn from that sentence? I learned not to think about the right answers but the right questions: do I love what I do? Am I learning something? Am I helping someone?

Nothing else matters.

For many years I have been working in the field of Personnel, also called Human Resources. While carrying out my work, I have been able to confirm how it is much more important to start by asking the right questions, rather than trying to guess the answers. I have been able to follow hundreds of careers and I have asked myself: 'How come only some of us are successful, many are limited to just getting by and many, too many, fail?' Have we chosen a job based on our passions and our talent? What are we good at? Did we understand the rules of the game, the organizational culture, to avoid being lost in translation? Have we learned something new every day? Have we managed to build trust and whom can we trust? What price are we willing to pay for our career? When is the right time to leave? How do we evaluate professional success? How do we stay free? What really matters? What would we do if we were not afraid? Which legacy do we want to leave? What does having a successful career mean?

This book attempts, by using questions, to provide meaningful reflections, helpful tools and practical suggestions to have, or rather 'be' a successful career, defined according to parameters established and decided by ourselves, not by others, and certainly not just based on profit and building a career at all costs, without reflecting on the consequences. There are two tools I use: the **Compass**, an instrument focused on our inner and deepest values that allows us to maintain a certain direction on our journey, and the **Radar** that helps us discover the obstacles, the dangers as well as the opportunities we will encounter.

I know some people will think I'm crazy or, even worse, spoiled and choosy and will remind me that it is already a miracle just to have a job. These arguments are understandable: even if you only think about choosing a job, given the extremely high unemployment rates, it may seem like a utopian mix between the luxury of the past and an unrealistic, if not impossible, dream. I, on the other hand, am convinced of the exact opposite: *only by choosing and building a career aligned with our values, our goals and our deepest motivations, will we be able to do great work and consequently have success and rewards.*

If we consciously choose the right job and culture for ourselves, *we will not do a job but we will be the job we do.* I attended a retirement party for a person who had spent twenty-eight years in the same organization. His last sentence was 'I came to the office for almost thirty years, but I always left my heart at home.' This is a tragic tale, a professional life thrown to the wind, a wasted talent, so many years of mediocre performances, and what's more, paid pretty badly. Was it worth it?

If we choose a career on the basis of criteria that are incorrect or established by others, we'll eventually be forced to perform in a squalid comedy written by others in which we only have an insignificant bit part. When we go to a restaurant who chooses what we eat? We do, right? Well, if we're perfectly able to make autonomous decisions for marginal issues like a dish at the restaurant, that's even more reason why we have a duty to choose our career. In this regard, Viktor E. Frankl, author of the book *Man's Search for Meaning*,[2] has left us with a fundamental lesson: they can take everything away from us but not the possibility of making autonomous choices, even in the most desperate situations.

The book is composed of storytelling, stories taken from various sources, such as Greek mythology, sport, US politics, history, short corporate and personal cases, short case studies, news and selected management and coaching concepts and theories, along with many quotes from books, movies, songs, articles, videos, speeches and web pages that have contributed to the narrative.

I've worked and lived abroad since 1992: twelve years in Washington, nine in London and four in Geneva, where I live now. I've been lucky to work with extraordinary people, in more than 80 different countries. This experience has certainly contributed to my particular perspective, including the lenses through which I observe Italy, which, as Leonardo Sciascia said, *from afar hurts less.*[3] My professional experience and above all my human experience has convinced me that everyone has at least one particular talent just waiting to be discovered, encouraged and used. I'm certain that I can help, offer support and persuade you not only to not give up but also to use strategies and paths that you didn't know existed. The stories you'll read are all true: I'll reveal secrets, I'll show you tricks, I'll offer you tools, hoping they can be useful, pragmatic and even fun.

At the same time, I'd like to make it clear that I won't be the one to provide you with *The Answer* you are looking for, nor to tell you what you should or shouldn't do. What right would I have to do that? My role is to help you formulate the right question and to accompany you on the journey by making the Compass and the Radar available. Nobody can provide us with the correct answers; we must find them within us. Professional success isn't a miracle or a stroke of luck. If we fail to achieve this success, we can't blame someone else: we're the ones who guide our lives; we always have choices to make, as free people, knowing that happiness comes from the journey, not the destination. We'll never be alone on the journey; it'll be up to us to choose our companions of fortune and the right tools: the Compass and the Radar.

The book is divided into three sections: Passion, The Compass, and Freedom.

The question that characterizes the first chapter is: 'How do we find out what our Passion is?' I discovered it from a street artist, Gerardo, who painted watercolours on the main street in Antigua, a beautiful colonial village in the highlands of Guatemala. On this road there were lots of artists who painted landscapes, but the works of Gerardo stood out: they had a particular light. During a day of torrential rain, I noticed that there were no artists on the street except Gerardo, who continued to paint undisturbed under an umbrella. I went up to him and asked if I could buy one of his watercolours, but he only had the picture he was painting. I asked him how much it would cost, he replied: 'fifty dollars'. I tried to get a discount because it was not finished. Gerardo replied that he usually sold his watercolours for twenty-five dollars, but for the one I wanted to buy I would have to pay fifty. I didn't understand. Gerardo told me: 'I'm charging you double because *you'll deny me the joy I get from finishing a job I love*'. I gave him the fifty dollars, happy to have learned an unforgettable, priceless, lesson.

The second part of the book, The Compass, will help us to orientate ourselves and is divided into various chapters based on a series of questions such as 'How do we understand which Village is the one, the right culture for us?' After a theoretical introduction to what culture is, you'll be provided with practical tools to help understand the culture of an organization.

Next, we answer the question: 'How do we get to where we want to go, get our chosen organization to hire us?' You'll receive many practical and useful suggestions, such as writing a CV, preparing for an interview and knowing if an organization is telling you the truth.

The fourth chapter answers a key question: 'How do I gain trust, knowing that this is the most important ingredient in every relationship?' Here you'll find a formula with all the elements that contribute to creating, or destroying, trust.

The fifth chapter will focus on two important questions: 'Whom can we trust? How do I understand the rules of the game?' We'll visit a zoo – or maybe I should write jungle – where we will find various types of animals that we must absolutely learn to distinguish. I'll surprise you by showing you that we're surrounded by invisible heroes and have, here and now, the possibility of becoming one too.

The sixth chapter will pose a fundamental question, which will force us to dig deep into our soul: 'What price are we willing to pay for our career?' I'll share stories with you about people who have made a 'pact with the devil'.

The third part of the book, Freedom, will also be characterized by a series of questions.

The themes of the seventh chapter will be: 'How do I build a career? What can help us? What mistakes should we avoid?'

'*Should I stay or should I go?*' is the topic of the eighth chapter: when is the right time to leave an organization? How are we really evaluated?

The last part of the book considers 'What really matters? What does it mean to be successful according to our values as people, not according to criteria established by others? What is the real capital we're responsible for?' Before setting off on the Journey we need to make sure we have our Compass and Radar. If we only have the Compass we will go in the right direction, but we'll be unaware of the dangers and end up in a dead end or, worse still, won't be able to see either ambushes or opportunities. If we only have the Radar, we'll avoid dangers, but we'll have no direction and may end up becoming very tactical without knowing where we're going. We therefore need both the Compass and the Radar to discover and use our passion, heart, nerves, soul and, yes, love.

I trust you will have fun reading *The Compass and the Radar*: enjoy the journey.

Part One

Passion

1

The hidden treasure

'The two most important days in your life are the day you are born and the day you find out why.'
MARK TWAIN

The treasure and the journey within

The Gods of Darkness gathered to decide where to hide Happiness, the most precious treasure, from Man.

'We could hide happiness at the top of the highest mountain', one of them suggested. 'There's no point doing that', thought the others, 'sooner or later Man will climb the mountains and find it'. 'Then let us hide it at the bottom of the sea, at the deepest point'. 'There's no point doing that, because sooner or later Man will learn how to reach the bottom of the sea'. 'Then let us hide it in the most distant and inaccessible lands', but even that solution was discarded: there would be no point, sooner or later Man would reach those places too.

A long silence followed. Then the most cunning and evil of the Gods of Darkness spoke and said, 'I have the solution. Let's hide Happiness at the bottom of every man's heart: he'll be so caught up and busy by travelling across distant lands, climbing mountains and crossing seas that he'll never look into his own heart; let's condemn him to a treasure hunt for eternity!'

The Gods of Darkness were very happy and sneered smugly, convinced of their choice. They would have triumphed, while Man would have remained forever unhappy, in a perennial search for the hidden treasure, his own happiness.

Then one day in spring . . .[1]

Do we want to continue this story together?

The treasure is within us. The treasure is really within us.

Let's think together about the meaning of this sentence, even from a professional point of view. 'The treasure is within us' means that our happiness will not be the result of external circumstances, something or someone 'external to us' that we can't control. Happiness in our work will instead be the consequence of choices that we make 'internally': we will therefore be the ones that guide our professional destiny but with an important condition. We need to know who we are, find out what our true passion is, our talent and the values which we believe in from the bottom of our hearts. If we accept this principle, we'll become who we really are, we'll be authentic, we'll trust in ourselves and in those around us.

'Know yourself', as Socrates said almost 2,500 years ago, becomes the starting point of this journey that we will take together. If I've learned anything in 30 years of work and after about 8,000 interviews with candidates from all walks of life, it's that everyone has a precious talent to reveal, a real treasure. But it's not enough to just discover it: it must be used and put into practice, at the service of others. The world is populated with people with a huge talent 'gathering dust in the attic'; many leave without singing their own song. Mozart, Dante, Picasso, Neruda, Mandela and Gandhi have left us their works and their teachings; they didn't limit themselves to the complacency of knowing that they had an immense talent, a divine gift.

The most important, significant, fascinating Journey of our life is not the one at the top of mountains, in the depths of the seas or in the most distant lands, but the one inside us to discover who we are, what we want to do with our lives, what really matters. This Journey will not be easy, because we'll meet showmen and charlatans who will tell us – upon payment – that they have the answer ready for us; an answer that, however, *only we* can find. The Journey will be difficult at first; we'll feel a kind of anxiety comparable to that of a sailor who leaves behind familiar coastlines and lands to venture into mysterious seas and lands. We'll begin to explore hypotheses, possibilities, options and then, just like our sailor, we'll begin to see a point of arrival, and new roads and possibilities will emerge, which will then become our direction. We will discover, as Mark Twain wrote, that the two most important days in our life are the day we are born and the day we find out why.

The objectives of this book are threefold: the first is to discover our hidden treasure; the second is to find the organization and the job we want; the third is to remain free because we have understood what really matters. We will have the Compass and the Radar to guide us.

During this Journey that we take together I'll have two roles. Above all I will be – but only if you allow me – your coach and mental trainer. In addition, I'll advise you, putting my professional experience and my personal respect at your service, to find the job you want, to gain the trust *of and in others* as a respectable person, to avoid traps and wrong choices, to understand how to know an organization and who is part of it, to build a successful career.

You'll have the most important role: you'll be *in the driving seat, in control*. Being in the driving seat also means knowing how to choose who your travelling companions will be, a very important choice because you'll never be alone. For the journey to be successful, based on the right questions, we must create the following conditions:

- *Mental state: how to be creative, have time to reflect and trust in ourselves.*

- *How to discover and create our 'core identity', our personal identity, the basis of the search for our job? What do we believe in?*

- *How can we recognize and avoid obstacles during our journey? What could we do if we weren't afraid?*

Creativity

Many of us go to the gym, ski, play tennis or football, swim, practise yoga or run knowing that we have to train our body. But do we also exercise our brains to improve our way of thinking? We can't solve a problem with the same mentality that created it. If we've never had the problem, it gives us an opportunity to learn new skills, to train new parts of our brain that have not yet been used. To be able to find our hidden treasure we need to be creative. Before we start, let's do some warm-up mental exercises.

- *Exercise 1*
  Without removing the pen from the page, join all the points of this figure using only four lines.

- *Exercise 2*
  Calculate, in less than a minute, the sum of the numbers from 1 to 1000.

Figure 1.1 *Exercise 1.*

• *Exercise 3*

Explain the meaning of a *nanosecond*, a billionth of a second.

Resist the temptation to look up the answers and let's see if we can understand what happens in our head when we try to solve these problems.

In the first exercise, the one with 9 points, many people think they are looking at a square. The logical conclusion will therefore be to look for the solution inside the square, but the solution 'inside the imaginary square' does not exist if WE set the limits that only exist in our head. The solution will be to draw lines outside the square.

In the second exercise, we immediately start to count: 1+2=3, 3+4=7, 7+5=12; then, after a few more additions, we become confused and discouraged, knowing that at our speed and calculation capacity, one minute is not enough to add up the numbers from 1 to a thousand.

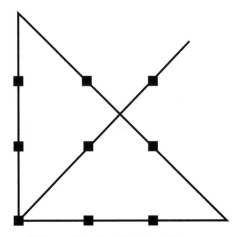

Figure 1.2 *Exercise 1 solution.*

Let's deal with the problem in Exercise 1 in a different way, visually, by putting the numbers on a continuous line.

1, 2, 3,..998, 999, 1000

Figure 1.3 *Continuous number line.*

We have a series of pairs of numbers, 1 and 1000 at the ends, which adds up to 1001, then 2 and 999, which also adds up to 1001, 3 and 998, again 1001. How many pairs? Half of a thousand, of course, therefore 500 pairs of numbers that always add up to 1001. The result will therefore be (500 × 1001) = 500,500.

The answer to the third exercise is that there are a billion nanoseconds in a second, technically the correct response. We can also move from the concept of time to that of space: the speed of light is about 300,000 km per second, so can we calculate the distance that light travels in a nanosecond? We divide the speed (300,000 km per second) by the time (1 billionth of a second) which gives the distance travelled, about 30 cm, the length of our foot: in fact, the nanosecond in physics is called a *light foot*!

These quick warm-up exercises help us to understand that we often frame problems with a rigid logic that does not allow us to tackle and solve them. What do we need to be creative about solving problems? To give you some practical and fun ideas, I want to reference one of my favourite books: *A Kick in the Seat of the Pants* by Roger von Oech.[2] The author tells us that when we make decisions, we must be explorers, artists, judges and warriors.

- **Explorer**: when we look for information, data or new roads for our job, we have to behave like explorers. Let's remember that, as the philosopher Emile Chartier said, nothing is more dangerous than an idea when it is the only one you have. The rules for being an explorer are: be curious, get out of your comfort zone, break mental patterns, ask why, don't impose limits that don't exist (for example 'seeing' a square that doesn't actually exist). What does this mean in practice? I'll tell you Jeff's story: he works as a civil servant in the tax collection department and has a good salary. Listening to his two children and their friends, who go to university, he develops a strong interest, almost a passion, helping university students identify their professional path. Jeff trains as a coach, and develops a plan, sending a presentation to the most prestigious universities and proposing a support and career counselling service for students. After about two years Jeff receives six job offers. A true explorer, he ventured into unknown lands and found his ideal job.

- **Artist**: when resources are transformed into ideas, we become artists. In this phase, we develop our contextual intelligence, the capacity to see connections to join the dots. Picasso wrote: 'Some painters turn the sun into a yellow dot, others turn a yellow dot into a sun'.[3] Can we visualize a different and better professional future? How do we link seemingly different elements? Which rules can we break or change? We often ask ourselves 'What would happen if ...?'. How do we manage to use our passion and talent in our work? We think of entrepreneurs who have created extraordinary products or services through their ideas but it is not necessary to be entrepreneurs to think like this. Look at what surrounds you; can you see how to solve a problem at work? Years ago, while working at the International Finance Corporation, I read a report that highlighted how some projects had generated huge losses because we didn't conduct a thorough analysis of the management of the companies in which we invested. I wrote a proposal, in order to integrate a new service to cover this failing, that was then approved, thus managing to combine my passion for travel with my professional experience. Three years of pure fun followed, every month a different project in a country where I'd never been before. A blast.

- **Judge**: when we evaluate the feasibility of our ideas in a strict and objective way, we become judges. To be feasible, our aspirations must be connected to our potential and be realistic. For example, at fifty years old it is impossible to become an athlete or acclaimed musician, if we haven't even begun, but we could become a manager of sportspeople or musicians, working in environments that bring us *closer* to our aspirations. We must evaluate data, weigh up the pros and cons, understand if the time is ripe, know what the basic assumptions are and listen to those close to us. A classic mistake is to confuse our passion with our talent. We can be passionate about music but this doesn't automatically make us singers with the talents of Pavarotti, Adele or Bono. The X-Factor television programme measures the distance between passion (all the competitors have plenty of this) and talent (only some of the competitors have real talent). By being judges of ourselves in the professional world we must continually evaluate our abilities and avoid arrogance. Napoleon said to his generals before Waterloo: 'Wellington is a bad general, the British are bad troops. We'll settle this matter by lunchtime'.[4]

- **Warrior**: if we've activated the explorer, the artist and the judge, all we have to do now is put our armour on and, as warriors, move forward towards our professional dreams, to translate our ideas into actions, into our new job. Everyone wants a good job full of satisfaction, but few are willing to fight to get it. This is nicely summed up by the expression *fire in the belly*: a kind of inner drive that motivates us to never stop and never give up. When I met Lance Mackey[5] I discovered a true warrior: born in Fairbanks, a small village in Alaska, Lance was diagnosed with cancer at a young age. What did he decide to do? He entered the famous Yukon Quest sled dog race, about 1000 km at temperatures that reach as low as 40 degrees below zero. Lance won four years in a row, from 2005 to 2008. In 2007 he entered the Iditarod sled dog race, the hardest of all, about 2000 km in Alaska, in winter. Lance again won four years in a row, from 2007 to 2010, achieving at the same time – something everyone thought to be impossible – victory in these two races in the same year. I asked him what it feels like to be able to do something thought to be impossible. He replied: 'I certainly didn't define it that way; I wanted to prove to myself that it was possible'. He also told me that he had succeeded above all thanks to his sled dogs, whom he loved. Lance told me a secret: 'It's very simple, they love me too, because they know I'll never abandon them and that I eat after them'. An extraordinary leadership lesson: a leader does not abandon anyone and eats afterwards, not before. Lance is a true warrior who inspires respect, as opposed to others who eat first and leave only the crumbs for everyone else. This discipline is elegantly called Executive Compensation. The question: are we willing to fight for our work? I also ask you to re-read the word IMPOSSIBLE: it can also be read as I -M – POSSIBLE. I am possible. Do you think it's a coincidence?

Reflection and confidence in ourselves

The world around us is changing at an amazing speed, faster than we are able to change ourselves. To find the treasure within us we must stop and, if the speed increases, we must take a break, reflect, ask ourselves important questions. What have we learnt? Let's read *very slowly* the first verses of the poem by Pablo Neruda 'Keeping Quiet'[6]:

Now we will count to twelve
and we will all keep still.
For once on the face of the earth,
let's not speak in any language;
let's stop for one second,
and not move our arms so much.
It would be an exotic moment
without rush, without engines;

we would all be together

in a sudden strangeness. [. . .]

To find the treasure within us we need silence, space and deep reflection. The term *mindfulness*, meditation, is proving an enormous success: it means to be present *here and now*, to feel a sense of psychological freedom that can only be perceived when we're at peace with ourselves? or mentally?, without making judgements. We think about our work, the moments when we're totally immersed in what we're doing, when we lose track of time, happy to use our talent to do something we love. Let's reflect on the common thread of the professional decisions we've made: if, for example, we've always opted for jobs and occupations based on income and earnings, have we overlooked anything important? Let's reflect on the professional choices we've made: aware of what we know now, would we make those same choices again? Have we ever tried to prove that we are right – for example with our colleagues – even when we were wrong? Is it better to try to be right or be happy?

Confidence in ourselves: on a scale between 0 (= I have no confidence in myself) and 10, what would we give ourselves? To prepare this chapter I counted how many times in a month I had listened to people who expressed a total lack of self-confidence, stopping after many, too many examples. 'I'm not good at languages', 'I'm not good with numbers', 'I don't understand much about politics, technology, computers, 'I'm not a good boss', 'I don't have the time', 'I've never been a good lawyer like . . .', 'I could never make a speech in front of so many people', 'I'm not good at leading people', 'I don't have the energy to manage the project', 'I'm not going to apply for that job because there'll be too many candidates, they'll never hire me', 'I'm not able to be a good father and a good colleague', 'There are younger, better candidates than me', 'I can't afford it and I have no time to learn and study', 'I don't have the courage to try', 'It's too late, I'm too old to start now', 'I'm too young, I have no experience, I could never do it', 'Nobody cares about me, better to let it go'. 'I'm scared ...' I could continue with more examples; the problem is if we say any of these phrases three times, we really will believe it and after a while others will believe it too.

Let's do the opposite: let's think about when we accomplished something instead. An exam passed at school, a job well done exceeding our own expectations, a sporting competition, a goal achieved, a language learned, a challenging book understood, a person with whom we managed to establish a good friendship, a job offer, a transfer to another country, a complex project completed. We must have confidence in ourselves; no one will offer us a job if we don't have faith in our abilities. Like children who are learning to walk, we will fall a few times, but they will not be failures but attempts to walk alone, with our legs. Failure is not the opposite of success but the process – which is sometimes painful but that, as we well know, leads to success. In my professional experience I've met many candidates and colleagues who didn't trust in themselves *for no reason.* Have confidence in yourself, it's worth it!

Some time ago I had the opportunity to listen to a presentation by a well-known *National Geographic* photographer. The photographer showed us some fabulous photographs taken on a Caribbean island: amazing beaches, crystal clear sea, palm trees, blue skies, exactly what we imagine when we visualize a beach in the Caribbean. Then the photographer showed us some pictures, of the same places, but taken with other lenses at different times of the day. The places were unrecognizable, not better or worse, but the perspectives, light and angles had all shifted. The photographer then asked us: 'How many lenses do you have in your life? If you always use the same lens you will always get the same pictures'.

Let's try a brief visualization exercise. I'm going to ask you to imagine a world map; now close your eyes for ten seconds until you can *see it in front of you.*

Now open your eyes: did you imagine *this map* of the world?

I'm ready to bet that, just like me, you didn't imagine *this* map. The reason is that, since primary school, we've only ever seen and studied maps drawn with a particular perspective, the one with Europe in the middle, Africa in the south, Asia in the east and the Americas in the west. If a European goes to Australia for the first time, the maps might seem 'upside down' but upside down: upside down with respect to whom? So, it is worth considering whether we have only one lens, whether we've analysed problems from a single perspective or if we can read the maps – in other words, the reality around us, with different lenses and perspectives. The profound beauty of diversity is precisely this – seeing the world from different perspectives.

Personal and professional identity

I'm now going to ask you to take a pencil, sit in a comfortable quiet place, and treat yourself to an hour of undivided attention without interruption. Turn off your smartphone, the television, close the door, stay connected *only to yourself*. Are you ready?

1 **Choose the 5 words that best describe *who you are*, not what you do:**

    –

    –

    –

    –

    –

2 **Heart: complete the following sentences spontaneously and honestly:**

    – I have a passion for . . .

    – I like to . . .

    – I would like to do more . . .

3 **Soul: complete the following sentences spontaneously and honestly:**

    – The most significant experience of my professional life has been . . .

    – I would like to experience . . .

    – I feel alive when . . .

4 **Your 5 most important *strengths*[7] (defined as the talent you've got multiplied by the investment you've made to develop it) are:**

    –

    –

    –

    –

    –

5 **What has given you the most joy and energy in your past
and what did it mean to you?**

Examples: 'First salary means economic independence'; 'Getting
a job offer means recognition of my professional skills'.

–

–

–

–

–

6 **What are the 5 value-principles and words with which you
identify yourself, which inspire you and motivate you the
most?**

Examples: Collaboration, Competence, Challenge, Helping
Others, Sense of Responsibility, Autonomy, Freedom, Status-
Visibility, Family, Wisdom, Respect for Oneself and Others,
Wealth, Order, Knowledge, Fame, Sense of Adventure,
Competitiveness, Compassion, Courage, Personal Development,
Power, Influence, Reflection, Dynamism/Speed, Trust.

When doing this exercise, write down the three that are most
important to you and evaluate how the presence or absence of
such values and principles might affect your professional
happiness. Here's my example: I greatly value the feelings of
autonomy and trust. Once they gave me a very large pay rise
but the new boss turned out to be a real tyrant who didn't
trust anyone (zero trust) and who controlled what I did on a
daily basis (autonomy reduced to a minimum). Despite an
improved salary, my morale was at historic lows for months. I
suffered like a dog because they had taken away my main
motivating factors.

7 **Ask 20 to 30 people you know well to describe you with ONE word.**

Which word did they choose? Are you surprised? Happy? Disappointed? Do not react but listen instead to what your inner voice is *whispering* to you.

8 **How do you spend your free time, which hobby do you have or wish you had more time to devote to? What did you like when you were a child?**

Before moving on to the last question, let's pause for a few minutes to carefully reread what we have written. What did we observe? Which topics and principles come up frequently? Have we learned anything new about ourselves, pausing to reflect on what emerged from this brief introspective analysis? In question 1 have we chosen words similar to those in question 5? What are our strengths? Have we connected the words that describe us best, things which give us energy and joy, the words and values that motivate us the most: what picture have we painted? As a first 'gut' reaction can we see how certain occupations and professions are closer to us than others? Why? Can we see an emerging trait, a common theme, a visible trace? Before moving on to the last question, I want to tell you a story.

What do we believe in?

Edward R. Murrow was a famous American journalist who, between 1951 and 1955, hosted a radio programme on CBS called *This I Believe*.[8] In this programme, people were invited to write a short essay that could be read in less than five minutes; in the text they had to indicate what they believed in, a teaching they wanted to share with others. The essay couldn't deal with religious or political themes and couldn't be written 'against' anyone. The programme was an extraordinary success and was later replicated. The stories, available online or collected in books and anthologies, are real pearls of wisdom written by people like us. I was struck by the story of James T. Harris,[9] President of the prestigious University of San Diego. When he was 17, to help pay for school, James cleaned the toilets in a factory near his home. The thing he noticed about this was that he had become invisible: people ignored him; the indifference of others hurt him and he swore to himself that he would never treat people as *invisible*, even those who do the most humble jobs. That's what he believed; that was his story.

Let's now spend an hour writing our short essay, our story. After writing it, we'll read it aloud and record it (there are free applications available to do this). What do you believe in? What are your values? What are your roots? You may want to start by writing 'I believe in . . '. Again, looks awful. Make sure it is something positive and constructive, not something 'against' someone.

In the zone

Think of the last time you were so absorbed and concentrated in an activity that you forgot about the time that flew by, in which you were neither bored nor stressed but, sucked into a magical whirlwind, completely present and concentrated, full of energy and enthusiasm. Look at children playing, an artist painting for passion, a person listening to music or focused while reading a compelling book: these people are – according to the Hungarian psychologist Mihaly Csikszentmihalyi – in a state of grace called 'Flow'.[10] During the *flow* state, also known as being *in the zone*, we focus on what we're doing, with a genuine motivation linked to the pleasure of doing what we're doing, with no ulterior motives. If you want a real indicator to help discover your passion and your talent think about the times when you've been *in the zone*. In a professional environment there must be three conditions for this to happen: clear objectives, an optimal balance? between opportunities and abilities, combined with immediate, constructive feedback that allows us to learn and improve ourselves. Think about days at work: some fly by without you realizing it, others never seem to end. If we reflect on the difference between these types of days, we realize the presence of moments of flow in the first type and boredom, defined as a lack of attention, in the second type. For me, being *in the zone is pure happiness*. Minor clarification: being *in the zone* should not be created by using drugs or artificial substances, that's another thing entirely. Another way to discover flow, and therefore our treasure, is to observe how easily we do certain things (for example, sports, learning languages, speaking in public, mathematics . . .). If we succeed naturally or much more easily than other people, we are approaching the treasure.

The others helping our growth

We're not islands; this means that in order to find our treasure we need other people, those we trust and who know us best. Let's start by sharing the answers we have found in this chapter with two or three people, for example our best friend, our partner, a family member. What do they tell us? Do our answers coincide with those of the people who know us well? Listening to their opinion, asking for their feedback will be a very important step towards discovering our level of *self-awareness*.[11] If, for example, we've said that a word that describes us is 'kind' and the people closest to us look at us in amazement, we've just learned a lesson.

To help us understand the importance of others in discovering the treasure within us, we can use the Johari window, invented in 1955 by two American psychologists, Joseph Luft and Harry Ingham (the name of the window comes from combining their first names). The window[12] consists of a square, divided into 4 quadrants. The horizontal dimension considers the degree of knowledge that the person has of themselves, for example in terms of personality, attitudes, impressions and emotions transmitted to others; this last type of knowledge can be known to the person only through interaction with 'the outside': a way of identifying the value on this scale is, therefore, the frequency with which the subject explicitly asks for feedback from others on their behaviour and the impressions it has generated. The vertical dimension, on the other hand, indicates the degree of knowledge that others have of the person. The combination of these two variables leads to the identification of four areas.

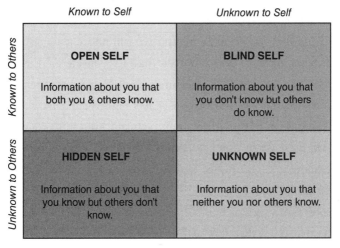

Figure 1.5 *The Johari window.*

The first quadrant (OPEN SELF) is the 'Open' area, also called 'Arena': here the information – understood, comprehensively, to be the set of personalities, knowledge, emotions and personal abilities – is known both by the person and by others.

The second quadrant (HIDDEN SELF) is the 'Hidden' area, or 'Façade', in which information is placed that is known to the person, but which he/she does not wish to share with others.

The third quadrant (BLIND SELF), called the blind spot, contains information about the person that is known to others, but not to the individual. The only way he/she can acquire information related to this area is through direct feedback from others, expressly requested or not.

The fourth quadrant (UNKNOWN SELF) is the 'Unknown' area, representing the information that is unknown both to the subject and to others because it is buried in the subconscious, and is revealed only in particularly emotional situations. There is no way to directly acquire the information contained in this quadrant.

The larger the blind spot area, the greater the need to increase our awareness and the need for feedback to get to know ourselves better. This is when an effective coach can help. It is not about judging – it's about increasing your self-awareness. Sometimes we'll find the treasure within us because a neutral eye will notice a talent we don't suspect we have, a possibility we haven't considered through a question, an observation, an encouragement. Help from experts given in good faith will help us enormously in our growth and in discovering both what we need to improve and the talent, even in its rough state, that we have when doing a certain activity. A clear sign is when someone makes you notice that you are good at 'x', or that not so effective at 'y'.

The treasure is therefore within us. In order to find it we must use our creativity, turning us into explorers, artists, judges and warriors;

we took a moment to reflect, aware that we had to trust ourselves. When answering some key questions, we then clarified what our professional and personal identity is, focusing in particular on our values and the importance of others in our human and professional growth. Our journey can continue.

Part Two

The compass

2

Before setting off.
Understanding which is
the right Village for us

'If you don't know where you're going, any road will get you there.'

LEWIS CARROLL, *ALICE'S ADVENTURES IN WONDERLAND*

What is culture?

In the first part of our journey together we learned a simple but vital secret: the treasure we've always been looking for, treasure which we sometimes doubt exists, has already been found. It's hidden within us. In our heart, in our mind, in our eyes. *The right path to discover the treasure is the one that leads to new questions, instead of guessing old answers.* To paraphrase Proust, the real voyage of discovery consists not in seeing new sights, but in looking with new eyes.

Therefore the time has arrived to look outside, to open the windows and see the Village which is right for us on the horizon. In other words, we'll try to determine which culture is best suited to our values or, conversely, if our values are in line and can be adapted to the culture we're a part of or would like to be a part of.

As I've already mentioned, I've been working in a Human Resources department for almost twenty years as HR Director. I've interviewed between seven and eight thousand people, listened to and discovered personal and professional stories and *I've learned that everyone has a 'treasure within' but only those who really understand the culture of a particular organization have a serious opportunity for growth and development within it.*

Almost everyone who works is well prepared and motivated, but few go on to become successful. I'm convinced that the decisive factor is the ability to fully understand the culture which one is a part of, and avoid ending up *lost in translation*. Everyone knows the proverb: 'When in Rome, do as the Romans do', which emphasizes the essential ability to adapt to a reference system and a culture which is different from their own. The problem is that nobody knows what the 'Romans' really.

But what do we mean by culture, especially in the world of work? Company culture is what *the organization is, as opposed to what it does*, sells, has or earns. If we pause for a moment to reflect, we'll admit that we conduct the same kind of analysis when we choose our dearest friends and our partners for life: we must first understand who they are, not just what they do or what they have. Therefore, in this chapter we'll focus on understanding how organizations are, an indispensable condition for finding a significant meaning in our work.

The term 'culture' is undoubtedly inflated: everyone talks about it but it's very difficult for two people to agree on its definition. Even the definitions found in a selection of dictionaries highlight very different aspects of this word that cover aesthetics, morality and anthropology. The key characteristic of culture, in its anthropological meaning, *is that it doesn't necessarily have to be explicit.* A group can live according to its own model of culture without being aware of it or realizing how much it differs from others. When they leave the confines of familiar surroundings, people react in different ways to new cultures. Studying culture is therefore essential for personal and professional survival and growth. Define it.

There are three definitions that are, in my opinion, relevant here. In *Cultures and Organizations: Software of the Mind* by the Dutch social psychologist Geert Hofstede, culture is the software of the mind, our *operating system*, or the way we are partially or completely programmed subconsciously.

Peter Senge, founder of the Society for Organizational Learning and author of the book *The Fifth Discipline*, defines culture as a *mental model*, made up of assumptions, generalizations, and images that allow us to decipher reality and take decisions according to our own individual rules. What is a mental model? It is **what you pay attention to.**

Finally, I've always considered personal culture as a *lens* through which we observe the world. So the third definition, in organizational terms, is to consider culture as the *invisible glue* that holds together a society or an organization. *Lenses and glue: it works!* Take for example the royal wedding of Meghan Markle and Prince Harry: close to 2 billion people watched it on TV all over the world, admiring the beautiful display of pure British culture, which culminated in God Save the Queen, sung by all people present at the ceremony. Culture is what brings people together: the social glue, remembering what unites us despite all the differences.

How to understand the culture of
an organization

Andrew Pettigrew[1] adds another element to the definition of culture as a glue: 'Culture is a system of publicly and collectively accepted meanings operating for a given group at a given time', emphasizing how these values can change, and generally do change when the leader of the group changes or the group is faced with a crisis. To decipher the culture of a Village, understood as an organization, we must therefore observe the symbols, the heroes, the rituals, the written and unwritten rules, the stories that circulate and the values shared by the members at a specific moment, asking: 'Are they compatible with our values and our cultural background?'

But what are the factors to consider, to evaluate our compatibility? Among the hundreds of studies and analysis on the concepts of culture, Hofstede provides an extraordinarily effective interpretation. In the book *Culture's Consequences: International Differences in Work-Related Values*, various characteristics are listed, such as: individualism, inequality, power distance, uncertainty avoidance. Let's look at them in detail.

- **Individualism**: In an individualistic culture one is expected to take care of oneself and exalt concepts of life based on absolute autonomy. The culture of the United States is strongly oriented in this direction: it's an example of the continuous proliferation of the heroes produced by Hollywood or the chronic resistance to any form of arms control, perceived as a limitation to freedom. On the contrary, values such as order, security, family, the common good are more relevant in a collectivist culture. People are born and grow up in large families or clans that protect them in exchange for their loyalty.

- **Inequality**: The concept of inequality is defined according to the level of tolerability within a nation, or an organization. Consider, for example, countries such as Mexico or Russia: there are a few hundred extremely rich people, while the overwhelming majority of the population have seen their economic and social conditions worsen. What does this mean? Do we accept, with a contagious indifference in our way of thinking, that a growing degree of inequality is normal and acceptable?

- **Power distance**: Another important dimension for understanding cultures is the power distance, which indicates the extent to which a society accepts that power is distributed unequally. I remember that years ago I had a boss from India, who belonged to a privileged caste: he didn't miss the opportunity to remind everyone about this, expecting the same privileges abroad as he would have enjoyed in his homeland. He had no problem using his position to ask everyone, including myself, for personal favours, private jobs, to bring him coffee. At first I went along with his requests, but after a couple of months I was forced to tell him that I wouldn't do anything that was not part of my job description. He reacted with genuine amazement to the fact that I was rebelling against a well-established routine. In another scenario, many years later, I found myself in the completely opposite situation, this time with a Swiss boss. One day he left work very early, but I saw him come back to the office about two hours later because he'd forgotten his house keys. I told him that he should have called me and that I would've gladly brought them to him, since I was going home anyway and we lived very close. 'We have abolished slavery in Switzerland; I would never have asked you to do that', he replied. These examples help describe different concepts of power distance, understood as the degree of social acceptability of inequalities: India has a very high level of acceptability and Switzerland, on the contrary, has a very low level.

- **Uncertainty avoidance**: High uncertainty avoidance – to be understood as economic, working instability – involves a high level of aggression, which translates into an impulse to work hard and to be intolerant towards deviants. Uncertainty is perceived as a constant threat to one's own stability, for which one must fight. The rules, both written and unwritten, must be fully observed and respected. Observe the way people dress or talk who are part of an organization. Are they all the same? How are the people treated who don't adapt to these rules?

On the basis of Hofstede's characteristics, we can understand the identity of an organization and ask ourselves if we really want to be part of it.

If we think of *culture as an instrument that helps us to live,* according to the masterly definition of Jomo Kenyatta, President of Kenya from 1964 to 1978, we can use what we have learned from Hofstede. It will be easier to get a quick idea of the degree of inequality accepted in organizations. For example, the architecture and size of a company's offices, has always been a visible sign of its power and importance. At the African Union, the equivalent of the European Union based in Addis Ababa, each Commissioner, the highest hierarchical rank, has an entire floor at their disposal. At the World Economic Forum, nobody has an office; everyone works in an open space. At the World

Bank the size of the office is linked to the hierarchical level of the individual. What is the office policy or tradition in your company: what do you notice?

From theory to practice

In 1951 I started my career in Japan at a prestigious company, with great hopes and aspirations. I found there were strict and unwritten rules for work – or not for work – such as never leaving the office before your boss and taking part in endless drinking sessions with your colleagues. In this environment new ideas were not accepted; the only thing that mattered was the absolute devotion and loyalty of the subordinate to the boss who, in turn, would protect them. In this environment there was no space for talented women, not only in terms of a career but also for survival. Even for a man like me, I saw no future . . . Things have not changed in Japan. Fortunately, after years enduring *suffocation and suffering,* I was hired by an American company in the Japanese branch, where I worked for the rest of my life, before happily retiring to the United States.

This is the message sent by *Economist* reader Muneyuki Nakano and published in the weekly magazine on 19 April 2014; in just a few lines we understand the real suffering of a person who felt suffocated by a culture that he could not accept.

Here is another example. Written in large letters at the entrance to a lobby were the following words: Integrity, Communication, Respect, Excellence. We were at Enron, where almost all the leaders ended up in jail for fraud. The company no longer exists, having declared fraudulent bankruptcy. Yet they displayed these exact words, called *value statements,* for all to see. It's clear that it wasn't exactly like that.

Many companies use similar words. It's up to us to identify the true values, the real culture of the organization, not what is being proclaimed.

So how do we understand which culture is the right one for us? In this chapter I reveal some useful tricks to discover the *soul* of an organization and avoid potentially costly mistakes.

In the introduction I have already pointed out to you how fundamental it is to evaluate a job on the basis of criteria that we've established ourselves. To guarantee we have the possibility of making the best possible choice, we must observe, understand and study certain characteristics of the organization where we intend to work:

1 How do the interviews take place?

2 What language do they speak?

3 Who is hired, promoted and why?

4 What happened to the person who did the job before us?

5 What are the incentive systems?

6 What are the numbers to pay attention to?

7 What are the rules of the game, written or not?

By observing these aspects, by asking pertinent questions, we'll obtain useful information that will help us make the right decisions, like a proper compass that guides us in the correct direction connected to a radar to avoid obstacles and pitfalls. To understand if a Village is the right one for us, we don't need a degree in management, we already have everything we need. In fact, I'll go further: if by chance we do have a degree in management, let's forget what we think we know. We just have to notice, observe, ask key questions, do some research, use intuition, find a middle ground between the archaeologist, the researcher and the explorer. To better explain what we're dealing with, I'll tell you some stories, real-life experiences, to which a lot of these questions are connected.

How do the interviews take place?

Let's start with the interviews. The stories used to illustrate this are from my own personal experience: the candidate for the job interviews is me. At the end of each story, some questions will follow that, while underlining some of the elements observed in the interviews, will help you to understand if the culture of that organization is compatible with your values and your way of being.

Close encounters with security guards

I just received an email: I've been asked to go for an interview in the United States in two weeks. Naturally, I change all my plans so that I can go and, after about nine hours on a plane, I find myself in a hotel room, where I see an envelope is waiting for me containing instructions for the next two days. The following day I have to show up at 8.30 for the first of nine interviews that I have to attend during the day, and then go to seven more the next day. In all, 17 interviews with people whom I only know by their last name; I don't know what they do, what level they are at, in what capacity they are there to interview me. I have an hour for each interview and about 20 minutes for lunch. On the morning of the first day I arrive at 8:15, a reasonable margin. I'm about to go through the main entrance, when I begin an endless tour, bounced from one armed security guard to another. Each guard directs me towards a different entrance. But even once I've managed to get into the building, a little nervous now because it's 8:22, I begin the process to get a pass, delayed by a queue created by a large delegation and the coffee break of one of the employees who takes the photographs for the ID document (it's safe to say it's not my lucky day!). Having completed all the entry procedures, I start running: at this point it's almost 9:00. Another armed guard tells me where to go and I pass through a large entrance like Victoria Station in London. Finally I find the person who's been waiting for me since 8.30, unaware of the obstacle course that I had to overcome. We walk quickly down long corridors, where I see large beautiful offices, maps of various countries and very small workstations, where three or four young people are grouped together. The first session starts at 9.15 instead of 8.30. I had to get past seven security guards, who were all very friendly. When I finally get started, I'm told, 'Welcome, but you're really late'. Disorientated by the time zone, by the near sleepless night and by the 45 minutes spent hunting for the right door, the greeting sounds ironic and sarcastic.

- What can I learn from the observation of the building, its architecture and the layout of the offices, the average age of the employees, the number of people encountered and the length of the selection process?

- What is the effect of seeing lots of armed guards and airport-style security systems just to enter the office?

Cappuccino and blue sofas

The train journey is very short. I arrive early and, as soon as I enter the building, I see six beautiful girls dressed in orange and white. One of them approaches me, offers me a seat at a bar table and asks me what I want to drink. I ask for a cappuccino which is quickly brought to me. After a while Mark arrives, the person I have an appointment with. He introduces himself and shows me around the offices where small groups of people are working in an informal but disciplined environment. There are bright coloured sofas for everyone and some black armchairs which are slightly isolated to favour concentration for those who need space and silence. After two interviews, they take me to lunch with a group of five employees who, openly, explain to me why they chose to work there instead of other companies where they would have earned more. They look like they're having a lot of fun, they're a tight-knit group and full of energy, young but mature in their behaviour. Later, I'm left with the person who holds the most senior position, perhaps the youngest. I spend almost two hours with her, a really smart woman: it's an interview, not an informal chat, she's evaluating me, but she puts me at ease. It's been eight hours since the morning cappuccino and I almost didn't notice the time go by.

- What impression did we get from the people we met?
- Making a comparison with the previous story, what does it mean when the manager comes down to pick us up in the lobby instead of letting us go through countless security checks?
- Did we get the impression that the staff work in a close team, where skill and competence count?

The Dubai tiger

Guys, what a hotel! After paying for me to travel first-class, they also came to pick me up to take me to a five-star hotel. The next morning I go to the company headquarters where I'm due to be interviewed, and I'm asked to wait in the lobby. While I'm waiting I notice a tropical garden behind me, protected by thick glass. After a few minutes I hear a roar; I turn around and see a tiger walking about. I stop worrying about the interview: the tiger is far more disturbing. A few minutes later; to my amazement, a small door is opened to the garden and a poor animal (maybe a small goat) is thrown into the cage and devoured by the tiger in a matter of minutes. During the first meeting, I ask what a tiger is doing in a tropical garden in the desert and why they let everyone watch him enjoying his bloody meal. They tell me that the tiger's meal is visible to everyone to *motivate employees*, to give them energy and turn them into real fighters. In total I meet nine managers: all the same nationality, wearing the same clothes, the same age; I understand that even if I worked with them, I could never be one of them. I ask the managers if there is not a lack of diversity; they sarcastically answer that as far as they are concerned diversity means Italian shoes, French wine, German cars and Russian women. Laughing, they offer me a beer. It's only 11 in the morning. I did not join them in the laughing and the mid-morning drinking. I felt immediately that I did not belong 'there'.

- What conclusions can we draw, if we're not comfortable with the way the talks are conducted or because of stupid or vulgar comments?

- Are we, or can we become, 'one of the group'? Do we drink beer in the office at 11am? If they offer us a lot of money, a nice house and a German car, can we accept the offer?

Two beers together to celebrate

I send off my CV and two weeks later I get a reply saying that the HR director, Franco, wants to talk to me. We talk on the phone, he finds my profile interesting, he asks me a lot of intelligent questions which are realistic and honest. When presented with some real problems, I respond twice that I have no idea how to deal with them, but that I usually learn quickly. At the end of the conversation, he informs me that he will send me the description of the position, the organizational chart and the salary that they are willing to offer, and informs me that, should I be interested in having an interview, I must reply within two days. I accept the interview and the following week I meet Franco; he accompanies me to his office and explains to me who I am going to meet and the kind of questions that they are going to ask me. About nine hours later, at seven o'clock in the evening, I go back to his office, he asks me if I have any plans for the evening and he invites me out to dinner. 'So, how did it go?' I reply that I had fun – which is true – but that I've lost my voice after all those interviews. 'So when are you coming to join us? I have already talked to everyone you met and we'd be delighted to have you on our team. What do you say?' He opens his bag and hands me the contract. 'Read it carefully, call me when you want and we'll see you soon'. Before paying the bill, he orders two more beers. 'To celebrate', he tells me, and congratulates me. He adds that there will be difficult days and a ton of work for me from the moment I start at the company. We're in the middle of July, it's a beautiful sunny day and, when I go out, I feel like I'm walking on cloud nine. I cannot believe my life is changing again and I start thinking about my wife, the umpteenth move we'll have to make.

- Have they been clear, fast, honest?
- Did they do what they said?
- How did we feel when we were with our future boss?
- Do they inspire trust?

At the end of these stories, have we asked ourselves the correct questions? It's a question of both analysing what we observed and 'listening to our gut', with regard to the sensations we had while we were at the interviews.

Before continuing with more stories, let us reflect and take stock of our personal experience. Retracing our steps, we'll find a lot of good ideas using some of the questions we've asked ourselves.

It's important to remember that job interviews work both ways. On the one hand there is the interview that potential employers give us; and on the other there is the interview *that we give and must give them*. The more prepared we are, the more we observe, the more we take note of what is around us, the more we'll be able to make the right decision.

It may seem strange, but the main objective of an interview is not to get a job at all costs, but to understand what the job is and in what kind of organization, culture and environment it will be carried out. Many people regret their choice during the first days of a new job: they were so focused on getting the offer that they didn't ask themselves the question of whether or not they really wanted it. It's therefore necessary to understand the organizational culture, to know 'when in Rome, do as the Romans do', meaning that when visiting a foreign land or 'territory', we should follow the customs of those who live in it. When we are in an unfamiliar situation we should follow the lead of those who knows the ropes, the 'Romans', the locals. In other words we must always keep our mental radar fully active.

In cases where you don't have the opportunity for a direct experience or an interview, the best strategy is to talk to people who already work in that structure, contacting them for example through LinkedIn. Or spend a couple of hours surfing the company's website and reading what they write on www.glassdoor.com, a source of inexhaustible wealth for information on companies, their culture and how they manage candidates and employees.

Smart use of social media can be helpful: you can often find friends of friends who have worked in a company. I'm not talking about the recommendations, a bad habit best avoided, but of contacts that can help provide perspectives and information which are relevant to your decision.

If possible, I suggest entering the company lobby discreetly, to look around: you'll learn a lot. I sincerely believe that you can find out more by observing the entrance to a company building than reading the last strategy document, which is often a series of clichés written for the use and consumption of investors or to please a distracted board of directors.

What language do they speak?

Gary Chapman, in his book *The Five Love Languages*,[2] explains that each of us has our own language to communicate with the people we love, using messages that continually reinforce this love. Difficulties arise when the languages of two people are not the same. If, for example, in a relationship the man buys lots of gifts for the woman and verbally repeats how much he loves her, using affectionate language, while she expects more specific actions to help her, such as taking care of the shopping or taking the children to school, therefore a language linked to specific acts, the two are destined not to understand each other. A bit like when we are faced with a person who does not speak our language and to make ourselves understood we speak loudly and slowly: we'll continue not to understand each other, only making more noise.

Organizations are constantly evolving living organisms; they have their own language that we must literally translate and learn to avoid being lost in translation. The American psychologist David Kantor[3] explains that languages can be traced back to three groups: that of power-action, that of feeling-affection and that of meaning-principles.

In other words, to understand an organization we must listen to the words, paying particular attention to the verbs. For example, again according to Kantor, referring to a corporate restructuring plan, the phrase 'We have to make sure that everyone works hard!' belongs to the language of power, action and control; 'I wonder how people will feel about the decisions we have made' is part of the language of affection, relationships and feelings, while 'We have to communicate that the decision is the right one because it's in line with the strategy' is part of the language of meaning, theory and principles.

We must try to listen and translate the language of an organization based on these parameters, reading interviews with the senior management of the organization, observing their website, videos and anything else available. In this way we'll become 'translators of languages'.

Daniel Pink, in the book *Drive*,[4] suggests an additional simple methodology to understand, through the language, the culture of an organization. Do employees speak about the company they work for using the pronoun *They* or *We*? 'They' obviously suggests a form of detachment, of indifference, if not antagonism. Using 'We', the effect is exactly the opposite: people really feel part of an organizational culture with which they identify. When I started working at the World Economic Forum, I noticed how people didn't refer to the 'Forum' but would say 'in the house', hence giving a very strong and personal connotation of not being part of a company but of a family, with all the aspects that this entails.

A second fundamental step is to learn to recognize our language and to carefully evaluate how compatible it is with that of the organization. Once I was called for an interview by a company that had to drastically reduce staff numbers in a short space of time. When they told me about their restructuring plan, I shared my thoughts with them regarding the fact that it would devastate the trust and morale of the employees. At that precise moment the interview ended;

I had used language related to relationships and feelings, while that of my interlocutors was the language of action, power, of cost reduction: in short, we weren't made for one another.

Another example of the importance of understanding language comes from personal experience. When I started working at the World Bank I had to translate their elegantly bureaucratic and cryptic language: 'We'll evaluate the problem as soon as possible' meant 'We hope that the problem will sooner or later be forgotten by everyone'. 'We need to analyse the problem in depth' was another way of saying 'We'll spend the next few months collecting data and information, even if it's useless, so that no one will ever be able to criticize us for a lack of analysis'. 'We have to create consensus' was used for 'We won't decide anything until we all agree' (highly improbable outcome).

Another effective methodology for understanding and de-coding the culture of an organization is – quite simply – to read their job descriptions very carefully. Which words do they use to describe themselves and what they do? Let's try an exercise: read this list – in strict alphabetical order – of a few world-famous companies, where you will find the most frequently used words in their job descriptions. Ready?

Amazon: 'wickedly', 'fast-paced environment', 'maniacal'.

Apple: 'comfortably', 'maintaining control', 'empathetic'.

Facebook: 'our family', 'ruthlessly', 'storytelling'.

IBM: 'digital transformation', 'technology solutions', 'innovation'.

Google: 'first-rate', 'prove that', 'tackle'.

Microsoft: 'driven person', 'insatiably', 'competing'.

Netflix: 'weed-out', 'bull by the horns', 'disciplined'.

Salesforce: 'work hard', 'play hard', 'hungry for', 'building alliances'.

World Bank: 'mission driven', 'sound analysis', 'development impact'.

World Economic Forum: 'speed', 'agility', 'community-networks'.

What do you *feel* by reading these words? Which one is closest to your values?

Who is hired and promoted and why?

If you think that hiring people, especially managers, is a purely technical task, based on skills, you're mistaken. Hiring people in organizations means above all managing and building a system of power. The concept was well understood by Bertrand de Got, Archbishop of Bordeaux, who was appointed Pope, in 1305. He chose to call himself Clement V, and in his first act appointed nine cardinals, all French like him. The Papacy of Avignon lasted until 1377 during which the nine successive Popes were, by happy coincidence, French, just to make it clear who was in command.

Kim Jong-un would almost comes across as funny, were he not the despotic and terrible dictator of the most mysterious, dark, poor and isolated nation in the world: North Korea. He became the leader of this country in 2011 inheriting the sceptre from his father who, in turn, had inherited it from his grandfather. Devilishly perfect nepotism, fruit of the skilful creation of a radical fanatic-religious cult built around a person, the figure of Kim Il-sung. I'll spare you the long list of honorary titles given to Kim Jong-un and I'll limit myself to mentioning only one: he is affectionately called *Abogi* by his fellow citizens which means 'God'. Thank goodness that Korea is thousands of miles away from us! Imagine if we behaved in this way . . . Or not?!

In his book *Give and Take*,[5] Adam Grant explains how one can understand an organization not only by reading the numbers, but by looking at photographs, images of the supreme leader or president, and how big they are in the company corridors and in the annual report.

In your experience, have you ever observed behaviour like that shown by the Papacy of Avignon or North Korea? Let me give you an example. Cinzia, a career woman, journalist and ghostwriter, wrote speeches and articles for the vice president of an important company. She was very competent in her position and everyone recognized this. The president was told about her, and asked her to work directly with him. After about two years, she was rewarded with a promotion to a position that was not suitable for her. Although this was clear to everyone, confirming Peter's famous principle that some people are promoted to the fullest level of incompetence, she was promoted again in a short space of time. And not only that: amid the general bewilderment, after less than two years she became the right-hand person of the president, with responsibility for programmes and functions about which she knew very little but on which she would pontificate constantly with solemn tones. Three promotions in less than five years and here she was at the top, feared and frowned upon. I happened to work with Cinzia on various occasions and I observed the diligence and generosity with which she made decisions and gave on-the-spot guidance on dozens of different topics. One day, when I heard her talking, I surprised myself by thinking that North Korea was not that far away. I realized that North Korea is not just a geographical place but a way of being or, better said, *not being*. To finish the story, when a new president was elected a year later, Cinzia was asked to leave and my colleagues and I spontaneously met up in a bar and drank late into the night.

Compare Cinzia's story with that of Fabiola where merit, competence, integrity, experience, qualifications, creativity, passion, diversity and heart are the ingredients for a career.

Think of Fabiola Gianotti, the first woman asked to manage CERN in Geneva: a scientist of undisputed world renown, to whom the *Times* dedicated a front cover in December 2012. Now she is leading around 10,000 scientists from all over the world and is living proof of how Europe can achieve wonders when working together with intellectual honesty on a fundamental mission. When we work in an organization where the manager is a Person, a word spelt deliberately with a capital P, like Fabiola Gianotti, we know how much merit and skills count and we'll be very far from North Korea.

Observing and understanding how people get to the top of an organization is important when assessing a company. Are they competent, good, credible? Or the opposite? Are they there through nepotism? What happens when a person is promoted too often and too quickly to a role that is not commensurate with their experience? How will this person be treated when they leave? Where do you want to work? Do you want to know if you are in tune with your company and its way of thinking? Read the list of people promoted in the last two years. If it makes you sick, you're in the wrong place. As we have learned from ENRON it is not the elegantly written value statement that counts but rather how the company truly behaves: in order to understand it look carefully at who is at the top and how he/she got there. Don't confuse elegant external narrative with harsh internal reality.

What happened to the person who did the job before us?

There may be various answers to this question. The first is that the person who preceded us has been promoted; this, in general, is a good sign but could also prove to be a negative factor if the promoted person becomes our boss and, suffering from 'withdrawal syndrome' from *their* toy, constantly tries to put their nose in our work.

The second answer is that the person was fired. In this case, we need to find out why, if possible, by talking directly to them. It could be, paradoxically, good news in the event the company decides to bet on us and turn the page, but we must understand what the *mistake* was. The news would, however, be very bad if getting rid of people was common practice at that place. For example, there are some football clubs in Italy where the chairman changes the manager at least three times a season. Apart from the fact that those teams never win, would we like to go and manage one?

A third possibility is that the person has left of their own accord and, even in this case, we must understand why. A friend of mine received a good job offer but later learned that the three people who did the job before her had had a nervous breakdown in less than six months.

We must then ask another question: is it a new position? If the answer is yes, it's necessary to assess the difficulties related to creating a new role in spaces occupied by others and the fact that this always creates internal tensions.

In this regard, it raises another related question: are there internal candidates applying for the position we hope to get? Let me immediately give an example to clarify the concept: if we went to a restaurant and noticed that the waiters, chefs and restaurant managers ate only food they brought from their own homes, what would we infer about the quality of the restaurant's cuisine? I would run away! If no internal candidate is interested, there will be a reason. But what? We must find out. In retrospect I should have used this rule myself. Once I gladly accepted a role that, on paper, looked prestigious. Within a few weeks, by learning that nobody from that organization would have even considered applying, I realized that I had made a mistake.

If, on the other hand, lots of internal candidates are interested in the position, we immediately know that we'll be competing against various masked enemies, who will often try to demonstrate how completely inadequate *we* are. In which case, it's plausible that we'll be *eaten alive by the locals*, who can't wait to have us for breakfast, not as guests but as the main dish; perhaps we'll even have to bring a portion of fries. The world is not populated with people prepared to recognize the talent of outsiders. And, to be honest, sometimes they're also right.

What are the incentive systems?

Here we need to understand what the real question to ask is. It's obvious, when asking ourselves the question 'Do I want to earn more?', everyone's answer would be clear: 'Of course!' But perhaps compensation alone is not the only element to consider.

Once I interviewed a very good candidate. At the end of the selection process, I had to negotiate a salary with him and of course I asked him how much he earned. He replied that he didn't know. I didn't believe him because everyone knows how much they earn. He excused himself for a few minutes, then returned to my office and told me that he'd called his wife, who had told him how much he earned: it was a rather low figure, but he specified that even though his basic salary was barely enough to cover the bills, if he reached his sales targets, it increased significantly; the incentives far exceeded his annual fixed wage, totalling up to an incredible figure, which almost made me fall off my chair. He added that he worked at least 80 hours a week, that he had not had a holiday in three years and that he would be returning to the office after our interview, even though it was already seven o'clock in the evening. He was under forty but looked over fifty.

On another occasion, I met an employee of a very bureaucratic organization, where salaries increased in relation to seniority, every

18 months, regardless of performance. He told me that he left every day at 4pm and that he would never be fired.

These are two extreme examples, of course, but relevant in order to recognize some distinctive features of different organizations. In pay systems, for example, it's important to know not only how much you earn, but also how earnings are structured. In the first story it's understood that, to obtain an adequate salary, the employee is required to make a big effort: it will be up to us to assess how feasible it is to achieve the target. If we prefer stability over a competitive system that rewards results, then we are probably better suited to work in less dynamic and in some ways closed systems. Therefore, in this case the absolute value of compensation must be evaluated not only in numerical terms but must be related to our preferences and our propensity to risk.

That said, there could be positions that literally offer nothing, but that provide wonderful opportunities to learn and then capitalize on later. If offered an internship at Google even without pay, many people would jump at the chance. Or again, there are jobs that in theory offer an excellent compensation plan, but in practice the targets are unattainable, or keep us stuck at the same level for 10 consecutive years.

In other words, choosing a job on the basis of a number may be a mistake: as always, more information is needed to make a decision. If you buy a car, the price is definitely relevant information, but certainly not the only factor.

When evaluating an organization, it's a good idea to take into account the difference between the highest salaries and those of the lowest positions: the wider the gap, the greater the tendency to generate a lack of trust, a sense of injustice, angry employees, inequality and the power distance we mentioned at the beginning of this chapter. Bear this in mind when the time comes.

What are the five numbers to pay attention to?

Economic results, number of employees, average age, employee turnover and diversity are the five important numerical elements when evaluating an organization. Don't worry, I won't bore you with data and numbers. We'll ask ourselves only one question, starting from this hypothesis: after much research, we have to decide between two job offers for similar positions, in two different companies, with the same salary and both less than 30 minutes from home. How do we choose?

The first option is a company that is part of a global group with 200,000 employees, listed on the stock exchange, with a small office in the UK that employs about 500 people and a high turnover of staff. The company has just hired a very dynamic general manager with an excellent reputation, who wants to hire young employees but has only two years to make the company profitable after five years of losses.

Option number two is a company with a single location in our region, about 2,000 employees who come from the same geographical area, which has been operating for thirty years. Due to the growing competition from Asia, it has seen profits decrease quickly and hard times or even big losses are expected in the next two to three years. The company has been firmly in the hands of a very rich and powerful local family for many generations, and the three sons of the founder and their wives are all employed at the company; obviously in high-level positions. No one wants to leave this company; they don't have unions and never hold strikes. The employees are fifty years old on average, they can pass their job on to their children when they retire and they get generous benefits to help with the family expenses (subsidies for buying food, reductions on the purchase of a car, etc.), provided they have been employees for at least 10 years.

As I said, same job, same salary, same distance from home but, on closer inspection, these situations could not be more different.

Where will we choose to go? How will we evaluate the risk of going to work for the two companies? What does it mean to be part of a large group, but in a branch office, or a local company with only one office? What does it mean to work for a company where the staff have an average age of less than 30 or more than 50? How are the company's current results and what expectations do we have for future ones? Does it matter to us that we'll never reach the top, a place reserved for family members?

Knowing the average age in organizations is important, as is the turnover and diversity of the people. It's all data and information that will help us understand the culture.

What are the rules of the game, written and unwritten?

During the eighteenth century, French philosophers and political scientists such as Rousseau, Voltaire and Montesquieu contributed significantly to the study of the concept of power, reflecting on its typologies, its holders and its management. In particular, Montesquieu in his masterpiece *The Spirit of the Laws* wrote in 1748 that a government should have legislative, executive and judicial power very well separated: when, for example, legislative and executive power are united, there cannot be freedom. I believe the Middle Ages ended when 'the rule of Law' finally replaced 'the law of the Ruler'. However, in many states and companies we are still, in terms of governance, in the depths of the Middle Ages.

The same principle must apply to organizations. Do they have clear rules? Who establishes them? Will they give us a contract of employment according to legal guidelines or are we at the mercy of rules which are unclear, not shared or, even worse, are we in the presence of fathers-godparents who make and break the rules as they please, despots and petty dictators? Compliance with the rule of law thus becomes the cornerstone of an organization, like a healthy society. Opacity and manipulation create chaos and toxic environments. Montesquieu was right but it seems that we have forgotten his lesson.

3

Destination identified. Arriving at the Village that's right for us

'Life is a story that we invent.'
BEN ZANDER, *THE ART OF POSSIBILITY*[1]

An encouraging story

In the first chapter we looked inside ourselves, to understand what we want, what our values are, our weaknesses, our passions; in the second chapter we became explorers, to find out what *cultures* are the right ones for us, to find the *Village* in which we feel 'at home' because it corresponds to who we are, not just what we do. In this third chapter we'll deal with a very practical topic: how do we *enter the Village*, that is, get hired by the organization we have chosen? To help you understand how the motivations and strategies that drive you towards getting hired by an organization can be essential, I want to share a true story.

Rama is an Indian woman who works in my team. Lots of colleagues have talked to me about her, so I invite her out to lunch to get to know her better. I ask her why she works at the World Bank and she tells me her story: she is less than 30 years old and about three years ago she worked in the administration department of an American company in Mumbai; she met a guy from her own country of origin, India, but he lived and worked in Washington. They got engaged with the idea that Rama, after the wedding, could join him in the United States. She had never left India before, spoke mediocre English and had only one year to prepare, but she was an independent woman, with a deep intelligent look in her eyes, and the idea of being a housewife didn't suit her. She then decided to follow a clear strategy to find not just any job, but the job she really wanted to do. For two months, she carefully researched the employment opportunities offered in the Washington area. The World Bank was the only place that interested her. Despite the opinion of her friends to the contrary, she spent many hours conducting research on the World Bank and improving her education, English and studies to the required standards. When she arrived in Washington her first step was to purchase the World Bank telephone directory, which listed the names, telephone numbers and other details relating to about 17,000 employees. Selecting the surnames from her area of origin in India, she managed to get the email addresses of 50 people, who she then contacted with personalized letters asking for 20 minutes of their time to get advice from them. In a week she received 22 replies and within a month she had met all the people who answered.

These first contacts generated others, until eventually she met a manager looking for a collaborator with similar qualifications to hers; she was offered a contract for only three months, poorly paid, but Rama was available immediately, the next day, and tells me that 'she wanted to be the first to arrive at the office and the last one to leave'. Despite the amount of work, she was determined to make a good impression and even managed to help other colleagues; in the meantime, she kept asking questions to learn new things.

When her contract expired, due to lack of funds, she was offered the chance to stay but with poorer conditions. Furious, Rama accepted knowing that at that moment she had no other real choices. After another three months they finally offered her a fixed position with acceptable conditions. Rama signed the contract on the condition that she could participate in a project that interested her a lot. Her boss accepted this and a year later she was promoted and started working in my team.

At the end of our lunch, I offer her my sincere congratulations. Rama tells me that she would like to see me again, just for 20 minutes, because she has some suggestions on how to improve a procedure that would save us time and money. The next day I receive a thank-you email from her and two pages full of ideas. She was right; her suggestions will save us time and money? When Rama proposed herself as project manager, I gave her the role and after a year she was promoted again. This time I'm the one asking for a meeting, because I want to thank her again.

The story of Rama, a very determined person, is an effective example of a winning strategy to get a job. *Looking for a job is a job*, if done seriously. Rama made a lot of good moves but also a mistake, when she proposed her project to me, bypassing her own boss, and a risky mistake before this, when she focused everything on a single company during the job search phase, when common sense would dictate that you have more than one option. However, her undoubted ability to quickly understand where there was opportunity, together with a bit of luck, made sure that she succeeded.

So how do we get the job we want? It takes realism, a bit of luck, but above all an effective strategy. We'll follow step-by-step the path to get where we want, to be hired and get a contract. On the next few pages, we'll see how to use social media to increase visibility, how to evaluate the real possibilities of employment, how to write our curriculum vitae and basically our story. We'll investigate who can help with research and what mistakes to avoid during the interviews, and we'll try to identify some tricks used by companies to eliminate candidates.

We'll evaluate the five main interview techniques and how to position ourselves in relation to each of them. We'll also talk about the interview *we'll give the company*, to find out if we are talking to Pinocchio. The following pages partly reflect the structure of a 'textbook' manual on job hunting, *What Color is Your Parachute?*, written by Richard N. Bolles more than forty years ago and updated every year.[2] Before we start, it is important to fully understand that looking for a job is a job: as such we need to tackle it with inner conviction and sound methodologies and helpful tools.

Internet and social media

What's your favourite food? I love ice cream. As an example, let's pretend that ice cream is available at all hours directly at our house. All this for free, 365 days a year. It seems like heaven, right? At least for those who, like me, love ice cream.

Now, let's replace the word 'ice cream' with 'data and information' and we'll understand the extent of the technological revolution underway. The difference between data and information is simple: data becomes information when it helps us to decide. To state: 'Today is the tenth of June' is just a piece of data, but it becomes precious information if it reminds us that tomorrow is the birthday of a loved one, giving us the chance to buy a gift. The internet has made available data, potential information. Not only that: the information has become *always* available, stored in the cloud, that is to say in ever-expanding virtual warehouses, and usually for free. Understanding which of the billions of available pieces of data can become relevant information becomes the true business of the future.

We're at the beginning of the Fourth Industrial Revolution that is profoundly transforming everything we do in all sectors, who we are, the way we look at the world.

An area that has been changed radically by technology is the labour market. While, on the one hand, we have plenty of news on available jobs – if we look, for example, at www.monster.com or www.indeed.com, there are thousands of positions open all over the planet – on the other hand, any organization or company can obtain information about us without our knowledge. Google allows anyone, at any time and for free, to know almost everything about us. The concept of privacy is very different from 10 years ago, especially for the new generations, the millennials, born after 1990. We must be very cautious when deciding what to put online, because we can be sure that what we publish on the web will never be a secret. So, in my opinion, we have moved from the Information age to the Reputation age.

Some time ago, as HR director of an organization, before sending a job offer to a candidate, I thought about checking out his profile on Facebook. From the photographs I noticed that every year he celebrated his birthday with a fancy-dress party. So far, nothing wrong; the problem was that for six years in a row he had chosen the uniform of a Nazi general as his costume, complete with swastika, flags and portraits of the Führer hanging in his room, all 'spiced up' with indescribable comments. I decided not to send him the offer.

We have to learn to use social media with intelligence and prudence, while at the same time we can and must use it to our advantage. A professional profile on LinkedIn or on BranchOut, Crunchbase, DataFox and InsideView, for example, helps to create many potential opportunities provided it's done properly, starting with a professional photograph that avoids cheeky, ridiculous, pompous or simply tacky poses, which do more harm than good. In general, negative online comments about your employer are to be avoided and always remember that even our emails are at risk of violation of privacy.

Internet and social media should not be feared – unless one has published inappropriate material online – but used well. A profile written intelligently on LinkedIn or on Monster.com can help to get yourself known and 'wanted'. A CV, even if well written, is not enough. We have to also show what we do, for example by managing a blog, showing photographs of the products we sell, adding phrases and comments from customers who have used our services, sharing articles we have written. The goal, on any social media site (LinkedIn, Facebook, Twitter etc.), must be to gain quality contacts, not just to accumulate contacts to achieve a number. Our social profiles must tell a story and explain in what way *we are different – not better –* than the rest. Think of yourself as a product: if you can't set yourself apart, nobody will be interested in 'buying' you. We only need a few, well chosen, words to explain who we are, what we do, why we can add value, while trying to be specific. We can also add information on activities we have done, such as volunteering or other small jobs to earn money, to demonstrate our ability to be selfless or to take the initiative.

Try doing an experiment: open the profiles of a series of people on Linkedin and 'decide' who you would offer a job to solely by looking at the photograph for less than three seconds. Then, calmly, reflect on your decision. Who have you chosen, why? Who did you discard? What do your choices have in common? What made you realize that a candidate didn't present a professional image that inspired confidence?

Evaluate the chances of success

'The only important thing you learn at Harvard is that it's easier to create a new job than to find an old one' (from the film *The Social Network*, directed by David Fincher in 2010).

Even before thinking about how to write our CV, we must consider whether there's an available position and to whom we send it. All large companies publish web pages with any available positions, regulated by information platforms. We must be able to understand which job to apply for and how and who will make the final decision: this is important information to help us write our job application. The labour market in Italy, for example, is very idiosyncratic, for example because about 80 per cent of companies are small or medium-sized and in many cases they are family-owned companies; therefore it's even more important to know who makes the decisions relating to recruitment. For many people, the Personnel department (also known as Human Resources) is generally avoided like the plague. I think it's a mistake because the people who work there can help and provide useful information, and maybe even lend a hand to help us understand how the selection process works.

If there is an available job, as mentioned in Chapter 2, we need to know why. In general it could be good news: it means that the company is growing or at least they aren't reducing the workforce. If there are no jobs available, we need to try a less traditional, more creative approach. We could offer our services for a shorter period, linked to a project, or make a proposal that the company might consider. And here, we need to be realistic and recognize how many possibilities are available.

The story of Rama at the beginning of this chapter is encouraging, but we must be realistic and specific. Would we like to work at Facebook? Though it has more than one billion three hundred million users and about one and a half million customers, Facebook has only 8,000 employees chosen from among the thousands of potential candidates who dream of working there. If we really want to work in Silicon Valley in California, we could focus on Salesforce: the largest cloud computing company in the world, where 15,000 people work and numbers are constantly growing.

The realistic possibilities of being hired should be considered not only on the basis of statistics (for example, there are 30 candidates for every two positions available), but also on the basis of the risk perceived by companies when hiring. Let me explain: the following matrix[3] shows two parameters (job/occupation that I currently have and would like to do, the sector in which I work now and in which I would like to work) with four different possibilities.

Looking for a new job in our sector and doing the same job (quadrant 1) – for example, a financial analyst who stops working at one bank to go and work for another – means the chances of success are high. On the other hand if we decide to do the same job, but in a new sector (quadrant 2 and 3) or to look for a different job in the same sector, we would have partial or limited possibilities of success. Finally, if we wanted to change both sector and job (quadrant 4), the possibilities would be reduced to zero, as companies would believe they are taking on too big a risk.

So, when we send off our CV, we evaluate which quadrant we are in and where we would like to go, following this matrix.

To all this we must also add a third parameter, represented by the geographical dimension. For example, it's unlikely that an organization will take the risk of sending a new graduate or school leaver to work abroad if he/she has never left the country before. We must therefore put together a plausible personal story to show that we have already done it: for example, during language study trips or volunteering projects abroad.

To be credible, we must be convincing and prevent companies from considering us as risks; we want them to see us as opportunities to be taken on the spot.

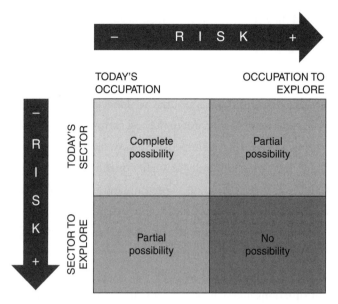

Figure 3.1 *Occupation and sector matrix.*

Write a CV or tell your story?

When we write our CV, the most important question we have to answer is: 'Did we manage to tell our story?' According to a study by the National Citizen Service, the British organization that supports young people seeking work, CVs are read and evaluated in less than a minute. We are witnessing the *Tinderization* of the labour market, a term coined by the newspaper *The Independent*, in reference to the dating application Tinder, which allows users to accept or reject the profiles of potential partners in just a few seconds. Many companies use software that automatically deletes CVs which are longer than two pages. In short, we must have the gift of incisiveness to communicate who we are and above all to convince people what we're able to do.

I would like to give some encouragement and two concrete suggestions. The first: be yourself, don't act. The second: don't feel blocked by the syndrome 'I don't have a perfect CV', if there is such a thing. Of course, some candidates can exhibit a very respectable 'pedigree', in terms of the studies they've done at the best universities and work experience carried out in the best companies. I often realized how candidates of this calibre had it easy, facilitated perhaps by belonging to a powerful family or highly qualified, with a significant investment in their education. Congratulations, but obviously not everyone has the same opportunities and luck.

The majority of candidates, in fact, weren't, as they say in English, born with a 'silver spoon in their mouth', but just wearing a nice pair of boxing gloves: they've had to fight for everything, coming from difficult situations and having to adapt, for example, to perform tasks traditionally considered menial. Have you ever worked as a dishwasher, babysitter, waiter, tour guide to pay for your studies? Well done! Not only should you not hide it, but talk about it to show that you don't give up, that difficulties don't scare you. Personally I prefer to give a chance to candidates who have struggled or even suffered to conquer what they have or want to achieve, demonstrating what is called 'PTG (post-traumatic growth)', the growth that follows traumatic events.[4]

There are basically two types of CV, the *chronological* and the *functional*. The chronological CV, more traditional, is a list in temporal order of the positions and roles held during one's career, starting from the current one, the most recent. The functional CV summarizes in a few points, from a minimum of 3 to a maximum of 7, the skills acquired during the career, limiting itself to providing basic information on where we've worked. For example: let's say we've always worked in sales for a technology company. At the beginning of our career we were in a shop, then manager at that shop, then sales director for the city, the province, the region: ever-increasing responsibility but always in the same sector. The functional CV could therefore state on one line: 'Long-term experience in the sales sector, including the management of sales force of n. people, achieved results of x million euros in annual turnover, with profitability of y%'.

Both types of curriculum are good for companies, provided we understand *what we should not do or write*. In light of my experience (I think I've read thousands), I would like to point out very frankly the 10 most 'serious' mistakes and therefore the chronic mistakes to avoid at all costs. Many of these seem obvious and yet candidates continue to commit them. Let's see what they are:

1 **CV too long**: nobody reads more than two pages. Better a single page, but well written.

2 **Spelling mistakes, incorrect punctuation:** makes the same impression as a sauce stain on your shirt on your wedding day.

3 **Lies**: they are a guaranteed 'suicide'; dismissal is a certainty even if you are hired. For example, you can't write 'graduate of such and such University' if you have only attended a two-month course or stopped after some exams. It's surprising to note that many candidates are convinced they're getting away with it. Scott Thompson, CEO of Yahoo, was forced to resign just 4 months after his appointment, when it emerged that he had not completed the computer science degree indicated on his CV.

4 **Black holes**: i.e. periods in which it's not clear what a candidate has been doing and the CV contains no indication or clarification.

5 **Unverifiable data**: that is, they indicate vague results or objectives, such as 'increased the reputation of the department I headed'.

6 **Confidential information**: legal, financial, personal.

7 **Irrelevant or obsolete information**: don't enter old news from twenty years ago like 'volleyball player in secondary school in 1998'.

8 **Explicit or exaggerated salary requests**: for example, 'minimum monthly salary requirement'. In Chapter 4 we'll talk about how to negotiate wages?

9 **Triumphal and purely subjective tone** of the descriptions used in the CV of the type: 'exceptional professional with a global vision for all international strategic, social and economic problems'.

10 **Multi-colour effect**: coloured pages, photographs, disorder, strange drawings.

The World Economic Forum receives about 35,000 job applications every year. Ninety per cent don't pass the first hurdle for precisely one of the reasons listed above. As we've mentioned, a CV should not be just a collection of activities carried out, but a page that informs who we are, the results we've achieved, what we're interested in doing and why. Now we get to the famous *cover letter*, that is to say the letter of presentation that accompanies our candidacy which must be sincere and convince those who read it that it's worthwhile to meet us.

Think, for example, of what we did when we met the person we love: did we give them a generic 'I need a man/woman' or did we say 'I only love you'? Companies are in some ways comparable to people: they want to know *that at that moment* the candidate 'wants' to be there, but without the connotation 'as a mercenary' ('I'll come on condition that you give me . . .'), with a lack of real interest or out of desperation.

Who can help us?

What is the role of headhunters or agencies? How can you *network* with recommendations and references?

We begin by describing the role of the famous *headhunters*, that is to say firms that deal with the selection of medium-high level executives for companies. Since 1980, there have been seven companies that dominate the market: Egon Zehnder, Korn Ferry, Spencer Stuart, Heidrick & Struggles, Boyden, Russell Reynolds, and Odgers Berndtson. The rest of the market is fragmented into thousands of small companies specializing in certain markets, segments, professions and even customers.

Let's remember that headhunters are paid by the companies which have assigned them the task (for example: 'Find me the new head of finance'), not by the candidates. Understandably they'll be working on behalf of their clients: they'll tend to convince us to apply if they have to cover a position in line with our profile, or ignore us completely if they don't have an open position corresponding to our skills and inclinations at that time.

However my suggestion if they were to call you for a position is to listen to them. And if they ask you: 'Do you know anyone who could be interested in this fantastic opportunity?' lend a hand in providing ideas or suggestions: in general, they don't forget who was available and kind. At the end of the day: can they help? Yes, provided we solve *their* problem first. For non-managerial levels, the use of employment agencies can be helpful. A serious agency will try to *introduce us* to a company and will only be paid when the candidate is hired. Examples of such agencies can be found on the portals www.indeed.com, www.monster.com, www.subito.it, www.infojobs.com, but a simple search on Google will give us access to many other websites with information on available jobs. Then there are organizations such as www.adecco.it, www.manpower.com or www.michaelpage.com that constantly provide hundreds of postings for jobs that are available maybe only for a few months.

Malcolm Gladwell, author of the book *The Tipping Point*, explains how important the role of connectors is,[5] that is to say of people who have a very extensive and efficient network. Gladwell cites a study conducted in the Boston area, which showed that as early as the seventies, 56 per cent of people had found a job thanks to personal contacts. The percentage should not be surprising: we all need to become effective at creating an informal network of personal contacts and we know how important it is to cultivate it. What surprised the researchers, however, was that the people who had helped the candidates find a job were not close friends but simple acquaintances. Gladwell coined an effective definition for this phenomenon: 'the strength of weak ties', the strength of weak connections, that is, of people who are part of other social groups and who have access to new and different information.

I think it's important to know what it means to *network*, a term that indicates the ability to build and maintain a network of contacts. Very often we think of using it only when we need to: we're wrong. Networking essentially entails *giving more than taking*, trying to be useful in solving other people's problems, making connections between people with similar interests. The book *Give and Take* by Adam Grant,[6] already mentioned in the second chapter, explains that those who establish a solid reputation as people who 'give' are also the best networkers in the world. Adam Grant tweeted 'A Taker is someone who helps when the personal benefits exceed the personal costs, while a Giver is someone who helps when the benefits to others exceed the personal costs'. If we can create a solid reputation as people who are available and sincere, we'll be able to use the network we have built.

Exactly like a bank account: first we make a deposit, we accumulate credit and then we can withdraw, not the other way around. I've helped many colleagues who were in trouble, knowing that they were good and that they would surely find work. They didn't forget it and it was they who helped me when I was in difficulty. I truly believe that constantly cultivating professional relationships is a fundamental key to having useful contacts in the future. As a result, it's absolutely crucial to continue investing in what will become our relational capital, capital of inestimable value. Ask yourself on a daily basis: have I helped someone today? If you help one person each day for three years, you will increase your relationship capital enormously.

And now we come to recommendations, letters or pressures from powerful or well-known people, sent to those who then decide whether to hire us. Never use them, without exception! Recommendations are to be avoided at all costs, for a very simple reason: if we enter an organization thanks to a *nudge*, we'll never be free but in constant debt to someone and we'll never know exactly what the 'payment' will be. They're generally favours that carry weight and can jeopardize integrity and careers. Moreover, even if we had some success at a company which we'd entered thanks to a recommendation, we'll always suspect that our career is due to something else or someone else, not related to our abilities. Personally, as soon as I smell a recommendation I automatically reject the candidate.

Providing references, on the other hand, is different; on the contrary, it's possible and desirable; indicating, for example, 'I worked directly with Mr. X, you can ask for my references' is a totally legitimate and professional practice. We need credible people who can testify who we are and what we can do, not godparents who will ask us for the 'cost' of their support.

Interviews: necessary
but not sufficient conditions

What are the necessary but not sufficient conditions, those which are necessary and almost sufficient and the final obstacles – often not visible – to be in pole position and get 'our' job?

In 1970, 95 per cent of the musicians in the top five symphony orchestras in the United States were men. Did they play better or was there a prejudice against women musicians? The recruitment system was changed, using the so-called *blind hearing*, in which the musicians played behind a screen that hid their identity, they even asked the candidates to take off their shoes so that the ticking of the heels from the women's shoes could not be recognized. Following this simple measure, the number of women recruited increased by between 25 and 46 per cent.[7]

Another very interesting experiment was conducted by the Australian National University. They sent out 4,000 CVs that were exactly the same for the same number of junior level jobs, the only difference being the candidate's name. To obtain the same number of interviews, candidates with Arabic or Chinese names had to send 64 or 68 per cent more applications, with an Italian name '*only*' 12 per cent more; the best results were obtained from candidates with Anglo-Saxon names.

Everyone has prejudices, most often unconscious: it's a fact. I confess that even I discovered I had one that I didn't know of: I received a candidate's CV for an important position, I read it carefully and then I wrote: 'No, too old'. I quickly realized that what I had written was horrendous, not to mention illegal, for a candidate who is two years younger than me! I was so ashamed, I called him for the interview and we offered him the job. He was good, not old.

The ancient Romans believed that '*Mens sana in corpore sano*'; the Jesuits professed the 'cura personalis', professional sportsmen know that they have to train to walk onto the playing field concentrated, fresh, focused. Having an interview can be compared to living as a player, not a spectator, a sporting event to which we must devote the same concentration and energy that we would dedicate, for example, to a tennis final (this is not about doing team sports).

The book *The Inner Game of Tennis* by W. Timothy Gallwey[8] illustrates what kind of mental state we should aspire to, in order to be at our best for important events. And an interview is one such event. We must arrive fresh, concentrated[9] and relaxed. What do we generally do to relax? A walk in the park, a swim, do we listen to music? Well, do it the day before, avoiding 'studying' until three in the morning to get ready. It seems like obvious advice, but no company will offer a job to a candidate who arrives upset, stressed or tired. If we just have a few minutes, let's dedicate them to deep breathing exercises, with our eyes closed: even if you're not an expert in meditation techniques, even three minutes will be enough to adopt a positive attitude. Watch the speech of the social psychologist Amy Cuddy on TED,[10] seen by millions of people to understand how our body language influences not only those who observe us but also our own behaviour.

Now, with our heart beating slightly faster, we'll begin the first interview. Let's remember that we'll never have a second chance to make a good first impression. In 1892, Sir Arthur Conan Doyle, giving voice to his best-known character, detective Sherlock Holmes, wrote: 'By a man's finger-nails, by his coat-sleeve, by his boots, by his trouser-knees, by the callosities of his forefinger and thumb . . . by each of these things a man's calling is plainly revealed. That all united should fail to enlighten the competent inquirer in any case is almost inconceivable.'[11] You will be well aware of the fact that you'll be observed and studied, so present yourselves at the interview with a plan. Here it is:

- **Punctuality**: arrive about 10 minutes before the appointment, to have time to catch your breath and study the environment.

- **Absolute courtesy** with everyone. Always.

- **Proper clothing**: must make sure that no one remembers you because of how you were dressed for the interview. Classic, elegant but not opening night at the theatre or a wedding. Carelessness must be avoided, eccentricity must be evaluated according to the context. It's important that nobody refers to you as: 'the candidate with the Mickey Mouse tie' or 'the candidate with the laddered tights' or 'the candidate who looked like a clown'. The best way to understand how to dress is to take a look at the company's web page and dress like the executives. There's always a picture of them: 9 times out of 10 we'll find the men are wearing a red tie, dark suit and blue shirt, women will be a little more imaginative. Be in tune with the company dress-code. If you were going to work at Ben & Jerry's,[12] an alternative ice cream chain, then have a 1960s Californian hippy wardrobe.

- **Handshake**: firm, convincing, friendly, not cold, dead fish. No sweaty hands.

- **Visual contact**: always maintain eye contact with the person speaking to you.

- **Face relaxed**, smiling.

- **Don't interrupt**, listen and listen again.

Necessary and *almost* sufficient conditions

We've got into the semi-finals, just by following a few rules of common sense and good manners. Many competing candidates have been eliminated precisely because they haven't applied these basic rules. Now you have to face the actual interview.

Daniel Pink, in his book *To Sell is Human*,[13] reminds us that everything we do requires sales techniques such as the need to interact in harmony with those listening to us, with flexibility and clarity. I can't argue with that. During the interview, you should be *persuading someone to buy the candidate, that is you*. What are the rules for concluding this 'transaction'?

From a behavioural point of view, start by being genuinely authentic: it's better to be the best version of ourselves, rather than a bad copy of someone else.

Then be prepared: Michael Jordan, the greatest basketball player ever, when asked how he had managed to win continuously throughout his career replied: 'I knew that if I failed to prepare I would be prepared to fail'. So let's see how to prepare and be in tune, flexible, clear, authentic.

1   Do lots of research into what the most relevant characteristics are for the position. If, for example, the position requires great analytical skills, provide specific examples of how you have successfully used those skills in the past. Avoid phrases like 'I'm very good at . . .': it's better to show that you already have the required experience, perhaps developed in different environments. Use specific examples, stories supported by numbers and data, not personal opinions, which are worth zero here.

2   Describing your job enthusiastically is fine, provided you can build a bridge to the new one. Therefore continually make logical steps between the current job and the new one. For example: 'Our company is changing rapidly' deserves a response in which you refer to all the changes you have experienced and what your contribution to these changes has been.

3   Many candidates try to get a job by explaining the benefits that they want, without clarifying what benefits the company gets. It's tantamount to trying to convince a person to buy a car by talking about the advantages *we gain by selling it.* Instead put yourself in the shoes of those who are listening and be convincing and empathetic. For example, explain how one of your ideas has been adopted and has brought verifiable and quantifiable benefits.

4   They will almost certainly ask you what your strengths and weaknesses are. Prepare a clear and convincing answer for both. For example, with weaknesses it's necessary to be honest and demonstrate that you have improved, that you've understood the lesson and that any difficulties have also been opportunities for learning and professional growth. Another question that you'll almost certainly be asked, is: 'Where do you see yourself in 5 years?' You must have a true story to explain what your *plan* is.

5   If you have 'holes' in your CV, that is to say periods when you have not worked, be open and explain why: it could prove to be an advantage if you have a true story to tell, for example, 'I always dreamed of travelling to Africa for 6 months and I managed to do it after 25 years of working'; 'I started studying again'; 'I took up an old hobby which had been neglected over the years' or simply 'I wanted to stop for a bit, recharge the batteries and spend some time with my loved ones'. Always tell the truth, sincerely.

6   Answering 'I don't know' is generally acceptable provided that you complete the answer on a positive note, like 'but I usually learn quickly' or 'On similar occasions I did . . .'

7   You need to have some questions ready to ask, to try to better understand the type of work. Many candidates, in

fact, are only prepared to provide convincing answers, without thinking about the possibility of obtaining valuable information through incisive questions I suggest preparing some of these questions. For example: 'If I were hired, what would be the three most important goals to be achieved in the first 12 months?'; 'How would you define the culture of this company?'; 'What advice could you give me?', 'Would you tell me your personal story at the company, what do you like about your job?', 'What do the people who have succeeded at this company have in common?'.

8   To better understand the culture of the organization, ask the question 'How is this organization different from the others?'.[14] Then listen to what they have to say through their own story. Stories about an organization are always unique; for example, questions about the character of the boss, the possibility of reaching the top or being fired, will present a useful narrative to better understand if your values are compatible with those of the organization.

9   As I mentioned before, never say 'I'm better than ...' but rather show that you are different in that you have relevant knowledge and experience. Communicate your energy and strong interest in working for that company but never show desperation or instil pity. You want an opportunity to show that you're an asset, not receive a commiserating pat on the back.

So, you've passed the initial phase, avoided mistakes, answered their questions honestly and competently and asked incisive and intelligent questions: will the job offer arrive? Not yet; two key aspects are missing. The first is determined by you and is connected to your ability to demonstrate emotional intelligence; the second depends on factors related to the company that may hire you.

Emotional intelligence

Organizations today want to know not only if we are competent, but if we have emotional intelligence (EI), a concept developed in the 1990s by Daniel Goleman in his volumes *Emotional Intelligence*[15] and *Working with Emotional Intelligence*.[16]

For decades the intelligence quotient, IQ, was considered the most relevant indicator to measure the possibility of success in life and was used by companies and universities as an element to select 'the best'. There's no denying that there is a correlation between IQ and career, but it has been estimated at around 25 per cent: that's to say that *75 per cent of our professional success has nothing to do with this indicator.*

Companies have become increasingly interested in the parameter of emotional intelligence precisely because they have realized that focusing exclusively on the IQ of people or their degree of technical experience is not sufficient for the purposes of an overall assessment of their employees and, even more so, in the selection processes of candidates for a job. The scientific and empirical evidence of the studies conducted in the field of emotional intelligence has pushed organizations to take this factor seriously, leading to EI becoming a cornerstone of the evaluation and professional development of employees.

According to Goleman, there are five components of emotional intelligence:

1   **Self-awareness**: very often we are faced with people who have enormous self-esteem ('I am the best . . .') but very little awareness. Being aware of ourselves means knowing how and to what

extent our way of being has an impact on others; moreover, it means always being aware of what we are doing while we are doing it.

2   **Self-regulation**: manage emotions, do not suppress them. The interview is a very effective test of this. We don't expect direct questions about our emotions, it'll be easier to examine us through our body language.[17]

3   **Motivation**: think of a profession in which you have to sell a product or a service. Even in times of difficulty or discouragement, a motivated person will continue to try to sell; the less motivated will become demoralized.

4   **Empathy**: the ability to put yourself in the shoes of others is an extraordinarily effective quality if, for example, you manage a team or have a customer-facing role.

5   **Social skills**: are we able to interact with others in a productive and effective way?

How do companies work out/determine if we have strong emotional intelligence? They ask questions about what inspires us, the words that best describe us or about our work relationships.

During the interview, what counts is not only what we say, but also how we say it. The tone will make the music, and we can control this tone. Regardless of the work we are going to do, we'll be evaluated on the basis of the emotional intelligence we demonstrate.

Some companies, especially large ones, use other interview tools such as assessment centres: candidates are evaluated through individual or group exercises, often simulations of organizational situations that are inspired by the reality of the company to highlight the psychological and behavioural traits that they want to observe and scrutinize.

For example, regarding teamwork, the American company IBM believes that the ability to cooperate is the most important aspect when evaluating its managers; therefore, in their interviews they listen to how many times the candidates say 'I' and how many times they say 'We', how often they refer to a team game or if they seem to prefer working alone. A typical question I have asked many candidates is 'describe your achievements'. People that do not even mention 'others' e.g. their team, peers or their bosses have the prima donna syndrome. Game over.

Obviously, we will also observe the body language of the interviewer: if our interlocutor touches their chin, for example, they're making a decision; if they have their arms folded and fists closed, this shows hostility.

Now we can tackle the interview, but we need to know what kind of interview it will be.

Interview techniques

There are various interview techniques and we'll look at the characteristics of the main ones.

Interviewer (I) Good morning and welcome to our company: let's start the interview for the position you have applied for.

Candidate (C) Thank you for inviting me here, I'd like to know if . . .

(I) We ask the questions here. And we only have 30 minutes instead of an hour: there are a lot of candidates available for this job, you know? Let's start with your profile. We took the liberty of checking the information relating to the secondary school where you have – so to speak – studied. We understand that you consumed alcohol, cocaine, marijuana, right? . . . you certainly weren't a model student.

(C) Yes but, as you have certainly read, I have stated that it was my biggest moral failure. I apologized and repeated hundreds of times that I shouldn't have done it. In this regard, I'd like to add that . . .

(I) I remind you that we don't have much time and that we ask the questions: let's talk about your university choices. We acknowledge that you've attended prestigious universities, but you have taken courses in the humanities and we have a preference for technological or scientific studies. Why did you make – shall we say – such a debatable choice?

(C) To be honest, I'm . . .

(I) Sorry to interrupt you, but have you not been honest until now?

(C) Actually yes, I was just saying that, as I wanted to become a lawyer, it seemed logical to study law, don't you think? And then, as you can see, I actually became a lawyer, allowing me to defend the rights of the weakest . . .

(I) We know this story; the fact is that you've never worked in the private sector, a very important element when evaluating candidates.

(C) Sorry, but I don't remember that experience in the private sector was mentioned in the description for the position you published in the newspaper.

(I) You're not wrong, but I remind you that four months have passed since we published the advert in the newspaper. The world changes quickly and you seem anchored in old ways of thinking.

(C) Old? I was just pointing out . . .

(I) Tell me about your failure in 2000, when you lost.

(C) Certainly. I wasn't even 40 years old but that experience helped me a lot for what happened in 2008 where, as we know . . .

(I) Let's forget about it, the other candidate threw it away all by herself: let's talk about the very coveted prize you received in 2009. A lot of us have asked ourselves whether you're convinced you deserved it: after all you had just started in your new job and you and I are well aware that there are people who work all their lives to get that prize and then not only don't win it, but are not even taken into consideration for the recognition.

(C) As you know, it wasn't my decision, but a recognition given . . .

(I) You've never worked abroad.

(C) I've been abroad I think at least 50 times in the last eight years, meeting and working with important people, dealing with difficult issues . . .

(I) The fact remains that you haven't worked abroad, you've only taken numerous trips, which is very different. That brings us to the last question: do you speak a second language?

(C) No, but I think I know how to perform in the field of communication; for example, with the speech I gave in 2007, when nobody knew me . . .

(I) As far as we're concerned what counts is what one can do, not what they say or how they say it. In conclusion, during your years of studies you didn't take any courses in scientific subjects, you've never worked in the private sector and never in a fixed position abroad; you also don't speak a foreign language and have received a prize that you probably didn't deserve. Do you have any questions?

(C) When will I know how the interview went?

(I) We'll let you know in the next few days. Thank you and goodbye, Mr. Barack Obama.

The interview is obviously imaginary, held after the end of the second and final term of Barack Obama, the 44th President of the United States. Obama used light drugs, but then he apologized numerous times; he studied Law at Columbia University in New York and then at Harvard, two of the most important universities in the United States; he chose to defend the rights of the weakest, rejecting attractive positions where he would have earned much more. In 2000, he lost the Democratic Party's primary election for the office of Senator in his home state of Illinois. But he regrouped for 2005, winning the Senate elections for the same seat. In 2007 he gave a speech at the Democratic Party Congress that brought him to fame; in 2008 he surprisingly won the primaries against Hillary Clinton and, later, the historical elections against the Republican candidate McCain, becoming president of the United States at only 47 years old. In 2009, after just 10 months as president, he won the Nobel Peace Prize. The rest is history, as they say.

This 'interview' is an example of a **stress test,** a technique deliberately designed to destabilize us, to see how we respond to an interlocutor who interrupts us, who dismisses whatever results we have achieved with a shrug of the shoulders and asks irritating questions. How should we behave then? Cold blood above all, under no circumstances should we apologize because it makes us look like doormats and even less get irritated which shows we don't have self-control. It's a good idea to respond calmly, explaining our arguments with a smile, not a sneer, and looking our interlocutor in the eye. This will demonstrate that we're able to handle stress, difficult clients or colleagues, unfair criticism, comments which test the limits of tolerability. Keep in mind that this kind of interview is like a comedy in which we want to buck the part of the predestined victim, while trying to get the leading role, as a 'positive hero'.

A second type of interview, very commonly used, is the *behavioural* interview, related to the analysis of our **behaviour**. During this type of interview we'll be asked questions which aim to understand how we've acted in particular situations, to evaluate our decision-making processes and our degree of judgement and maturity. We can expect questions like:[18]

- 'What's been the most difficult moment of your career?'

- 'Can you describe a time when you've had to make a decision on the spot?'

- 'Can you describe your greatest professional success and your greatest failure? What lesson did you draw from it?'

- 'Can you describe a situation where you managed to anticipate a problem?'

- 'Can you describe a situation in which you had a problem with your boss? Or with a colleague at the same level as you (peer) or with one of your subordinates?'

- 'Can you describe a situation in which you disagreed with your boss and how you managed it?'

- 'Have you ever had to give bad news to a client?'

This type of question will give you the opportunity to excel, provided you use a well-defined scheme. This methodology is called STAR.

- **S** for Situation: in the first part of the answer, in which we have to be brief, we present the situation in which we found ourselves.

- **T** for Task: what did we have to do, what results did we have to achieve?

- **A** for Action: what did we do?

- **R** for Result: what did we achieve?

A third type of interview is the standard, classical, **evaluation,**[19] in which – as in school – scores are assigned based on pre-established criteria such as relevant experience, appropriate communication skills for the position, a positive attitude, the right level of professional or academic training. If the position requires 10 years of experience gained in a similar context, we'll know that this criterion will be decisive; if we have only five, we'll be *weak* candidates in this particular dimension, but we'll nevertheless be taken into consideration. This methodology of interviews is somewhat mechanical: it really feels like being questioned at school. As candidates, we must therefore be flexible in our responses and very specific in the examples we provide.

A more detailed version, but in some ways similar to the evaluation method, is the interview based on **skills**. In this methodology the company has defined the key skills – generally from 4 to 7 – and you'll be asked numerous questions for each of these. There may be more than one interviewer and each will have the task of evaluating a particular skill; for example, people in Human Resources will examine issues related to emotional intelligence, whether we are good managers or if we're people who work in harmony with others.

For many traits this methodology can resemble the behavioural technique: often the questions are about character, but the interviewer will want to evaluate our degree of technical competence, our level of responsibility, also including some behavioural aspects such as, for example, our ability to work in a team.

The last example actually consists of the absence of any methodology at all. In this case we are dealing with an interviewer who is not very experienced, who will simply ask rather generic questions like 'Tell me what you do'. This is a **descriptive** interview, which we'll have the opportunity to direct where we want, providing examples and following the STAR methodology described above; in this way the interlocutor will understand our capacities, both technical and behavioural, and how they adapt to the criteria established for the position.

I'm going to use a short story to look at this further. Steve Jobs, the founder of Apple, wanted to hire a CEO in 1983 and considered Pepsi Cola president John Sculley as a candidate. What did he ask him? 'Do you want to spend the rest of your life selling sugary water or do you want to have the chance to change the world?'

The most prepared interviewers will not only know the different methodologies or interview techniques, but will also be able to ask *the question that will make us reflect*. We must be ready, have that mental flexibility, also called *contextual intelligence*, to grasp the meaning of that question.

Lastly, many organizations use online tools to obtain assessments on candidates or, for senior positions, send candidates to appropriate assessment centres where they will be observed by psychologists and/or managers.

If we were to find ourselves in a situation like this, no problem: we remain calm, focused and authentic when giving the answers we feel are 'ours', not those that we think may be best.

Discovering Pinocchio

During the interviews we must above all listen carefully to what we are being told, not just try to answer the questions. We should prepare some questions and be ready: don't accept set phrases or rhetorical sentences without having specific evidence of what they refer to. Here are some classic examples:

- *At this company we have training programmes for new employees.*

   What are they? How many days? What's the company's investment in training courses? Is it possible to speak with someone who has attended these courses?

- *There are great opportunities to build a career.*

   Do they have pre-established career plans? What are they? What are the times? Is it possible to talk to someone who has been promoted recently?

- *We review salaries every year.*

   When? What was the average salary increase over the last 3 years? According to what criteria have salaries increased?

- *With the bonus you can double your salary.*
   How many people have been awarded a bonus? Is it possible to talk with someone who has achieved this goal?

- *You can work from home whenever you want.*

   Are there internal rules that regulate the application of this option? Could I meet someone who works in this way at the company and/or some people in the team?

It's not about being arrogant, but about getting clarity on fundamental points to avoid unpleasant surprises (or lies) and superficiality.

Employment contract?

We made a good first impression, we were able to respond effectively to technical questions, we demonstrated emotional intelligence and conducted an excellent interview, aware of the techniques of the interviewers and the possible 'pitfalls'. Can we expect a job offer? No, or rather, *not yet.*

The moment a company makes a decision is very complex because factors are involved that don't depend on us, but that will weigh on the final decision: does the company that wants to hire us still have the budget to do so? Have they changed their mind because maybe an open and transparent recruitment process is, after all, being sidestepped? Has hiring been put on hold due to a corporate crisis?

Furthermore, we must be aware that we all have, in the eyes of the company, at least one negative factor going against us that could affect the final choice: be aware that age, gender, geographic origin, schooling, sexual preferences, religion, our accent, how we are dressed, name and surname are elements that could somehow make the difference. During my more than twenty years' experience working abroad, for example, I have always had to deal with certain annoying clichés related to my Italian origin, from the Mafia to the mandolin, to pizza and to the shady politics.

After having 'overcome all these obstacles' and having provided the references to guarantee our seriousness and competence, if all goes well, the job offer will arrive. What should we do at this point? My opinion is that negotiating our offer is not the last action of the candidate, but the first, very important, action as an employee and will help to create our future reputation in the company. I always say that I hire missionaries, not mercenaries: people who have a higher purpose than just their wallet.

In fact, the first steps we take in the new village will be crucial to know if we'll succeed in our new job. We need the Compass and the Radar like never before.

4

Entering the Village.
How to gain trust

'Love all, trust a few, do wrong to none.'
WILLIAM SHAKESPEARE[1]

Trust, a fundamental lever in organizations

In this chapter, equipped with a fully functional Radar, we'll face a fundamental aspect of building our success in any organization: how to *gain trust*. We all know how important it is. Here it's not a matter of seeking a perfect academic definition, but rather of developing specific actions related to meeting *the locals*, our new colleagues and supervisors – an area that will be developed in the next chapter – and of fitting into a new culture and work environment. How do we build a lasting relationship of trust in this context?

I believe that *building trust* is the central issue in organizations, as well as the backbone of a person's success at work, regardless of level, sector or company.[2] I've learned that companies can *forgive* a lack of results, even if only for a limited period of time, but become merciless if the relationship of trust is broken or even if it just cracks a little. In fact – and not surprisingly – trust is also the main ingredient of any productive coaching engagement.[3]

Trust is not something that one owns but something that is built, maintained and learned. Vaclav Havel, the poet and philosopher who became President of the Czech Republic,[4] said in a speech after the Velvet Revolution: 'We must learn to trust each other'. Nelson Mandela, on the day of his inauguration as President of South Africa, after spending 26 years of his life in prison because of the local apartheid policies, of racial segregation, invited the same prison guards who had oppressed and humiliated him for years as guests of honour. The message was clear: 'If I can trust them, then we can all do it, thus starting a process of national reconciliation to rebuild the country'.[5] Great leaders don't start with strategic plans and budgets: they unite, they don't divide, and they always start by building trust. We'll do that too.

We'll start with the negotiation – and the cooperation – necessary to obtain a contract of employment, or letter of appointment, that is satisfactory both for us and for the company. Getting the long-awaited contract of employment is the last step in a selection process that can last a long time, even several months. From an *emotional* point of view, the negotiation of the employment contract represents a significant milestone: the moment when we begin to establish our reputation and the way we'll be perceived at the company. Therefore, it's a key moment to getting ourselves known, for starting to gain *trust*; a number of variables come into play, not all controllable, including three errors of cognitive bias, which is very frequent among candidates in this phase, called the *anchoring effect, halo effect* and *ladder effect.*

In the second part of the chapter, we'll deal with how to build a relationship of trust with the company or organization we are going to join. I'm referring not only to the technical aspects of a position but to a much deeper and longer-lasting aspect. Whether it's a job in a big company or a fruit and vegetable shop around the corner, there are, and there always will be, some fundamental ingredients to establish the relationship of trust, a *sine qua non* condition to prevent failure. I will describe them one by one, with true stories, and then I will unveil a *magic formula*. I'm not joking: there is a real mathematical formula that can help us to decipher, understand and implement a plan to gain trust, the basic element for a successful professional or personal relationship.

I'm convinced that trust is the most important indicator of the quality of relationships between people, between groups of people or between a person and an organization. We must also be aware that trust will always be conditional, we'll never have a 'blank cheque', unlimited credit, and that's a good thing. We've learned from history what happens when a nation or organization blindly trusts only one person, it usually ends badly. If you're not able to gauge the degree of trust that exists in an organization, observe the degree of control. The more extensive and detailed the procedures and the control manuals, the lower the degree of trust that exists and the higher the dis-functionality of the overall social system. Unconditional trust for a leader coupled with blind obedience from followers is a recipe for disaster: we have learned that from history, haven't we?

Negotiation of the contract

The interviews are over, the references have been verified, we have the feeling that the interviews were positive. The following days alternate between anxiety and contentment. We don't say anything just in case. Then finally the good news arrives, by phone, text message or email: they've decided to offer – just us – the position. A piece of advice, use caution: all this doesn't constitute a work contract *yet* and only a proper document duly signed by the company has legal value; so we'll need to keep the champagne on ice for the moment. When the draft contract is sent to us, we need to read it carefully, not just once, at least three times. If you have another job, don't resign immediately: you need to wait; there are still a few steps to go.

In particular, we have three aspects to consider during the negotiation phase: the information available to make the best decision, the right timing and finally the modalities, the *tone* in which we do it. *Est modus in rebus*: there is a method in all things, our ancestors wrote. They were right.

Contract: salary and other factors

Let's think about what we did the last time we bought a car, rented a house or decided to take a trip: very quickly we became experts in that field. We all become *researchers*, we ask friends and acquaintances questions, talk to specialists, spend hours on the internet, read specialized magazines.

We now have to apply this methodology to get the best conditions. The company will often try to save money, even more so during times of crisis, while we'll try to get the maximum possible. The dancing begins and we'll need to prove we are experienced dancers, without treading on the toes of those we are dancing with, trying to coordinate our movements and to collaborate.

It is not easy to obtain exact information on salaries, even if some organizations share them online, such as the United Nations.[6] As usual, the internet provides us with useful information. For example for professions or sectors, keeping in mind, as we well know, that some sectors pay better than others on average: i.e. the financial sector traditionally pays better than the tourism sector.

Another inexhaustible source of information is www.glassdoor.com, where data on companies are provided anonymously by those who work there (the same principle as TripAdvisor, applied to businesses); on this platform, candidates and working people freely express their opinions, adding the most positive or negative aspects. Stories about interviews, the list of questions that are asked and the things that companies expect are particularly amusing. We can select the organizations we are interested in and receive a weekly email with various comments, both from candidates and employees.

If we're interested in working in the United States, we could consult www.salary.com, www.salaryexpert.com, for medium-high levels, or www.jobstar.com, a veritable mine of information. With a simple search on Google for 'Jobs in London', we would discover dozens of web pages to find work in London (sites like www.careerbuilder.co.uk/london) or to understand how much you can earn in the British capital (for example www.reed.co.uk/average-salary). In addition, dozens of new 'specialized' web pages are created every month for professions or sectors, almost all available for free with data that is continuously updated. A further step is to carry out *targeted personal* searches. For example, we can check if any of our LinkedIn contacts is working for the company that offered us the job and – very politely and delicately – ask for 10 minutes of their time to find out the information we need.

As candidates who have reached the final phase we must avoid three typical mistakes: the *anchoring effect, the halo effect* and the *ladder effect.* Let's look at them one by one.

- **Anchoring effect**: *anchoring* indicates a cognitive bias that leads us to decide on the basis of what we consider to be the only relevant information.[7] In my professional experience

I've noticed that many candidates have a number, a fixed
figure in their head: for example, a candidate who earns GBP
30,000 a year[8] has the sole objective of obtaining a salary of
36,000. Even if they succeed – and I really hope they do – this
candidate should also consider other aspects: the new
company may not offer insurance cover or doesn't have a
canteen, may only offer two weeks of holidays instead of five
or may not give any pay rises for the next three years. Or
again, the workplace may be at a considerable distance from
home: our time has an immense value that we must keep in
mind and evaluate accordingly. Anchoring on a figure set
subjectively by us can turn out to be a false objective. In fact,
as noted above, even if the salary proposed is higher in terms
of an absolute figure, we might find ourselves with worse
conditions. We must therefore make an overall assessment of
what is offered to us, including factors that are not easily
calculated in economic terms. We must also understand how
much room for negotiation we have. If our supervisor earns
GBP 40,000 per year and our colleagues between 25,000 and
32,000, we'll know what the available pay band will be and
we'll know our manoeuvring limits. The last aspect to be
evaluated is purchasing power which, as we well know, varies
according to the place. GBP 36,000 a year is a low salary in
London, but it would have a different impact, for example, in a
small town in Scotland. A colleague of mine has moved from
Geneva, one of the five most expensive cities in the world, to
go to work in South Africa, one of the least expensive
countries; initially stunned to see that in his new job he
earned about half in absolute terms, within a short time he
realized that his economic conditions had actually improved.
To get a better idea of the concept of purchasing power, we

can consider the so-called Big Mac index,[9] that is to say an indicator that provides a guide to the purchasing power in various countries. Also the consulting firm Mercer provides updated and useful information to help understand the differentials of cost and purchasing power between various nations.[10]

- **Halo effect.** The second mistake to avoid is the *halo effect*.[11] The term was coined by the psychologist Edward Thorndike in the 1920s. Basically this is an effect related to the first impression that leads us to suppose that a person or an organization that possesses a certain characteristic must automatically possess other similar ones. Is the candidate friendly and brilliant? They must also be intelligent as well as a great worker. If we want to work for a prestigious company, we deduce that our work will have to be equally prestigious. Are we really sure? As mentioned in the previous chapters, a company with great prestige and reputation manages to attract the best candidates, but the high-sounding name may be misleading. External reputation and internal substance are two different things.

- **Ladder effect.** The third error, the *ladder effect*, is linked to a framework that we are commonly unaware of. This derives from the *ladder of inference* model,[12] conceived by one of the great masters of management, Chris Argyris, one of my heroes. Our mental frame of mind leads us to select information among the many available; this is interpreted according to our reference scheme, from which we draw conclusions, our interpretative key and then act accordingly. In other words, *we quickly climb the ladder*, without having analysed the problem in depth, hostages of the mental model that we have unconsciously developed. Instead, we should listen to our reactions, pay attention to others and *descend the rungs of the ladder to understand what led us to draw certain conclusions.* Did we ignore obvious data? Did we give weight to just one piece of information? Do you remember the film 'The Sixth Sense'[13]? Only at the end is the spectator able to 'reread' the film and the full meaning of the story.

As candidates, therefore, in this delicate and important final phase, we must avoid the *anchoring, halo* and *ladder* effects and obtain information to evaluate the job offer in a broader context: never forget that salary is a relative figure, calculated according to purchasing power: while important, it shouldn't be the only factor on which to base our decision.

Timing and methods

The selection process is in some ways similar to a long, prudent, intelligent and respectful courtship in which you can't make hasty or wrong moves. After an initial phase of curiosity, we move onto mutual interest, to get to the phase of knowledge, then to that of 'I like them' and finally to the final phase, in which – hopefully – the interests of the company converge with those of the candidate. As part of my professional activity I have negotiated more than 1,000 job offers in numerous countries and with people with different experiences: from postgraduates without experience to former prime ministers. The following suggestions apply to all.

Our golden rule must be to let the company speak first about money. We'll then be asked this question: 'What are your salary expectations?' Being a question we must respond to, we can consider three answers, presented in order of preference.

- 'Since you are the experts in terms of both the market and your company, I imagine that you have in mind the remuneration bracket for such an important job: could you please indicate what it is?'

- 'My compensation is x, to which y must be added; so, if I had the opportunity to work with you, I think it's realistic to expect an overall improvement of z ...'

- 'I thought about an overall salary of between 35,000 and 38,000 per year, but I would like some further details: do you have an annual salary review, what could I expect in the future in terms of pay rises, what perks do you offer, for example medical insurance or loans at a subsidized rate?'[14]

The interviewer could be pretty tight-fisted and say: 'In the event of equal professional qualifications, we'll choose the least expensive candidate'. How do we respond? It happened to me: I replied that it was a legitimate choice but, given the importance of the position, had it depended on me, I would have hired the most qualified candidate, not the least expensive candidate. They acknowledged I was right. And they offered the job to the other candidate.

Other factors that will influence the choice are the internal rules and the corporate culture. First of all, some companies have no problem negotiating: for example, family businesses, where the owner makes the decision, or the commercial banks, where they almost seem to expect that a candidate will negotiate hard. Other organizations, on the contrary, just can't do it, like public administration, where salaries are often established by law.

Another factor: if we look for a job when we don't have one already, we'll be in a condition of relative weakness unless we already have a job offer, in writing, from another company. I caution you against lying; of the various times when the candidate told me that they had another offer in hand, only 20 per cent of the time did this turn out to be true. My advice is not to bluff, but always to be honest.

And again: if they contacted us, you'll be in a position of relative strength. Once I was contacted directly by a company because a former colleague had mentioned my name. During the interviews they told me directly that they were in the middle of an emergency, and were in a hurry because the internal candidate had resigned and the external candidate had changed his mind at the last minute for family reasons. I was, therefore, in a position of relative bargaining power; the company at that time had no viable alternatives available. Result? I asked for and got 20 per cent more than I had initially indicated. I did nothing more than apply the famous *rule of the combinations of speed, cost and quality.* If we want to obtain something quickly and not pay very much, it can't have quality; if we want quality and cheap, it can't be quick; if we want speed and quality, it can't be cheap. The same principle applies to the selection of candidates and could be a point to our advantage: we also need information in these situations.

The list of elements to consider in order to accept a job is long, but – careful – no contract in the world will provide us with the most important and significant information, without which any other condition is irrelevant. How much will we learn? Will we become more qualified professionals? Will we be able to increase our *value,* not only professionally but also humanly? We need to become *learning animals,*[15] as they say at Google,[16] and have an inner passion that ignores any financial or contractual considerations. Motivations must be intrinsic, deeply part of what we are and do.

Having said that, to consider a job offer we must remember the values that we believe in, as we saw in the first chapter. I recommend a useful exercise: list and rate each aspect on the basis of two elements: how important it is for us and our degree of satisfaction in relation to what is offered, for example on a scale between 1 and 5. We can add all the elements that interest us, some are easily quantifiable (salary), others less so, such as the degree of autonomy and flexibility that we'll have in our work. The visualization of this analysis will give us very good information on the correctness of our choice, provided that we don't lose sight of the passion we have and what we'll learn from doing a certain job.

Element to consider	Importance to us	Satisfaction
Salary		
Benefit		
Holidays		
Training courses/learning		
International environment		
Title and position		
Duration of the contract		

Let me share a little secret: every time I accepted a role I have asked myself this question: Would I become a better professional and a better person in a four-year timeframe? I fast-forward four years in my head and try to answer this question and visualize what my next job could be. What would I be able to learn? Which possibilities do I have to improve? Do I have a manager/team/peers who I can learn from? Once I take the decision to accept the role I stick to my 4-year plan and then leave if the learning-journey is over or stay if there are other opportunities. I do not have 'money' on my mind as that can derail my decision-making. Money is for careers what sex is for relationships. Exciting, yes. But it does derail and cloud judgement and rational decision-making.

I think, however, that it's simplistic to think of the negotiation as a zero-sum game, where one person wins and one loses. If we have decided to accept the job offer, we must move from negotiation to cooperation, a strategy that is generally much more effective than a *confrontational approach.*[17] I suggest writing, or saying, to your future boss something like this:

> *Dear Sir/Madam . . .,*
>
> *Thank you very much for your job offer: it is an honour and a privilege for me to become part of your prestigious organization.*
>
> *I have read your proposal carefully and I am grateful for the trust you have placed in me. Before signing the employment contract, I would be grateful for your opinion and advice on how to resolve certain issues related to the document. I assure you that I am flattered by the offer and that I cannot wait to start work as soon as these issues are resolved.*

The key phrase is *'your opinion and advice'*. This approach always works: the interlocutor wants to 'close' and will appreciate being part of the solution; with a pinch of humility, we'll try to gain an improvement on certain aspects related to the contract. If we were to say 'I'd like a higher salary' they'll respond with a firm and polite refusal, so we'll have to take a different approach, for example by saying 'If I were to stay in my current job, they would give me an increase in three months of between 3 and 4 per cent: I would very much appreciate it if the salary offered could be reviewed in light of this information'. Specific, factual, not emotional, clear. To finish with the comparison of courtship, if we've decided to *get married* it's not worth fighting over who will pay for the confetti.

This approach, the transition from negotiation to cooperation in the final stages, always works, I can assure you. Stephen Covey[18] says it encourages us to think about *win-win* situations where there are no winners and losers, but where everyone can gain something. By behaving in this way, we'll start to work with an ally, the person who has actively contributed to the solution of a problem and we'll begin to develop a reputation as a serious, firm, courteous, intellectually honest person.

If the conditions of the initial offer don't improve with the negotiation, we'll have to take stock and make a reasoned choice also considering the modalities and the reasons for the refusal. In my experience, more than 90 per cent of the proposals are accepted and, in the end, there is almost always a halfway point between the company and the candidate.

However, remember that only when we have the contract signed can we celebrate. As soon as we start the new job, we'll invite the person who has dedicated their time and their help for a coffee, and we'll thank them sincerely: they will become a precious ally.

First, however, we must bring things to an end with our organization, the job, the colleagues whom we have worked with for such a long time. We must do it with kindness, class, manners and respect. Time is a gentleman, never burn bridges or relationships built up over the years, even if it's impossible to maintain professional or personal relationships with everyone. We write the letter of resignation adding warm thanks to the colleagues and the boss, without artificial rhetoric, or worse, petty revenge. Sure, some decide to leave loaded with revenge, some even post their moment of resignation on YouTube and, in exchange for a few days of visibility, they damage their careers for good.[19] Let's leave with dignity, with our head held high, working late on the last day, thanking everyone, shaking hands, with smiles and sincerity. I always find it surprising how some people, perhaps after years of hard work, do little or nothing in the final weeks, damaging a flawless reputation. If we have enemies, let's remember that the best revenge is proving we are respectable people, always: we'll never lower ourselves to the vulgar level of those who hurt us. I speak from experience: professional life is a bit like a marathon; 42 kilometres is a long distance; there's no point barging our way through with a sprint, in every sense. Michelle Obama once said 'When they go low, we stay high'. I have applied this rule many times: the best revenge is deciding not to take any as you are in a different space and mindset.

Building trust in organizations

Having signed the contract, we now have a new job. We are rightly satisfied and happy. Now we want to start well[20] in our new job and the first question we ask is: *'How can I gain the trust I need?'*

Good news: if they offered us a job, they've already started to trust us. Like when we get married: we believe in good faith in our choice and we'll give everything we've got to make it work. So we start off from a good foundation but we don't have unlimited credit and it's better that way: trust yes, but not 'blind trust' no matter what. Starting with the 'magic formula' described in the book *The Trusted Advisor*[21] by David Maister, I propose, based on my experience, some instructions for use; as if it were a cooking recipe I will list the ingredients, including those not to be used, and I will add some components.

At this point, after internalizing the formula, we'll be able to start the new job.

Credibility and reliability

According to Giulio Gili,[22] credibility has a *cognitive root*, as a skill linked to qualifications denoting an expert, and an *ethical-normative root*, i.e. the sharing of perceived values, such as integrity. As candidates and as employees we must continually demonstrate both our technical knowledge and irreproachable ethical behaviour.

The concept of loyalty often assumes a 'practical' meaning: a loyal person is generally also valued as very *reliable*.

Gianluigi Buffon, legendary goalkeeper for Juventus and the Italian national team for more than 20 years. Steven Gerrard, Liverpool's iconic symbol for 17 years. Ryan Giggs, 24 extraordinary years at Manchester United. All great champions, idols to their respective fans, respected by players and fans from opposing teams.

Now let's consider other players who, on the contrary, change team almost every year, who behave terribly at times, have a great deal of talent that is seen in flashes but don't know how to get the most from what they have. If we were the Chairman of a football club and we could *sign* (recruit) one of these players, who would we want on our team, who would we offer the job to? How would we rate their loyalty and reliability? What do we think of a player, or candidate, who has changed team almost every year? These cases make it clear, for example, that talent is only one factor which influences a company's willingness to offer someone a job. Other elements are considered to be more relevant not only for the selection of candidates but also in the development of careers, a topic that we'll address in depth in the following chapters.

Reliability and loyalty are qualities which are much more appreciated than having perhaps great talent but being perceived as mercenaries or not loyal to the badge, be it at a football team or an organization. When we go to *play* for a team, do we want to be considered as one of the players from the first or second group? The same criteria that we use as fans are used by companies. Easy, right?

Proximity

The organization Missionaries of Charity,[23] founded in 1950 by the winner of the Nobel Peace Prize in 1979, Mother Teresa of Calcutta, with offices in more than 130 countries, and more than 4,000 employees, aims to be at the complete service of the poorest of the poor: refugees, AIDS patients, former prostitutes, abandoned elderly people, the disabled, the destitute, the rejects of a society that has no consideration for those who are weak, without protection. The employees of the organization work for free, operating in the field, living humbly alongside the people in need, forgotten by everyone, *making a moral choice before a strategic one.*

George W. Bush, President of the United States at the time of Hurricane Katrina, which hit the south of the United States on 28 August 2005, bringing the entire city of New Orleans to its knees, was on holiday at the time of the catastrophe, as were the top people in his administration. Bush got off the plane in Washington with his dog in his arms only after three days, just flying over the areas hit by the hurricane. This image caused irreparable political damage and deeply marked the collective imagination of the traumatized nation. Bush's indifference, mixed with a sense of total incompetence and improvization in the management of the crisis, caused his presidency to reach rock bottom: After 11 September, his approval rating had reached more than 90 per cent; after Hurricane Katrina this statistic collapsed to less than 40 per cent. One in two Americans had changed their mind and probably didn't vote for the Republicans in the next election, paving the way for the historic election victory of Barack Obama in 2008. The lesson does not seem to have been understood by Donald Trump, 45th President of the United States. After natural disasters, floods and storms in Texas, Louisiana and Puerto Rico,

Donald Trump decided to enjoy a day playing golf [24] and, generously, he dedicated the tournament trophy to the people who fought to survive, underlining how the situation was under control.

Here we also have two different stories. The presence of Mother Teresa, always alongside the impoverished, and the embarrassing absence of Bush and Trump or so many politicians when we need them – as opposed to when there are cameras present or to vote – are indicative. 'Show up', the Americans say: we must be present.

I'm not talking about working at the office until late every day. On the contrary, I believe that always spending 10–12 hours a day at the office is wrong and counter-productive on so many levels. We simply have to *be there*, where and when we're needed. If we want to be doctors, this can mean almost total availability; if we are teachers, we should be available when the children are at school; if we're managers, when important decisions are made. And for all the people who work with us, proximity is not just physical presence: it can take on the moral connotation of humility.

Proximity and humility count for far more than we can imagine. In 1990 I worked in Milan: one of the departments absolutely had to finish some tedious and repetitive administrative work by the end of the year. It was 30 December and we were seriously late; we were never going to get it done. The general manager, who had started by doing exactly that kind of work 25 years earlier, decided to roll up his sleeves and get to work alongside the employees, to lend a helping hand. We all followed him. It was 14:00; at 20:00 we ordered pizzas for everyone; at 7 in the morning the cappuccinos arrived, just when we had finished, exhausted. I still remember that night spent at the office, the proximity established at that moment made it clear to everyone that the general manager was still humble, one of us. Unforgettable, for everyone.

Conflict of interest and impartiality

According to the Wikipedia definition, a conflict of interest[25] is 'a situation that occurs when a high decision-making responsibility is entrusted to a person who has economic, personal or professional interests in conflict with the impartiality required by such responsibility'. In establishing a relationship of trust, the *perception* that there is, or may be, a conflict of interest will come into play. We must be vigilant and careful that this does not happen and avoid any shadow of a doubt that may damage us.

Paul Wolfowitz[26] was named President of the World Bank in 2005 by US President George W. Bush, a controversial appointment due to the role that Wolfowitz had had in the US entry into Iraq. He was forced to resign following an increase in salary granted to his partner in spite of the internal rules of the World Bank. The motivation for the dismissal was expressed clearly by the board of directors: 'Paul Wolfowitz didn't accept the rules on conflict of interest, trying to negotiate for himself a solution which was different from those he would have applied to any other employee of the organization for which he was selected as President'. Words as heavy as stones, the final epitaph of a career.

The lesson we've learned from our own experience is that conflict of interest, or the lack of impartiality that it produces even when only perceived, causes a loss of credibility and authority, understood in the deepest meaning of moral integrity.

Arrogance, hubris

When you think about it, history, literature and the news have told us the stories of numerous characters who become victims of their hubris and who then disappear into thin air without too much ceremony or regret.

Abraham Lincoln, the 16th American president, said that if you want to test a man's character, give him power. Many people decide to misuse power in an arrogant fashion. Better not to join them, as the queue is quite long.

Small secret: very often companies don't finalize a job offer to candidates, after observing how they behaved (badly) with the personal assistant and with the person at the reception desk, or how they answered the phone or an email.

Results and expectations

At the beginning of this chapter we talked about how to build trust. Trust is not given unconditionally: it is a balanced judgement between expectations created and results.

Felipe Scolari seemed to be the happiest and luckiest man in the world: after a successful career as a football coach, he'd already won the World Cup in 2002 with Brazil and was chosen again to lead the team for Brazil 2014. The tournament began, with plenty of controversy over the delays and huge expenses incurred to host the World Cup, but these problems were partly forgotten because Brazil, according to all the expectations, was set to win its fifth World Cup. Brazil got through to the semi-finals, not without a few scares, for a match with Germany, a game that will go down in history not just because of soccer but for the collective drama of a nation. The final result was a humiliating 7 to 1 in favour of Germany: Brazilian players left the game in tears, in disbelief, in shock. The President of Brazil made a speech on national TV to console citizens; some of them took their own life. Two days later a soulless Brazil lost the final for the 3rd place but at that point nobody cared any more. Felipe Scolari made a quick appearance in the pressroom, mumbled a few words, and vanished. Since then he has gone off the radar: he started to manage again at a mid-level club, Grêmio in Porto Alegre, then he went to manage in China, where he was buried by an avalanche of unfulfilled expectations.

When starting a new job there will always be expectations to face, even if we don't have to make promises or proclamations. The results obtained by our predecessor will always be compared to our performance when we start work at a company. Some expectations will be explicit, such as 'We must make a profit of at least …'; others will be more nuanced, if not hidden from us. Our results will always be evaluated in relation to the created or presumed expectations. It's always better to under-promise and over-deliver: failing to understand this is a classic error by people with little experience who tend to underestimate or have no idea about the internal difficulties of a company.

What should we do? I think the best thing is just to promise serious commitment and, as we say, 'fly under the radar', avoiding any announcement or promise … just work hard. Many agree that among the best political speeches ever made, along with that of Martin Luther King 'I have a dream' given in 1963 in Washington is the first speech given to the British Parliament by Winston Churchill on 13 May 1940, in the middle of the Second World War: '[…] I have nothing to offer but blood, toil, tears and sweat.'[27] What did he ask for? Unity among all the political forces, which he obtained. What did he want? Victory, to stop Nazism defined, rightly, as a monstrous tyranny.[28] Another leadership lesson from one of the greatest statesmen ever.

The formula of trust

So now we come to the mathematical formula that we must always keep in mind to win the trust of those around us. Before we look at the formula we need to bear in mind that to gain trust we need to be authentic and to have empathy, genuine interest in others and their feelings.

The trust we'll be able to gain is linked to the sum of our credibility, reliability and proximity. This capital represents our *reputation*, that is *what is said of us when we are not present*.

Our reputation will then be divided by the sum of conflict of interest and by arrogance or hubris. The result will then be multiplied by the difference between the results we have to achieve, and the expectations we must limit. The *ingredients* I've added are arrogance, results and expectations.

$$\frac{(CREDIBILITY + RELIABILITY + PROXIMITY)}{(CONFLICT\ OF\ INTEREST + ARROGANCE)} \times (Results - expectations) = TRUST$$

Figure 4.1 *Trust formula.*

5

Meeting the locals. Understanding the rules of the game

'Seek first to understand, then to be understood[1].'
STEPHEN R. COVEY

Welcome to the jungle

We are now facing a very important issue: once we enter the organization we are going to work for, who can we trust? Before we can respond we'll first have to get to know the people who are part of it. I'll introduce you to the types of individuals we'll meet and analyse how to manage the relationship with new colleagues. We'll enter a 'zoo' where we'll have to be careful to avoid dangerous animals and to ally ourselves with the 'right' animals. *Welcome to the jungle.*

In December 1642, the Dutch captain Abel Tasman led an expedition of two ships exploring the Indian Ocean and Oceania. They arrived in the northern part of New Zealand, the first Europeans to see the coastline, and decided to start exploring the bay in front of where they had docked. The men sent by the captain returned after a few hours, followed by natives who, from their canoes, began to produce guttural sounds and to play a wind instrument, a ritual which was incomprehensible to the Europeans. The Dutch also sounded their trumpets and the next morning tried to take part in an exchange of objects. All this made them assume that they were friendly practices and attempts to approach; Captain Tasman himself wrote in his logbook: 'These people, the locals, just seem to want to make friends'. A few hours later, however, the natives approached the Dutch ships with numerous canoes and attacked them, killing four sailors on board a small boat. From the two large ships they opened fire against the locals, who retreated towards the beach. Captain Abel Tasman decided to set sail immediately; that same evening he wrote in his logbook that in that inhospitable place the inhabitants were to be considered enemies. He called the place *Murderers Bay*[2] and no European set foot in New Zealand until 1769, with Captain Cook's famous expedition.

When we 'arrive at our destination', in the organization that best reflects our values, we must avoid the experience of Captain Tasman, who knew nothing about the place he had arrived in, didn't know the language, local customs or rules of the game, and could not communicate in any way. Tasman went from optimism (they want to be friends) to escape (they are enemies), losing four men. We must be able to find ourselves in much better conditions.

In the fourth chapter we learned how to gain trust, the most important ingredient for success. This chapter answers, now, two fundamental questions allowing us to start – and continue – our career successfully:

The first question is: *what are the most important qualities we should use when we start a new job?* Demonstrate how good we are from the moment we arrive? Talk about our achievements? Work 12 hours a day and go to the office even on Saturday and Sunday? Offer gifts to our new colleagues? Be friendly? Dress smartly? Be the first to answer questions? Make it known that we've already understood everything? None of this. Most importantly, we must remember the names of the people we meet, listen carefully, ask questions, be aware and handle with compassion and respect the emotions that always arise between people.

The second question is: *how do we understand the rules of the game, discover who we can trust?* We'll analyse people's behaviour based on two characteristics: their *political intelligence* and their propensity to act according to a *personal-individual* or *organizational* agenda.

Remember the names of the people we meet

The wonderful film *Invictus*, released in 2009 and directed by Clint Eastwood, tells the story of how Nelson Mandela – masterfully played by Morgan Freeman – used the South African national rugby team, called the *Springboks*[3], to unite a divided nation after years of apartheid and racism. During a match against England in 1993, Mandela realized that many of his fellow blacks were cheering against their national team because all the players on the pitch were white: the team didn't represent them. When Mandela became President of South Africa in 1994, he met the Captain of the Springboks, François Pienaar (played in the film by Matt Damon), asked him to read the poem *Invictus*[4], which Mandela himself used to read to other prisoners during his period of imprisonment at Robben Island, and convinced Pienaar that a victory at the Rugby World Cup – which would take place the following year in South Africa – could unify a still deeply divided nation. At that time the Springboks were only ninth in the world rugby rankings and the All Blacks, the famous team from New Zealand, were the big favourites to lift the trophy. Before the world cup, Mandela went to the team's training sessions and, during the car trip, he memorized all the names of the players. When Pienaar offered to introduce the team to him, Mandela approached each player on his own and, shaking their hand and looking into their eyes, he pronounced their name and surname. On 24 June 1995, South Africa won in the final against the All Blacks, in what is still remembered as an unforgettable match, becoming a part of rugby legend.

A small story, which involves me: when I was living in Washington, in 1996, a dear friend, Roberto, got me a front row ticket with an unlikely press pass, to see a basketball game, the Washington Bullets against the Chicago Bulls. There were 20,000 people there to watch the world-famous Michael Jordan, a legend rather than a player. A few minutes before the game started, the President of the United States arrived, Bill Clinton; he was just a few metres away from me, escorted by a dozen secret service agents. At the end of the first half, I asked one of the agents if I could say hello and, to my great surprise, I was given 10 seconds. I greeted the President, who asked me: 'Where do you come from and what's your name?' I replied: 'Paolo, I am Italian'; Clinton replied: 'Oh, Italy! Wonderful country'. I shook his hand and half-stunned with emotion, I walked away. At the end of the game, using my press pass badge, I sneaked into the locker room to see Michael Jordan up close. It was simply impossible even to try, he was completely surrounded by cameramen and reporters. Suddenly a secret service agent entered the locker room and shouted: 'All quiet and move, the President will be here in a minute'. I made myself small, I was practically through the exit door. Everyone remained silent, Clinton entered the locker room, he saw me and said, 'Hello Paolo, how are you?' Everyone wondered who I was and I don't think I've ever been so close to having a heart attack in my life.

What did I learn from this experience? The first thing is that in the United States, before 11 September 2001, it was easier to approach the President than a famous basketball player. The second thing I understood was the emotion you get when someone, especially if they're more important than you, remembers your name.

Let's therefore remember that it must be our duty to learn all the names of the people we meet when we start a new job. We're not the President of the United States, of course, but remembering the names of our colleagues will be appreciated as an act of respect and consideration, with an immense emotional value. If we've only learned the names of the important people, but not those of the people who hold less relevant positions, we should reconsider our approach and perhaps shake hands with the doorman we've seen every day for years, ask their name and offer our apologies, with a smile.

Ability to listen

When my daughter Sadika was about four years old she got angry with me: after telling me what she had done during the day, at the end, raising her voice, she said to me: 'Dad, now repeat to me what I told you!' She realized that I hadn't stopped reading the paper I had in my hands and glancing at the messages on my phone. Rightly offended by my lack of attention, she had challenged me. She was less than a metre tall, weighed less than 20 kilos, but her words weighed a ton. I apologized and, since then, I try to listen to her carefully or I ask her for a moment to finish what I'm doing, before giving her my attention. We decided that when we realize that someone in the family is not listening we say 'Rabbit', a code word to get us to listen again. Rabbits have long ears and, in my daughter's expert opinion, they hear very well. I think she's right and it works.

How often do we pretend to listen? Just to give an example: we're talking to a person and we receive a phone call; after a few minutes we resume the conversation and our interlocutor asks us: 'Where were we?' Panic: we have absolutely no idea what we were talking about, for the simple reason that we were not listening. This is level 1 of listening.[5]

We're in a business meeting and we know that sooner or later it'll be our turn to talk. We listen out for the best moment to intervene, looking for a phrase or a response that will make a good impression on those present. It's a kind of internal listening, directed at ourselves. While we pay attention to the words of the people around us, we think about how to apply them to our situation and what feelings and judgements we have in relation to what has been said; we answer according to our canons. We have thousands of examples of this kind before our eyes, thanks to the famous talk show format used on TV, which can literally be interpreted as *show yourself while talking*. In these situations, people don't listen to the speaker to have a conversation, but rather intervene to prevail over others. This is level 2 of listening.

The third level of listening is the one in which we are focused on listening to the person who is speaking to us, without interrupting or making judgements. We pay attention to the words, but also to the tone, the speed, the feelings expressed. We're at ease even if there are long silences, we dedicate our unconditional interest, there are no interruptions, we turn our mobile phone off, mouth closed, maintaining eye contact with the person speaking to us.

The fourth level of listening is the one in which we have a global, broader vision. We observe the body language of the speaker, mood changes, breathing, pupil dilation, energy, hands. We pay attention not only to the words and pauses but also to what is not being said, to unexpressed feelings, to looks, to the tone, breathing. We keep ourselves at a respectful distance, we don't interrupt to give advice, we listen by offering our own body language to inspire trust, respect, attention, but not judgement. We show compassion and respect spaces, autonomy. We are not therapists, we're not in a coaching session, we are simply listening unconditionally, without distractions. The Chinese ideogram for the word 'listen' is made up of many different parts and translates like this: *'I give you my ears, my eyes, my undivided attention and my heart'*; Listening carefully becomes, therefore, a profound act of total respect.

I'm convinced that we all have the ability to listen at the third and fourth levels.[6] Let's go back to the moment we met the person we fell in love with, to whom we gave our full attention, to our ability to listen to spoken and unspoken words. Or think about the attention we give our children. So, when we enter an organization we must be at least at level 3: listen, prepared to *understand before being understood*. If every time we met someone we gave them our unconditional attention even for only four minutes, our life would change radically[7]. We live in the era of distractions, noise, interruptions, a thousand messages, a thousand digital friends that we have never met or even heard before. We have lost the ability to listen, but we know that it's possible to re-acquire it. As the American writer Wilson Mizner said[8], 'A good listener is not only popular everywhere, but after a while, he knows something'.

Asking questions to learn

It's often said that, during the first three months of starting a new job, we are *on honeymoon* with the organization we're a part of. It's a time[9] when we'll have plenty of opportunities to ask questions, some of them a little naive, and we'll be forgiven with benevolent indulgence even when they're not particularly intelligent. In short, a wonderful opportunity to learn and to listen. There are millions of questions we can ask: the best way to navigate is, in my opinion, catalogue them into two types, as described in one of my favourite books: *Change your questions, change your life*, by Marilee Adams.[10] There are questions asked with the intention of judging, and questions asked to learn. If we behave *like judges*, with inquisitorial questions – 'Why do you do that?', 'How come ...', 'Whose fault is it ...' – we'll probably receive defensive answers that will not help us understand or establish relationships of trust.

I had a boss who told me that, every morning at breakfast before going to the office, he was thinking about the problems he had observed during the previous day by asking himself the question: 'Who should I blame?' He arrived at the office and every single day summoned 2 or 3 unfortunate subordinates. You can imagine how much fun it was to work with a person like that, unable to say thank you but very good at criticizing in a disconcerting way. At first he made me angry, then I started to feel sincere tenderness and sadness for him. I believe that he never understood the difference between being demanding – which is a legitimate prerogative of a Leader – with being demeaning – which is a horrible personal trait that does not belong to Leadership.

However, we have a better alternative. By asking open questions, denoting someone who genuinely wants to learn, such as: 'What are the facts, the data ...', 'What can be improved?', 'How can I help you?', 'Explain your point of view?', 'Did we miss an opportunity?' 'What have we learned' we'll open doors and possibilities that initially seemed impossible. Regardless of the role, everyone is generally proud of the work they do and will tell us with pride about their passions, expectations, hopes, frustrations. Asking the right questions is a key to being in tune with them; to introduce a question with the phrase: 'I need your help' or: 'I am interested in your opinion about ...' opens the space to conversation, if we interact with sincerity. Conversation is a word that derives from the Latin, composed of the particle *cum*, which means 'together' and the verb *versare*, which means 'to go'. Conversation means, therefore, going together in the same direction. I believe that asking the right question is one of the most important, yet under-rated, skills we can have. If you don't know which question to choose, start by asking 'What do you think?' by paying attention to the tone you use. Every person will immediately understand if it is a sarcastic question or a genuine one seeking to understand the person in front of you.

Remember the names of the people we meet, listen carefully, ask the right questions like people who want to learn. Here are three key points to start well in a new job, to build the foundations for positive coexistence.

Using emotions to build positive relationships

The book *Beyond Reason: Using Emotions as You Negotiate* by Roger Fisher and Daniel Shapiro[11] is – rightly – considered a kind of sacred text for those involved in diplomacy, difficult negotiations, full of emotions. I had the opportunity to put it into practice at a very tough moment of my career: I had to manage the closure of an office of 20 people in a country in Africa where a job represented much more than a salary, as it was the difference between providing a future or not for your family in an economic context without hope for better alternatives. I didn't know what to do: I was rationally aware that closing that office was a decision that was understandable and justified by the numbers, but people are not numbers. I felt very strong emotions which had to be processed and managed; I was sick at the thought of communicating to those people – whom I had never seen in my life, in a country which I had never been to before – that they would lose their jobs. What could I have done? I decided to apply the rules of Fisher and Shapiro: the first step is to understand the point of view of others. It's not just a matter of courtesy, though useful; it is literally to put yourself in the shoes of others, to listen to their opinion – which does not mean to agree with them – and to communicate that we have understood, not only with the head but also with the heart, through our words and our actions.

During the first two days, after communicating the bad news that the office would be closed within three months, I listened to all the people individually to understand their point of view, their reasons. It was certainly no fun, but it wasn't difficult to find objective merit to their arguments, to discover details and new data, not considered by those who had made the decision in the space of an hour, 6,000 km away. At the same time I looked for authentic, real affinities. We all have affinities with others; we discover them every day: sometimes we meet strangers on a train and after a few minutes we discover that we grew up in the same city, we studied in the same university, we support the same team, we have children of the same age. Everyone, always, instinctively seeks things in common. If we talk about the weather, traffic, television programmes, restaurants, we already know that these conversations will maintain an emotional distance between people. Family, emotions, dreams, hopes, ideas are topics that reduce the distance. Listening to these 20 people, I discovered many deep affinities. At the end of the second day, although I had arrived with really bad news, I had the feeling that I was no longer considered a stranger, but a person they were starting to trust. However, my role could not be limited to listening: everyone was expecting specific proposals to alleviate a desperate situation. One evening I was called down to my hotel reception, where I found some of the people who were going to lose their jobs in a matter of weeks. We went out for dinner and they put forward some practical and interesting solutions which the following week, back at the office,

I proposed to management, who accepted them. The office in that African country closed, but after a year instead of after three months. Six people, at their request, were transferred to a neighbouring country, three people were given early retirement, some were hired in another organization thanks to the experience and contacts gained at our company; the remaining people were offered money, training courses and impeccable references, which helped them find a new job. Thanks to the advice of a colleague, who had managed a similar situation, I was also able to negotiate a continuation of the employees' medical insurance for two years.

In rereading the book by Fisher and Shapiro, I was struck by the actions required to be accepted into a new group where it's possible that there's diffidence, if not an open conflict: *listen to understand the point of view of others, build affinity, respect the autonomy of roles and their importance, choose a position and perform congruent actions.* These are golden rules, applicable to everyone for a positive start. They work: they allow you to have authentic conversations and open up new opportunities.

Entering the Village to understand the organization

A study carried out in 2011 by the British consulting firm Revelation indicates that '95 per cent of people believe that manipulation and hidden agendas at work have influenced their personal life'[12]. The thing that surprises me about this study: *how come it's only 95 per cent?* The book *Rumor Psychology*[13] illustrates effectively the role of gossip and rumours, if not slander, present in all organizations. The informal network of communication knows no crisis: on the contrary, I believe it is a thriving industry, especially in organizations where narrative and communication are confused and non-credible. When the primary market doesn't work, the secondary market thrives. We all know that organizations have a political aspect that is part of their culture: our task will be to understand what really happens, who's in charge, who's part of it, how people behave, how they speak. We'll call this capacity *political intelligence*. 'Politics' is not actually a dirty word; it's part of a complex, human system, be it an organization, a church, a tennis club or a school, where people with different interests, values and perspectives interact.

First we must understand that the official organizational structure is not necessarily the real one. There are relationships and dynamics unknown to us that we must take into consideration. To have fun, let's take a look at the *real organizational structure* of a drawing. Sure, it'll make us smile, but this irreverent structure tells us a great truth: there are many, often not evident, relationships between people who

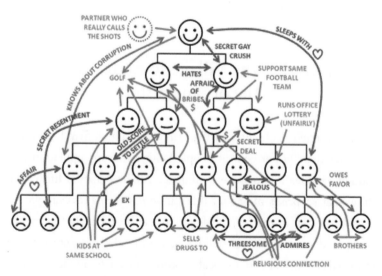

Figure 5.1 *The irreverent organisation chart.*

can facilitate or hinder our effectiveness: potential allies and hidden traps. We mustn't become paranoid but only continue to observe, listen and avoid ending up stranded between useless dynamics and struggles between opposing feuds, in which we can risk taking stray bullets or poisoned pills. In practice, we have to become experts in what Peter M. Senge, MIT management teacher, calls *system thinking*[14], that is the awareness that comes from analysing the whole system in its complexity, instead of *taking into consideration only some components*, disassembling them and trying to fix them individually. This approach involves the consideration and analysis of many different perspectives, the human intellectual curiosity to *understand, before being understood.*

Meeting the locals

When I arrived in Switzerland in 2014, as a new resident, I was given a free booklet, *The Swiss Confederation: A Brief Guide.* On the first page, Corinna Casanova, Federal Chancellor of the Confederation, said: 'The ambassador of an Asian nation had arrived in Switzerland for a few weeks. He was at Zurich station to catch a train that would leave for Bern within a few minutes. As he waited he saw a gentleman running with his tie fluttering in the air, trying to catch the same train. He was the President of the Confederation! He couldn't believe two things: that the President would take the train like any other citizen, or even less, that the train wouldn't have waited'[15]. It seemed interesting to me that this story was at the beginning of a guide given to newcomers, to explain to them how the Confederation 'works': in Switzerland there is no privilege, not even for the President, and absolute punctuality is conceived as a moral value, symptom and symbol of reliability and precision. This story helped me a lot to understand the country where I live and also the company where I work: since then I arrive on time.

Finally we meet the people who are part of the organization: as mentioned, we have to learn their names, listen to them, ask questions. Who are they? How do we figure out who to trust? In my first job I was lucky enough to meet a wonderful person, Luigi Porta, who was a mentor to me and to whom I'm still grateful, even though he passed away several years ago. After a few days at the office, he told me: 'There are people who work for the organization and people who work only for themselves. There are people who understand that the wind blows and people who don't, even if you explain it to them every day ... It's up to you to understand which category the animals of this zoo belong to...'.

Believe me, these words are still useful to me: I designed a square-matrix to understand the behavioural styles of people in organizations and I have been using it for twenty years. The two variables-dimensions are: the level of knowledge of the culture-politics of the organization, defined as *political intelligence*, and the *orientation to work for oneself or for the organization*.

In each of the four spaces of the matrix we'll find three animals with similar characteristics. In the first quadrant of the zoo we'll meet the inept or foolish: Donkeys, Chickens and Parrots; in the second the naive-innocent: Dogs, Bears and Lambs; in the third we'll have to be very careful because we'll find the dangerously cunning and in this category are included the narcissists and psychopaths: Wolves, Peacocks and poisonous Snakes; in the fourth quadrant, finally, we'll come across the wise creatures: Owls, Elephants and Lions, not by chance considered the king of the jungle.

But before entering the zoo, here are some stories to focus on, to understand what *political intelligence* and *individual or organizational orientation* mean.

Political intelligence

Anna was a brilliant career woman, promoted to senior positions before the age of 30, working at a large and prestigious international consulting firm. When an important client offered her a job, she accepted, flattered because it was a very interesting position. On the third day of work, Anna presented a project to her supervisor, which was accepted by the board of directors with enthusiasm; the following week, Anna gathered her team, about 70 people, to present the plan and explain that it had to be concluded at all costs within a period of time that seemed unrealistic to everyone. During the meeting some people didn't hide their doubts and a certain degree of resentment for not even being consulted; Anna showed that she was polite in her manner but inflexible in substance, ending the meeting with an aggressive tone, stating 'Anyone who is not with me is against me'. She worked 12–14 hours a day, openly criticizing those who went home before 7pm; her team hardly ever responded to requests to speed up, to meet her deadline. After six months, with the project severely behind schedule, Anna dismissed two people blaming them for errors and delays. At this point a large delegation of the team went – secretly – to Anna's supervisor asking for her to be replaced, and threatening a strike: 'either her or us'; Anna was fired the following day.

Peter was considered to be a kind of child prodigy by his supervisor John: much younger than all his colleagues, recruited by a prestigious bank, he worked with passion and skill. John asked him to conduct analysis of the team and of the work methodologies, considering – not without reason – that a team of about 30 people should achieve better results. Peter conducted the analysis and presented his findings during the weekly team meeting. During the meeting Peter indicated how the continuous requests for data, the long meetings and written reports requested by John had *heavily* impacted on the group's performance. At the end of the meeting John informed Peter of his transfer to a department nicknamed 'Siberia', effectively eliminating him from any promotion plan. Peter, enraged, resigned shortly thereafter.

These two short stories show how both Anna and Peter, although technically talented, well educated and serious professionals, had not developed a 'political' knowledge of the environment in which they worked. In just a few days Anna alienated her team of collaborators, who turned against her. Peter had highlighted the cause of the team's inefficiency, but had – in fact – blamed his manager who had immediately sought revenge: two chronicles of death foretold.

Individual or organizational orientation

Karl, the HR director, was desperate: he'd just received a message in which the third consecutive external candidate had declined a job offer for the position of vice-president. The President was very impatient and didn't understand why it was taking months to find the right person. Karl asked his team to check if there were no other candidates available among the employees. In fact, one person was: Veronica seemed qualified, but in hierarchical terms she was two levels below that of the required position. Veronica was interviewed and then *prepared* for the final interview with the President, who was satisfied and ordered that an offer be made. Karl prepared the letter but with a single promotion, since the rules of the organization didn't allow for a double promotion; the second promotion and a 25 per cent increase in salary were envisaged after a year exactly. Veronica refused the offer, asking for an increase of at least 70 per cent – in short, demanding the double promotion – victim of a very pronounced anchoring effect. Karl made her a counter-offer with a maximum increase of 33 per cent, providing her with some objective data, including the fact that she would be the highest paid person in the department. But Veronica refused again; at that point, the President, informed of the situation, ended the negotiation. Karl began his search again, while Veronica returned to her job and received no pay rise for two years.

This short story highlights how Veronica, stubbornly putting her own interests against the written rules of the organization, has shown extreme 'egoism' to the point that the company excluded her for two years from any reward, basically putting her in the corner, 'as punishment'.

Here we have the matrix with the variables: individual (egotistical) or organizational (altruistic) behaviour? Extensive or superficial political intelligence? The behaviour styles are calibrated according to these two variables, in four areas populated by very different animals. Are we or are we not in a zoo?

Styles of behaviour

Incompetent category: Donkeys, Parrots, Chickens

In 2012, the press reported that Franz-Peter Tebartz-van Elst, Bishop of Limburg in Germany since 2008, had travelled first class to India: an unfortunate choice, but formally not forbidden and, therefore, soon forgotten. In March 2013, Jorge Mario Bergoglio was the first Jesuit to become Pope, choosing the name of Francis in honour of Francis of Assisi, to underline that the Catholic Church was at the service of the poor.

Ignoring the new direction given to the Catholic Church by Bergoglio, Tebartz-van Elst carried on regardless, as if nothing had happened,

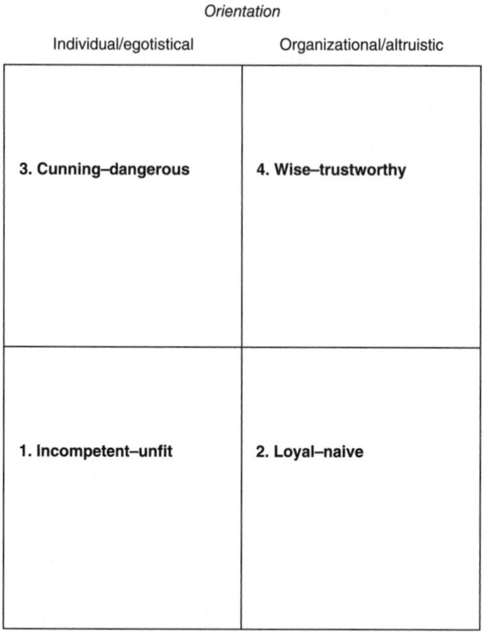

Orientation

Individual/egotistical   Organizational/altruistic

3. Cunning–dangerous	4. Wise–trustworthy
1. Incompetent–unfit	2. Loyal–naive

Figure 5.2 *Behavioural matrix.*

having various renovations carried out with costs that would have dwarfed the budget of a Russian magnate: EUR 200,000 to renovate his apartments, EUR 300,000 for the private chapel, EUR 20,000 for the bathtub, EUR 500,000 for his wardrobe, EUR 35,000 for a conference table … and the list continues; the final bill was just under EUR 31 million. Once informed, the Pope summoned him to Rome and had him wait for nine days before removing him from his post. I believe that Franz-Peter Tebartz-van Elst is a perfect example of a person who puts his own interests before the interests of the organization, in this case the Catholic Church, and that he can be deservedly included, with honourable mention, in the square represented by the *Donkeys*. People who ignore, or pretend to ignore, the behavioural rules related to an organization and who, moreover, do the opposite don't last very long and, in general, are also pilloried with more or less refined systems, based on the level of sophistication of the organization.

Parrots are ornamental animals that have the habit of mechanically repeating what they hear from their masters. We will find these birds in any organization we work for. They dress like the boss, they wear the same kind of glasses, they move in the same way, they grow their hair or beard and moustache in the same way, the best ones even speak with the same accent. There are so many *Parrots* out there and we almost feel sorry for them, unable to consider that they too *could* have a personal opinion. They are easily recognized because in meetings they never say: 'I think that . . .' but always 'as our excellent Managing Director would say . . .'. The parrot only works for itself, in love with his multicoloured feathers, generally gnawed by envy, ready to change master if it suits him. The list of corporate *Parrots* is long: it's not worth telling a story. Just a small warning: if the number of Parrots is more than 1 per cent in an organization, we have ended up in the wrong place; better fly away quickly before we end up in a cage.

Below, however, we have an example of the behaviour of the *Chicken*. Let's imagine a situation in which the company communicates to the employees a budget reduction and cuts that will be executed with the objective of making savings. The *Chicken* is the one who asks the boss the next day for a pay rise and the possibility of going on a refresher course at a tourist resort. A *Chicken* that will be roasted quickly.

Donkeys, *Parrots* and *Chickens* have a tendency to demand a lot in terms of time, attention, energy but give little or nothing in return. I don't think it's necessary to say that we must avoid prolonged contact with those who belong to this quadrant: a kind greeting will suffice.

Category of the naive and innocent: Dogs, Bears and Lambs

US President Harry Truman[16] said: 'If you want a friend in Washington, get a dog'. Dogs are famous for their absolute loyalty to their owners;

in the newspapers we often read moving stories about these animals, which watch over a sick master or wait for days for his return. Many people at organizations behave in the same way, demonstrating an absolute dedication to the *social colours*. Companies celebrate – and rightly so – these forms of attachment typical of loyal employees. The quadrant with *Dogs* should therefore be understood as an absolutely positive value: these are the people who keep organizations going, they usually work there for years or for all their lives as employees, without questioning the company mantra.

Sometimes, however, *Dogs* turn into solitary *Bears*, people who are very busy with their work but unaware of what is actually happening around them. This lack of interest in what is happening – an indication of low political intelligence – leads to the neglect of fundamental aspects of the culture of which they form a part and a degree of awareness that is limited *to their own back yard*. If there is new leadership, restructuring, an opportunity for promotion or a better paid job, they will be the last ones to find out about it, thus becoming sacrificial *Lambs*. After a while, organizations begin to see these people as if they were part of the furniture, going through the motions without passion, in the same way as a long-time married couple. Who remembers Giovanni Drogo, the main character of Buzatti's *The Tartar Steppe*[17]? A young lieutenant arrives at Bastiani Fortress full of hopes and expectations, he spends his whole life there where absolutely nothing happens, except crossing off the days that are always the same. By the time Drogo begins *to take one step at a time*, realizing that his youth is already behind him, it is too late. Often these people are forgotten in a corner or removed without much attention or, as in Buzzati's book, *die*, forgotten and alone.

The transformation from a *Dog* to a solitary *Bear*, to becoming a *Lamb*, occurs when these people are finally *sacrificed*. *Lambs* are people who have a strong orientation to work for the institution to which they belong but do not have an adequate level of knowledge about what is going on, maybe waiting for some kind of miraculous event. People in this category must be respected; they are often a source of technical knowledge and as they're very generous, they'll be available to give us a hand and dedicate their precious time to us. We could reciprocate by making them aware of what we know and help them gain a broader vision of the work they do in an exemplary manner, with pride and a strong sense of duty.

Category of the dangerously cunning: Foxes, Peacocks and Snakes

The first thing to know about *Foxes*: their image, visibility and formal reputation is more important than anything to these individuals. They are selective with information, they manipulate the rules to their advantage without scruples, they are so intelligent that they *never* leave a trace. They lie as a norm. When there's a dirty job to do, they delegate a *Lamb* or a *Dog* and then deny it was their idea, blaming the unfortunate perpetrator. They form alliances of any kind, even with historical enemies, just to win their own battle: think of the pact between Hitler's Nazi Germany and Stalin's Communist Russia of 1939[18]. *Foxes* have no sense of loyalty to any ideal, least of all to any person. People are mere tools of their will, like objects. They're very good at forming special, but not lasting, coalitions. If something goes wrong, they can immediately choose a victim to blame, usually a *Lamb* to sacrifice. They never make wrong moves in terms of appearances and formalities but are deadly in terms of substance. If they compliment you, be assured that a request for a big favour is coming or a destructive criticism, usually in front of other people as public humiliation is their preferred modality to provide feedback. From time to time they punish their *subordinates* – that's what they call them – just to remind everyone who's in charge and who's not.

They are disturbingly mellifluous, exquisitely polite and obsequious with the powerful, but they are dismissive and arrogant with everyone else; they never take a clear position on any subject, but they do take all the credit; they don't accept criticism, which they interpret as insulting, and punish publicly.

Welcome to the dangerous den of the *Foxes*: unscrupulous people, totally dedicated to their own cause, they are totally absorbed with themselves, with a textbook political instinct. The description of the *Fox* is very similar to Machiavelli's Prince or, if you prefer, the diabolical Francis Underwood, the main character in the TV series *House of Cards*, a power-hungry Mephistophelian politician played by Kevin Spacey. All of us have surely met a *Fox* – or maybe even voted for one, in a moment of weakness – because sadly some people at the top have exactly this kind of psychological profile. In general, *Foxes* choose to work with loyal people who are a little naive – the characteristics of *Dogs* and *Bears* – they devour *Chickens* at will, sacrifice *Lambs* and surround themselves, for their entertainment, with complacent *Parrots*. A tragic circus.

Peacocks are typically narcissists and put their appearance at the centre of everything. Obsessed with their own visibility, they're available for any wickedness in order to appear in the newspapers, on the internet, in conferences or in meetings. Their terror is to be forgotten. The big weakness of these people is their pathological and chronic narcissism. They're a bit like drug addicts, a lack of visibility and admiration leads to withdrawal symptoms. They are often surrounded by a higher than average number of *Parrots*, whom they use as consultants or advisors and of whom they ask the following question: 'Mirror, mirror on the wall who's the fairest of them all?' The *Parrots* play another very important role: laughing out loud at the master's jokes, even when they're old, embarrassing jokes. And, of course, they enthusiastically applaud their master as soon as he pontificates.

Sandy Hotchkiss wrote a manual, *Why It Is Always About You?*[19] to understand and cope with people suffering from pathological narcissism. In the final part of the book, the author describes the *Peacock*-narcissists in the workplace, who are particularly dangerous if they have power, lethal if they have absolute power. First of all, narcissists have a kind of seductive and manipulative power and, in their presence, the boundaries between private and professional life vanish. They expect us to be always available for them at any time, including Christmas. They call you in the middle of the night, expect you to be available when sick or when on holidays, they send emails as soon as the weekend starts, just to make the point. They do not understand the difference between paying people (salary) and buying people (obedience). Secondly, when a problem emerges they won't try to solve it but rather find the person to blame because, by definition, it'll never be their fault. Finally, as if this were not enough, *Peacock*-narcissists have a vision, which is messianic and vague. For example, a politician with these characteristics will never commit to approving a specific law to help young students in search of their first job but will pontificate, with apocalyptic tones, about the hypothesis of creating a million jobs, leaving the details of this plan to their faithful *Dogs* and *Lambs*.

The visions, the great plans of the narcissists, are often unattainable or unquantifiable, the result of unbridled ambition; they can only be realized by subjecting the people around them to infernal schedules, nervous breakdowns and burn-outs, in a whirlwind of productivity as an end in itself. Anyone who can't handle it any more is branded as weak, incapable and eliminated in brutal fashion.

Peacock-narcissists don't see people as human beings but just tools to get what they want, exploiting without reservations those who collaborate with them. Hence, they have no emotional intelligence, but only a sense of vague paternalism, which confirms their destructive power. *Peacock*-narcissists, like spoiled little children, are prone to huge mood swings and uncontrolled outbursts of anger; they obsessively seek unconditional admiration and they can't stand anyone who can, even remotely, steal the limelight from them. Anyone who thinks they're the number two, ready to take over, is very quickly and unceremoniously taken out of the picture. The number two is therefore relegated to play the part of, at best, elegant butler, or colourful clown; it depends on the occasion. They're not interested in facts, truth, data or statistics unless they confirm what they already have in mind. Paranoia becomes good judgement; it is their compass for decision-making. If one of their subordinates achieves a goal, they'll take the credit. They're terrified of ageing, they do everything they can to look younger, denying the inexorable passage of time, sometimes resorting to surgery or aesthetic stratagems of dubious taste.

If we can recognize the *Peacocks*, we also know their weak point: to live in peace we must let them take centre stage and let them believe that they really are the most beautiful of them all, never criticizing them. Michael Maccoby wrote a relevant article in the *Harvard Business Review* entitled 'Narcissistic Leaders'[20]. He believes that they have weaknesses such as being less inclined to criticism, an inability to listen, a lack of empathy, a fierce desire to compete all the time and with everyone. From my experience, I've realized that this kind of person doesn't give suggestions, they don't want to listen but they give precise orders to be executed urgently – only their agenda matters.

We'll sometimes find ourselves putting on an act in order to survive. Once I had organized a business seminar and a journalist contacted me to write an article with an interview about the event. Knowing that my boss was pathologically vain, I sent the reporter to interview him. As a result, Narcissus got his name in the paper with a lot of photographs. He was in seventh heaven and later I learned that he'd bought 100 copies of the newspaper to be distributed among his team, which was made up of less than 20 people. Sandy Hotchkiss gives us great advice in 'Why it is always about you?:

> Be careful not to do anything that offends or challenges the Narcissist's image or illusion. Remember that the Narcissist is not interested in truth, reality, or you. . . . never compete for attention with the Narcissist . . . unfortunately this means minimizing your talent and accomplishments and allowing the Narcissist to take all the credit. . . .[21]

Snakes exist in society and, therefore, in every organization as well. They're the psychopaths[22], people who totally lack any trace of empathy and are unable to put themselves in the shoes of others, without scruples and remorse, faithful only to themselves. Approximately 1 per cent of the population is certifiably psychopathic[23]: the highest percentage of psychopath can be found in jails and prisons and then at the top of organizations,[24] so chances are that, yes, there is one of them in the Senior Management Team. The first book to deal directly with psychopaths was written by a German doctor, J. L. A. Koch in 1891, entitled *Die Psychopathiscen Minderwetigkeiten.* This is where the label psychopath comes from. Then Hervey Cleckley, back in 1941, wrote *The Mask of Sanity,*[25] followed by the book *Without Conscience* by Robert D. Hare,[26] who conducted some experiments to find out who, among the inmates of a prison, was a psychopath. The experiment consisted of reading a few words with a high emotional content such as 'blood', 'knife', 'rape' and terms with a low emotional content such as 'tree', 'table', 'stone'. The psychopaths showed no emotions of any kind, totally indifferent to all the words.[27] Truman Capote, in his novel-investigation *In Cold Blood,*[28] described the mind of psychopathic killers. As far as *Snakes* are concerned, *the others are not people* but simply tools to be used, lemons to be squeezed, obstacles to be eliminated; they're very good at manipulating people and situations, obviously always to their advantage. The worst massacres in history were committed by psychopaths,[29] *Snakes* who were totally indifferent to the fate of their victims.

Many of the main traits of psychopaths are often confused with leadership skills: they are masters in impression management, they are polished, impeccable with formalities and decisive; they are good at reading people and manipulating them, at times for years. But, be careful: they also have very destructive skills: psychopaths are cunning, manipulative, parasitic and they feel no remorse or guilt.

I've known several *Snakes* but one in particular stays with me, imprinted in my mind. When I arrived at the office, I realized something had happened. Some people were crying: I was told that a colleague was dead but that the circumstances were unknown. Confusion, pain and tears followed; some police officers came to my office to tell me that the person had been killed or perhaps had committed suicide. When they left, I couldn't breathe; I asked for a glass of water and sat on the floor, staggering as if I had been punched in the face. When I recovered, I quickly went to talk to the general manager and inform him. With a broken voice and teary eyes, together with two other colleagues, we communicated the bad news. The *Snake* replied without batting an eyelid: 'Greg can replace him from tomorrow'. I couldn't believe it, the news of the death of a colleague didn't affect him in the slightest. A *Snake* or, worse, an anaconda that swallows people like candy, indifferent to any pain or emotion.

Once a nurse was interviewing a psychopath:[30] she showed him a frightened face and asked him to identify the emotion. He said that he did not know what the emotion was but it was the face people pulled just before he killed them.

Now, to be clear, I am not suggesting to create organizations where many paranoids are looking for the few psychopaths: this would be rather unhelpful. However, the subtle art of spotting psychopaths can truly save your wellbeing, career and in some extreme cases even your life. One way to spot one is to observe how comfortable is that person in an emotionally charged situation, for example giving a farewell speech when someone leaves the organization or the level of emotional intelligence displayed in delicate issues, for example in the case of handling dismissals. Psychopaths don't see the emotional side of these situations; they are simply brutal and they call it leadership, which could be somewhat funny if it wasn't tragic. The most sophisticated ones may seem, from the distance, even fashionably sensible: the truth is that they simply don't care about people and will never ever understand what they do to them as they are too busy building their brilliant careers, totally possessed by their narcissisms, obsessed by their power at the expense of everyone else around them. To survive, people can only become obedient servants, *Parrot*-like humans or just leave them behind.

So what should we do when we encounter *Foxes*, *Peacocks* and *Snakes*? We must keep our distance from them, provide as little information as possible and not open up. As they aim to control you, total polite indifference is the only option left. Indifference drives them mad as they cannot even consider that someone is not paying attention to them. They expect blind obedience, not independent judgement or any trace of critical thinking. They appoint in key roles only people they can fully control: weak pretenders, they never ever appoint real contenders who could challenge them. They have a mask, we have to wear a robust armour, with a gentle smile. *Foxes*, *Peacocks* and especially *Snakes* are *amoral*, unscrupulous people, whose behaviour doesn't depend on ethical values, since they consider morality as a ballast, useless baggage. If you can identify them, avoid them.

I think the best way to describe this category of *Foxes*, *Peacocks* and *Snakes* is by using the words of Guido Piovene[31] in the preface of his book *Confession of a Novice*:[32]

The characters in this novel, although different, all have one thing in common: **they all find each other repugnant when they get to know each other.** Each of us understands ourselves only when we need to, everyone keeps their thoughts suspended, fluid, indecipherable, ready to change according to their convenience [...] everyone seems to think of their own soul not as their essence but like another being with whom they coexist, following the rules of diplomacy [...] If we, more demanding or less sympathetic of it, want to give this behaviour the appropriate name, we would be perhaps forced to call it bad faith. Bad faith is the art of not knowing oneself, or rather of regulating our knowledge of ourselves on the basis of convenience [...] I say that a man is always, or never, in bad faith. Bad faith is not a state of the soul, it is one of its qualities.

The wisemen and the true leaders: Owls, Elephants and Lions

I got interested in *power*, or rather, *abuse of power* by reading George Orwell's classics and masterpieces when I was a teenager (*1984* and *Animal Farm*). Power is not a dirty word: it can – and should – be well managed. *Owls* are people with high political intelligence as well as behaviour oriented towards the success of the organization they are part of. They encourage the exchange of information to improve relationships and results and they emphasize learning, not criticism. They have no problem managing differing opinions, unlike the logic of the *Foxes* which is 'with me or against me'. They seek solutions in which everyone can benefit and try to protect people's dignity. They help others and make themselves available. Their most important characteristic is that they're driven by strong moral values and they don't betray people, unless they've been betrayed themselves. They never *shoot* first because they believe in dialogue; they shy away from deceit, ploys, tricks, lies. They defend colleagues and employees publicly and privately; they're very attentive; they don't speak much, but when they do speak everyone listens.

Owls become *Elephants* when they gain experience, *gravitas*.[33] *Elephants* have a prodigious memory and in organizations they're respected people not so much because of their position but because of their wisdom and authority. You can identify the *Elephants* in the organizations thanks to their moral weight: 'Have you consulted Mr. . . .?', 'Have you heard what . . . thinks?', 'First we must talk about it with . . .' are all sentences that refer to these characters and they can be useful to identify. The *Elephants*, also known as *opinion leaders*, are people with a degree of judgement that can influence the way of thinking in organizations. When we identify an *Elephant*, the first rule is to approach them with the proper respect. *Peacocks* seek adulation, whereas *Elephants* instil respect and sobriety. The second rule brings us back to our capacity to listen and ask questions, to ask for advice. The best strategy is to convince the *Elephants* to guide us, as Virgil did with Dante,[34] the moral and spiritual guide in the journey of *The Divine Comedy*.

The *Lions* are the only true leaders of organizations. Here comes the paradox of the leader who, on the one hand, must represent the values of the organization and, on the other hand, must succeed in changing the organization itself. When I think of this paradox, I am reminded of Pope Francis: on the one hand, the head of an organization, the Catholic Church, with 2,000 years of history, on the other hand leading extraordinary change in relation to corruption and an openness to issues considered taboo by the Catholic Church until recently. A true leader, who perfectly personifies the paradox.

What makes *Lions* different to *Owls* and *Elephants*? *The courage of their convictions*, whatever the cost, is the most important quality in a leader. I present you with two *Lionesses* and two *Lions*, each with a phrase taken from their extraordinary lives:

Mother Teresa of Calcutta, founder of the Missionaries of Charity, awarded the Nobel Peace Prize in 1979: 'I have found the paradox, that if you love until it hurts, there can be no more hurt, only more love'.

Rosa Parks,[35] American civil rights activist who refused to comply with the orders of a bus driver on 1 December 1955, who ordered her to give up her seat to a white man, according to the racist laws in force at the time: 'You must never be fearful about what you are doing when it is right'.

Mahatma Gandhi, Indian political-religious leader, who led his country from British colonialism to independence: 'First they ignore you, then they laugh at you, then they fight you, then you win'.

Giorgio Perlasca,[36] an Italian businessman who during the Second World War, with the help of Spanish diplomats, saved 5,218 Jews from extermination and deportation to concentration camps. When asked why he had done this he answered: 'But if you had the possibility to do something, what would you do when men, women and children are being massacred for no reason, except hatred?'[37]

We can be heroes . . . We can all be heroes

Lions therefore have the *courage of their convictions*: these people have absolute conviction in their ideals, and have been imprisoned or killed for them. Must we therefore follow the same fate which, however heroic it may be, is certainly not very palatable? I am convinced that everyone, except *Foxes*, *Peacocks* and *Snakes*, can potentially become *Lions*. Not only that: if we look carefully, there are thousands of *Lions* around us – perhaps we ourselves are already *Lions*, without knowing it.

A *Lion* is the middle-aged man who loses his job, and hence his identity, but has the strength to get back in the game, ready to start again from scratch, with dignity, just to survive. A *Lioness* is the single, widowed or divorced woman with a strong sense of responsibility who manages to keep going day after day to offer her children a better future. A *Lion* is the young man who, despite tremendous levels of unemployment, fights to get a decent job, continues to study or creates a business or a start-up. A *Lion* is the worker who breaks his back for a decent salary, working nights, taking the same 5am train for 30 years. A *Lioness* is the cleaning lady who works with dignity, starting before 8am and continuing after 8pm, making sure our offices are clean and tidy. A *Lion* is the immigrant who comes from a distant country, doing menial jobs or tasks with dignity even if perhaps he is a lawyer or teacher, sending everything he earns to his family. A *Lion* is the adopted child who was abandoned or the son of a divorced couple, who manages not to lose trust in adults, in their love, in life. Lions are the priests, nuns, monks, rabbi, iman, who help the deprived, the forgotten, the invisible. Lions are the doctors, the teachers, the judges, the nurses, the police officers who, often with modest salaries, concern themselves with the health, safety or education of others. A Lion is the entrepreneur who, despite endless bureaucratic obstacles or abuse from the Mafia, drives his company forward and offers work to those who deserve it. It is the Lions who, struck by a terrible event, work to help people who have had a similar destiny, teaching us that even hard times can be overcome. Lions are the journalists or artists who use their art and knowledge to tell, denounce, serve, cheer up, give hope. It is the Lions who protect our environment, our artistic treasures from unscrupulous speculators. A Lion is the pensioner who, after 40 years of work, receives a miserable pension, but lives with dignity and commits himself to be a good grandfather for his grandchildren. It is the Lions who, discriminated against because of their sexual, religious, racial or political preferences, walk with their heads held high and continue on their own path with conviction, without abandoning their dignity and identity. It is the Lions who don't tolerate exploitation, criminals, corruption, cheating, a rigged deck to the detriment of the more deserving. It is the Lions who devote their time to volunteering and helping abandoned elderly people, exploited women, forgotten children, prisoners, prostitutes, the lonely: our society has created too many disenfranchised, obliterated, invisible, forgotten lost souls.

The time has come to change our model of heroism. So that *being a Lion* doesn't become a mythical category reserved for the super-heroes in comic books or limited to a few legendary figures or, worse still, to *Peacocks* who spend all day in front of the mirror, or posting selfies on Facebook or Instagram or to *Foxes* and *Snakes* who surround themselves with groups of unhappy, fearful people to show they are winners. Being *Lions* is a process and a journey[38] that never ends and becomes our way of being: we don't need heroic acts or deeds but daily struggle and human dignity. Our work therefore becomes not just a mere occupation to get a salary but our deepest and most authentic identity, our moral compass, who we really are. I'm convinced that you're a *Lion* too or that you're about to become one.

Let's not forget: 'Walk tall or don't walk at all',[39] sings Bruce Springsteen.

6

The pact with the devil. The price you pay for your career

'The awful thing is that beauty is mysterious as well as terrible. God and the devil are fighting there and the battlefield is the heart of man.'

FYODOR DOSTOYEVSKY[1]

The price you pay

I want to draw inspiration from the titles of two famous rock music masterpieces to reflect on two fundamental questions.

The first song, *The Price You Pay*, written by Bruce Springsteen, leads us to reflect on the question: *what's the price we have to pay to make a career?* Warning: there will always be a price to pay; there are reasonable prices and others that are quite simply unacceptable. Sometimes, unknowingly, we make other people pay.

With the second song, *Sympathy For The Devil* by The Rolling Stones, the question arises: *have we made a pact with the devil to make a career?*

The chapter will end with a reflection on the art of negotiating with ourselves – and with those close to us – the price we are ready to pay for our career and avoid making a pact with the devil in exchange for something indispensable: our soul and our freedom.

I remain convinced that it's much more important to formulate the right questions rather than to guess plausible answers. In my work, a question that I've frequently been asked is: 'How can I get promoted?'

Problem: this isn't the right question. Performing your work with satisfaction and love is one of the profound joys of life and it is absolutely legitimate and right to seek advancement in your career. If you accept this assumption, you must also ask yourself: what's the price to be paid, not just the salary I'll receive?

I've often wondered why this concept, which is so clear in everyday life, is not applied to a wider range of issues. If, for example, we're in a pizzeria and we notice that the pizza margherita costs GBP 100, do we order it? Of course not; we'd perhaps be willing to pay up to GBP 15, if we're in a special location, for example, with a sea view, but GBP 100? Not a chance. Another case: it's Sunday evening, we've just noticed that we don't have any milk in the fridge and the only supermarket open is a 10-minute drive from home; it's raining, it's cold and it's already dark. After a quick cost-benefit analysis, we conclude that it's not worth it.

Why don't we apply the same methodology to our career? Why don't we work out to what extent *it may be worthwhile*? In short, paying a price for a career means balancing the trade-offs, the choices we feel like making – or not making – and the resulting sacrifices. Choosing means giving something up.

How much is enough?

Let's start with a general overview: Robert and Edward Skidelsky, father and son, one an economist and the other a philosopher, have written an engaging text together, full of food for thought, starting with a question: *how much is enough?*[2] How much is enough? How much do we really need to enjoy life? These two writers have examined the question from different angles, evaluating from the point of view of philosophy, religion, economy, distinguishing so-called *needs* (for example a roof over our head, hot meals), from *desires*. The difference is simple: needs are finite, quantifiable and limited while desires are unlimited. In short, *we need* 2,500 calories a day to live but *we want* to eat lobster. As Bruce Springsteen writes in the song *Badlands*,[3] 'poor man wanna be rich, rich man wanna be king, and a king ain't satisfied, 'til he rules everything', describing in one sentence a fundamental problem: the existential malaise of never being content.

If we take into account the correlation between an increase in income and the level of perceived happiness, in Great Britain, for example, between 1973 and 2007 the income doubled, while the level of satisfaction remained the same; at the same time the degree of inequality in the distribution of wealth has increased significantly, together with obesity, deaths from alcoholism and divorces. In July 2015 *La Repubblica* published an article entitled 'It was better when it was worse: happiness and growth don't go hand in hand'[4]: from a study by the Marche Polytechnic University on the correlation between economic growth and quality of life, it emerged that until the 1960s the trend was positive, while for almost 50 years it has been negative. Presented like this, these reports may seem like statistics that don't really affect us; but, in practice, what happens to normal people like us?

The relationship between stress and productivity has been studied since the times of the Industrial Revolution. As early as 1908, two American psychologists, Robert Yerkes and John Dodson, had empirically demonstrated the existence of a direct relationship between these two phenomena: without any stimulus, commonly called *stress*, productivity is low, but if we're excessively stimulated, that is, *too stressed*, productivity is reduced to nothing. The Yerkes–Dodson law states that *up to a certain point*, stress is positive because it helps us to focus and stay focused. Once this limit has been exceeded, stress becomes negative and jeopardises performance. What is this point? And what happens if we go too far?

To try and find out more, I approached Dr Jim Stricker, psychologist and therapist at the World Bank for 17 years. The first time we spoke, it was in relation to his candidacy as manager of a team that was responsible for measuring and managing the stress of around 17,000 employees. I asked him to somehow *quantify* the price, including stress and psychological costs, which the World Bank employees had to pay, considering that they always work under pressure. The analysis conducted by Stricker was rather enlightening. At the World Bank all the employees are highly qualified, they have university degrees and doctorates, speak three languages fluently and have good experience in their country of origin. In short, we are talking about a very competitive environment, made up of idealistic people, who have confidence in the World Bank's mission. In addition, the employees must travel frequently to work on projects all over the world. I myself was used to travelling about 150 days a year for work.

In terms of the price paid to make a career, all this means that people commit themselves up until their breaking point and sometimes idealism turns to cynicism in the face of the exasperatingly slow pace of some projects, or witnessing the rampant corruption in some countries, when jet-lag and the physical fatigue of long hours of travel takes over and the family at home starts to protest, and rightly so, for being neglected. At the beginning, any motivated and competent professional carries on, trying to manage the situation the best they can, but at a certain point there is the risk of a sudden collapse, the exhaustion of too much work, which leads to long recovery times and unpleasant consequences: depression, illness, divorce. This is the point that should never be exceeded, the price is too high to pay. For starters, a good deal of awareness and wisdom is required when managing time and energy. Having the right priorities, being able to count on constructively supporting friendships, knowing how to take care of oneself, in body and spirit. It's right to look for inner motivation and to work hard, but there are limits, including physical ones.

So, our goal is to understand how to keep our inner motivation steady without having to pay too high a price to bear.

For a more in-depth analysis of this topic of what is the *right* price to pay, in the next paragraph I will consult the help of two dear friends, one Russian and one Sicilian.

How much land does a man need?

How Much Land Does a Man Need? is the title of a story written in 1886 by a giant of world literature, Leo Tolstoy,[5] Russian writer and philosopher. It is the story of Pachom, a peasant obsessed with possessing as much land as possible. Looking for land to buy, Pachom learns that for a thousand roubles he can buy a plot of land equal to the perimeter that he can walk in a day. He goes to the place where the deal is to be concluded, showing up at dawn to face this challenge, trying to delimit as much land as possible and running as fast as he can for hours and hours. When the time comes to circle back to the starting point, Pachom sees a wood and, blinded by greed, he can't bring himself to give it up; he starts running again, even though he realizes he is getting further and further away, squeezing out the last drop of energy, because if he doesn't complete the perimeter it means losing the bet. He thinks to himself: 'I absolutely have to do it'. And he does it, he arrives just in time to win his land, but while shaking hands with all the villagers who want to congratulate him, exhausted by the fatigue, he drops down dead.

How much land does a man need? 'About two metres' is Tolstoy's ironic answer: just enough space for the grave at the cemetery.

Giovanni Verga, the great Sicilian writer, also wrote a similar story, *Property.*[6] The protagonist is again a farmer, Mazzarò, 'a man without both defects and affections, with a shiny head, a belly that is bloated and rich like a pig'. His obsession with accumulating property leads him to madness; when he is told that he should worry about saving his soul as he is about to die, he starts killing the animals on his farm, shouting: 'My property, come with me'.

How many Pachoms, how many Mazzaròs have we met on along the way? Have we behaved like them?

The rat race

The following story is a direct experience of mine. My boss informed me that a good colleague, Emily, has resigned and that, if I want, I can have her job, giving me a promotion, a big pay rise and a team of about 30 people to manage, as well as regular and frequent trips. I said 'yes' immediately, convinced and enthusiastic. A few days later I receive a letter with my new salary, a 20 per cent rise, and the prestigious title of vice-president. However, after a while I understand how the game works: I have to travel for two hours to get to the new office and work 12–13 hours a day; I have to travel twice a week on planes that leave at 6am, and my holiday is cancelled. A colleague tells me that Emily has not resigned at all, but is actually in hospital being treated for a nervous breakdown. I reached breaking point when, on one occasion, I left the office at 2am to go directly to the airport to take yet another flight: I'd just turned 30 but I felt as if I were twice as old, trembling with exhaustion. I felt like a total idiot accepting a job that I ended up hating; I was now completely exhausted and I bitterly regretted having made this choice without thinking, blinded by the 'bright lights' enticing me. I quit shortly after taking the promotion that I'd wanted so much.

Excessive pace even for the 'wolves' – people with a ferocious desire to advance in their careers[7] – can be too much. G.M., an American, worked for JP Morgan, vice-president in the technologies department; W.B., also an American, a former manager at Deutsche Bank, was to be promoted to head of high-risk investments, but the promotion was blocked; T.D. was communications director at insurance company Swiss Re; P.W., was head of finance for another Swiss insurance group. What do these people have in common? They worked in London, they had fabulous salaries, all four of them committed suicide.

The famous investment bank Goldman Sachs takes protective measures[8] by dictating the rules for interns who, every summer, go to work at the bank hoping to eventually be hired: you aren't allowed to arrive before 7am and you absolutely must leave before midnight. I guess they see it as flexitime, 'only' 17 hours a day: a kind of holiday!

Robert Reich was Secretary of Labour under American President Bill Clinton from 1993 to 1997, a university professor at Berkeley, California, author of compelling books and the maker of the documentary *Inequality For All*, which is a must-see. Like many people who love their work, he spent at least 14 hours a day in the office. Until one evening, during yet another phone call to the family to say he wouldn't be back in time for dinner, his youngest son asked if he could wake him up anyway when he got home, even though it wasn't necessary because they would see each other at breakfast the next morning. 'Wake me up Daddy: I just want to know you're here at home, with us'. These words made it clear to Reich that he had to quit his job: the price to pay had become too high.[9]

Henry is a dear friend; he spent almost 15 years working about 80 hours a week at a famous investment bank. His goal in life was to earn a certain amount, which in my opinion was crazy, before turning 45. I remember during a Thanksgiving dinner, he spent the entire time answering the phone, neglecting the table so carefully prepared by his wife, who was irritated and dejected. The good news is that Henry managed to earn the stratospheric sum he had set himself; the bad news: in 10 years he never spent more than three consecutive days with his family and has become a perfect stranger to his children. Obviously his wife left him as she couldn't take it any more and – ironically – kept almost all the money, after years of fierce legal battles.

Dying For a Paycheck is not the title of the latest horror movie but the compelling book from Jeffrey Pfeffer: he demonstrates the human costs of a life only devoted to work, always available to respond to emails, taking calls, working double shifts. We are becoming sleep-deprived zombies with our cognitive and emotional abilities dwarfed by unsustainable expectations. In short, a life exclusively devoted to work causes *dukkha*, a Buddhist term referring to the unsatisfactory nature of a life filled with suffering. *Total work* is a term coined by the German philosopher Josef Pieper just after the Second World War in his book *Leisure: The Basis of Culture* (1948). This is the process by which human beings are transformed into workers and nothing else. Corey Pein goes to Silicon Valley to study the working conditions of possibly the most highly paid professionals on the planet. His book is entitled *Live, Work, Work, Work, Die* and is self-explanatory. So, there seems to be overwhelming evidence that a life of total work drives people to the grave and creates dysfunctional families and societies.

Tolstoy's question remains engraved on our minds: *how much land does a man need?* The concept of *making a career* is easily comparable to the idea of the *rat race*. We are so worried about winning this race that we forget to be rats. If we think that a career is a ladder, which we have to climb, we must also ensure that the ladder is not leaning against the wrong wall.

One lunch together, in 28 years

Eugene O'Kelly, CEO of the consulting firm KPMG, with a dream job and offices on Fifth Avenue in New York, wrote a book[10]: so far nothing unusual. The thing that will leave you speechless is *the moment* when he decided to write it: the very same day the doctor diagnosed him with a brain tumour. The illness is in its terminal stage; nothing can be done. The first line of this text leaves us short of breath. Eugene writes: 'I was blessed: I was told I had three months to live'. The chapter is entitled 'A gift'. His story will stay with me for the rest of my life: Eugene describes the agonizing farewells that he dedicated to the people who had been part of his life: acquaintances, colleagues, close friends, family, children. The most emotional farewell is reserved for his wife Corinne, who also wrote the last pages of the book, when Eugene was no longer able to do so. In every line of this extraordinary story there is a feeling of pride for a career that is nothing short of splendid, but also the sense of lost time, unspoken words, kisses not given, skipped dinners, forgotten children, birthdays not celebrated, of the frantic times, of a life always spent in a hurry. I'm reminded of a beautiful sentence by the Lebanese poet and philosopher Khalil Gibran, who wrote: 'Between what is said and not meant, and what is meant and not said, most of love is lost'. Eugene's book struck me with a memory: 'In 28 years of work, I've only once had lunch with my wife on a weekday'. *Once in 28 years!*

Eugene was lucky when he discovered he had three months left to live. We're even more fortunate to have the opportunity to learn the lesson from an extraordinary man who has taught us with sweetness and compassion what matters in life. *Today* is the right day to have lunch with the person we love. Not only that: we must tell them that we love them deeply. Today, not tomorrow. Life is now.

Bronnie Ware has done a job for years that few have the courage to do: she's a nurse who cares for patients who are terminally ill.

She wrote a book which I read three times in a row. The book is entitled *The Top Five Regrets of the Dying* and tells of her experience accompanying these people, literally, until their last breath. What are the five regrets then? The first: not having had the courage to live the life we would've liked to live. The second: having worked too much. The third: not having had the courage to express our feelings to the people we love. The fourth: having lost contact with loved ones. The last: not having been happier. When reading this splendid book, I thought how lucky we are to know today what really matters.

Paul Kalanithi's book *When Breath Becomes Air* is a deep and emotional story of an amazingly talented young neurosurgeon who finds out that he has cancer.[11] His moving story is a reminder of what really counts in life. Even when terminally ill, Paul was fully alive, in love with his beautiful wife and newly-born daughter and his job. As Paul Kalanithi wrote: 'Literature not only illuminates another's experience; it provides the richest material for moral reflection'.

Randy Pausch, professor at Carnegie Mellon, was asked to give a lecture when he learned that he was terminally ill. Following this, he decided to write *The Last Lecture*[12] another meaningful book that starts with a powerful question: how to spend my limited time?

These four books have left me with a question that's got under my skin: which legacy do you want to leave behind?

The price of power

There are other prices to pay for a career, hidden costs in the frantic search for power. Jeffrey Pfeffer, in his book *Power*,[13] explains that having power increases visibility and puts you in the spotlight, like being famous. We know everything about them: where they go on holiday, how they dress, who they go out with, what they did yesterday.

As we advance in our career, gaining power, we'll be carefully observed, even when we're not present.

A loss of autonomy is another cost to consider. James March, a scholar of organizations and politics, said that one can have power or autonomy, but not both. In itself, power can cause dependence, like a drug where the dose must be increased, so it's always stronger and more intense.

Loneliness is a further cost to pay: one of the nefarious consequences of power is loneliness. Then there is the dilemma of trust: who to trust? Powerful people develop, understandably, a kind of armour with which they protect themselves; they tend not to trust those around them. It would be interesting to evaluate the correlation between the degree of power and mistrust towards others. Jennifer Chatman of the University of Berkeley has done experiments to evaluate to what extent adulation towards the powerful is effective. The study concluded scientifically that adulation always works, there are no limits, especially when it comes to working with a *Peacock*-narcissist. I imagine it as a kind of curse of power. On the one hand, power pushes us not to trust others, but at the same time leads us to believe their adulation. How sad it must be to get to the top only to listen to the flattering *Parrots*, jokers and fools and be wary of all others. Observing and evaluating the behaviour of certain modern imperial courts, also called management teams or boards of directors, we understand why adulation is held in such high esteem and used so frequently. I believe that in certain situations rebellion is a moral obligation or, at least, people have the option to stand up and gracefully walk away.

Organizations as frog farms?

In 1957 William H. White wrote a book called *The Organization Man*, a portrait of the United States that later became a manifesto of the social

transformation underway in the bureaucracy of that time, which aimed
to wipe out individuality to create perfect bureaucrats, able to pass
any test of conformity. If I could, I would make it obligatory to read
the article by Jerry B. Harvey, professor of Management at George
Washington University, entitled 'Organizations as Phrog Farms'.[14] Harvey
uses what appears to be a mistake, writing *phrog* and not *frog*, specifically
to indicate a process of modification limited to the human world but not
to the animal world. Changing autonomous individuals into obedient
phrogs, each croaking on their own lily pad in the pond, seems to be a
feature limited to organizations. The article is hilarious but explains that
we can also be turned into phrogs. For example, in several organizations
it is much more important to follow the chain of command than to
act sensibly, with judgement and maturity. In fact, it's just like that: one of
the deadly sins in any organization is to speak directly with the boss
of your immediate superior without the latter knowing.

I can't fail to mention a passage from Harvey's article:

> *There is a myth among phrogs that kissing another phrog turns that
> phrog into a prince. I think it should be noted that, in general, kissing
> a phrog only produces skin irritations. For those who decide to kiss
> anyway, I think they should also realize that, in all that fog, it is very
> difficult to determine which way a phrog is facing.*

A brilliant step to explain how the flattering dynamics in
organizations work. They are like a slow but inexorable genetic
modification of our behaviour.

Harvey then describes how the internal struggles are very similar
to the traps set in the phrog pond, as the phrogs frequently try to set
traps for one another. Stated differently, if you have to set a phrog trap,
there is no need to do so. *You are already in it.*

In addition, the phrogs have another feature to keep an eye on: the
fear of thinking independently. The phrogs let the others decide and

this renunciation presents some undoubted advantages linked to the total perceived absence of responsibility. How many times have we heard the phrase: 'I was only following orders from above?' Many times: for example during the trial against the Nazi criminals held in Nuremberg at the end of the Second World War or from the mouths of the accused in various corruption trials. These human beings, turned into poisonous frogs, said – and continue to do so today – that when they killed innocent people or stole in the name of the party, they were only obeying orders, as if it were impossible to say no. Do you believe them?

Trip to China

In September 2014 I visited, together with a group of about 60 young entrepreneurs,[15] the Central Party School of the Communist Party in Beijing, a fundamental institution in the complex Chinese political system. Once inside I was amazed, I felt like I was on a university campus in England or the United States: modern buildings, well-tended lawns, order, cleanliness, even a beautiful artificial lake. The School of Management is the place where the 1,300 senior managers of a nation with 1.3 billion inhabitants are trained and catechized, people who will occupy essential positions in Chinese society. To be admitted to this school, you have to overcome very competitive selection systems. I was struck by the very high level of openness and curiosity. For example, for many years the School has invited people from all over the world from the fields of finance, industry and politics to learn and observe. Certainly the ideology of the Communist Party remains absolutely firm and incontestable, the openness and interest in learning from those who come from outside is evident and the students didn't seem to be 'frogs in the pond' at all, to return to

Harvey's analogy, but thinkers – naturally, with a perimeter of thought well limited by an unquestionable ideology – ready to conquer the world with absolute determination, to admire and give you the shivers.

When we think of the price we are paying for a career we have to ask ourselves this question: do we work in an organization that looks like a frog farm? Do we enjoy large spaces but are *enclosed* by an ideology that cannot be discussed, as in the Communist Party School? Do we work in an organization where we can be ourselves, like a gym where we can train and develop our talent? If you hear croaking, or worse, you've started croaking, take a big leap and leave. History has taught us that there's very little chance of being kissed by a prince or a princess.

Three millennia of wisdom and authenticity

The price to pay is not just paid by us, but also weighs on the people with whom we share our existence. The question then becomes: what's the price we make others pay?

The Men's Club is a group of about 40 people aged between 65 and 90 who have been meeting in Virginia, near Washington, twice a month, on Saturdays, from 7.30 to 9 in the morning, over the course of many years. They became acquainted at the end of the '80s because they used to go to the same church; one of them proposed continuing their discussions together at his home and it became a tradition, to the point that even their wives began a similar tradition. Among the participants, in turn, two brought coffee, two orange juice and some bagels, the famous American doughnut. Everyone arrives punctually, each with his own chair brought from home. I was invited to participate by my friend and neighbour, Rick, an energetic and positive man who is more than 70 years old. I accepted more out of politeness than anything else; I was by far the youngest, but from the first day I didn't miss a meeting over the next four years. The group followed strict rules. First: no talking about work and no business. Second: we could talk about anything *that was in our heart*. Third: at exactly 9am the meeting ended with a prayer to give thanks for being alive, for still being close to the people we loved and to remember the people who are suffering. I didn't miss a meeting in four years because, besides making me feel really welcome, protected and respected, I was interested in understanding what regrets, dreams, aspirations these sincere men could have who had come to the end of their careers.

I didn't have to wait long. John, one of the participants, had got divorced years before and for a long time had only had occasional contact with his now 30-year-old daughter. One day the young woman called him on the phone with a sad voice but he, always working, was too busy and promised to call her back soon. He called her back after a few days but it was too late. His ex-wife informed him that their daughter had committed suicide, without any apparent reason. Having received the terrible news just a few days before one of our meetings, John decided to share it with the Men's Club for comfort and support. At the end of John's sad story, a few minutes of deafening silence followed, one of the longest of my life. The devastating story of our friend's daughter influenced our conversations in the following months. What price did we make others pay? Were we around and available when other people needed us? Did we listen not only to what they said, but also to how they said it? *People forget what they have heard but remember how they felt.* I realized that the men of this club, with different social backgrounds and religions, shared a regret for the time they hadn't spent with their wives, children and grand-children. Not once in four years did I hear these men talk about career-related regrets. I understood, with the heart before the head, that what worries us and occupies the brain at 30, 40 or 50 years of age ('I have to increase sales, reduce the budget, get a promotion, buy a car, go to the meeting, answer emails . . .') is not a major issue when we *really* take stock of our lives.

When it was my turn to host the meeting, I asked the group a question: 'Did you manage to fulfil the *dream* you had when you were young?' You can't imagine the intensity and the beauty of those conversations.

During these meetings I also laughed more than at any time of my life since my school days. During a meeting, Peter – 82, always wearing the baseball cap of his favourite team – told us all that he thought he had a prostate tumour, asking us to pray for him. Two weeks later, Peter came to the meeting and shouted out: 'Friends, good news: thank God, they're just haemorrhoids!' We all laughed out loud, shouting for joy and hugging him happily. In this case, I understood that being healthy is a source of happiness and how we can take it for granted. I realize how important it is to have a support group, people who listen to you and don't judge you. I understand the joy of being sincere instead of 'putting on an act' to convince others, to build an image that doesn't correspond to reality. You will learn that in life you will meet many masks and few faces, as Pirandello wrote.

When I left Washington, I hugged those 40 wonderful men, one by one, with affection and gratitude, trying to imprint those faces in my memory, knowing that it takes courage not to wear a mask.

Men's Club, I really miss those sincere people: we have to learn from human beings like them, a wealth of experiences and love. With their incredible stories, they taught me what really matters in life.

The orange taxi

My wife and I are celebrating our tenth wedding anniversary. I take Lalia out to a nice restaurant for the occasion. When the moment arrives for the toast, I kiss her tenderly, while thinking to myself that my wife should be made a saint for having endured someone like me. These have been ten wonderful years, thank you so much. Lalia points out: 'It's only been seven years, not ten'. I hesitate for a moment, then I reply that, no, it's been exactly ten years. Then, without any tone of reproach, she reminds me of my 75 business trips, lasting an average of two weeks: 150 weeks, three years away from home travelling to more than 50 different countries. She's right. What price did I pay? What price *did I make the people I love pay?*

At the airport, on my return from my next trip, I look at the fathers and mothers buying presents for their children. I also buy a useless gift, while inside I know only too well that my daughter doesn't want gifts but just wants to spend more time with me. I remember how my father, when I was seven, took me to the cinema to see a film and then we went for pizza together, just me and him. I remember absolutely everything about that day: it was 1971, it was raining, my father had brown velvet trousers, it was an occasion that was never repeated. He worked 15 hours a day; he did it for 35 years. In the same way, I'd once taken my daughter Sadika to see a film she had chosen, *Frozen*. Sadika, just five years old, had wanted to sit on my lap and I couldn't have felt happier.

Here at the airport I remembered that moment: remembering the sound of my daughter's breath, the warmth of her small body sitting on my lap, I decide to quit a job that I like, but which is keeping me too far away from my daughter. I decide to look for a job that doesn't require me to travel so much anymore, that no longer forces me to take the orange taxi to the airport on Sunday morning while all three of us make a huge emotional effort not to cry.

I thank heaven for having had this opportunity, and am so grateful to Lalia and Sadika, who are close to me and helped me understand with their love the price that we, as a family, were paying. Repentant? Yes, for not having done it earlier.

How much land does a man need? Do we really know what the price we have to pay is to make a career? How far can we push? Do we really want to win the rat race? Cost-benefit analysis should not only be economic, but also emotional and personal. Starting with the costs we force others to pay, often just to satisfy our own ego and vanity. How much land do we need?

The pact with the devil

What does it mean to make a pact with the devil? To explain it, we can't help but refer to two classics of literature: Goethe's *Faust* and Oscar Wilde's *Dorian Gray*. In the first, Faust stipulates a pact with the devil, Mephistopheles, not to obtain favours or riches, but to soothe the profound sense of dissatisfaction, which so precisely describes the soul of modern man. Faust sells his soul to Mephistopheles and is pardoned by God only at the point of death because of his continuous aspiration to reach infinity. In the second, the protagonist, obsessed with the cult of his own beauty and youth, stipulates a pact with the devil to remain eternally beautiful and young, while his portrait, hidden in the attic, bears signs of his physical decay and the corruption and moral depravity of his soul. Torn with remorse, Gray slashes the painting with a knife, killing himself. However, the following day the man is found dead, with the knife stuck in his heart, aged and ugly, while the painting portrays him as beautiful and full of youth.

Turning to history, and therefore to real events, I want to remember the story of Stanley Milgram,[16] an American psychologist who, unable to understand the horror of the Nazi concentration camps, in 1962, at the University of Yale, conducted an experiment that made the world tremble, and not just the academic world. Milgram wanted to investigate a question: if a person with authority asked a common, normal person to give an electric shock of up to 450 volts to another person, what would the normal individual do? The experiment was conducted with 40 volunteers, called 'teachers', supervised by a 'researcher' in a white coat, who gave 'students' electric shocks of increasing intensity when they gave wrong answers to pre-established questions. The electric shocks were actually fictitious and the 'students' were actors who were part of the experiment, but the 'teachers' were not aware of this. As the experiment progressed, the fictitious effects produced by the electric shocks created problems for the 'teachers' who refused to continue; at that point the 'researcher' in the white coat, would push them to continue using precise sentences: 'Continue, please'; 'The experiment requires you to continue'; 'It's important that you continue'; 'You have no choice: you must carry on'. In 65 per cent of the cases the 'teachers' continued until they were giving the most dangerous shocks. At the end of the experiment, 84 per cent of the 'teachers' said they were happy to have participated. How is it possible for people considered normal to become perverse or sadistic? According to the Yale study, the factors related to obedience are different, but in general the majority of people tend to obey in the presence of pressure exerted by a person or group with authority. Even more disturbing are the experiments conducted by Philip Zimbardo, completed in 1971 at Stanford University.[17] The experiment consisted of dividing university students into two groups: a group of prisoners and a group of guards, reproducing the dynamics of a prison. The experiment was terminated after six days – it should have lasted 15 – because it had become too violent and psychologically unmanageable by those who had organized it.

Although in the experiments by Milgram or Zimbardo, the electric shocks are fictitious, sometimes history has shown us how people who are considered normal can become accomplices in events that nobody should ever have been a part of. This is explored, for example, by Daniel Goldhagen's book *Hitler's Willing Executioners*,[18] in which the author wonders how many German people were capable of carrying out the most monstrous genocide ever. Blind obedience. Just the *thought* of a possible punishment leads to absolute obedience and to removing the principle that actually we *always* have a choice, that of *not obeying* certain meaningless orders. The legal aspect can be taken into consideration up to a certain point: almost everything Hitler did was *legal*, after he'd passed inconceivable and inhumane laws. We must therefore understand that what is legal is not necessarily also morally acceptable. Often it's exactly the opposite.

Finally we consider the extreme case of Eric Fair[19] and his inability to rebel against the authority that led him to perform horrible acts. Enlisted in the US army as an Arabic interpreter from 1995 to 2000, Eric worked in Iraq as a contract interrogator in early 2004. He was sent along with other colleagues to the prisons of Fallujah and Abu Ghraib (the infamous prison of Saddam Hussein) to interrogate 1000 prisoners. Twelve-hour shifts, 6 days a week. Eric had to keep them awake for hours, put them under pressure, wear them down, scream, humiliate them, in other words, torture them. And he did it. That experience and the regret of not having had the courage to rebel against those inhuman interrogation practices devoured him day after day and for this reason, in 2007, he decided to write a letter to the *Washington Post*[20] to denounce the nefarious things he'd done, his pain and the nightmares that haunt him. There's a sentence that struck me in his letter: 'I failed because I didn't have the courage to disobey malicious senseless orders'. By the law of karma, now it's he who no longer sleeps, who no longer enjoys life because he sold his soul 'to the God of torture'.[21]

Disobedience or choice?

Returning to Milgram, subsequent experiments demonstrated the importance of rebellion: when a subject publicly refused to obey,

90 per cent of the other study subjects stopped before giving the victims severe shocks. If we think about it, the history of humanity is made up of people who have disobeyed, who said NO. Rosa Parks, a civil rights activist, didn't get up from her seat on *that* bus, thus starting a movement that led to the end of racial segregation; Martin Luther King, too, didn't accept racial segregation; the Chinese student stood in front of the advancing tank in Tiananmen Square; Nelson Mandela didn't bend; Mahatma Gandhi didn't submit to British colonization; Giacomo Matteotti rebelled against fascism; and the Catholic Church, Falcone and Borsellino – and many others with them – didn't remain silent against the Mafia. What have we learned from these people?

Thank God, we're not in such extreme conditions. We're not at war, we're not hostages of fierce dictatorships, we're not held prisoner in places forgotten by everyone. These are stories that can help us to understand how even in normal work situations we can come to terms with the devil and identify our inner hell. For this reason, I want to share them with you.

At a conference I bumped into Pedro, a former colleague of mine who was also in charge of HR, whom I hadn't seen for about three years, as we had both changed employers during this time. He seemed older, grey, sad. We agreed to meet up for a drink after the business dinner, and he told me what happened with regard to his most recent departure from the company we were both working for. Pedro tells me that his superior had asked him to approve a pay rise for his partner; he replied that it wasn't a good idea and that he would have to wait for the annual salary review, but his boss insisted and Pedro ended up doing what he wanted. However, everyone found out about the famous pay rise and when the manager found himself in a difficult situation he blamed Pedro, who was forced to resign; only later was the boss fired. Pedro told me, trembling like a leaf, how the experience left him traumatized. He thought he had established a relationship of trust with his superior, but he hadn't hesitated for a second to blame him to save his own skin. Pedro confessed to me that he regretted obeying orders, instead of putting in writing that he wouldn't approve the unreasonable pay rise. Buckling under pressure from his manager, he'd signed his own sentence.

Some time after this episode, my boss asked me to hire a person at a high level and with a generous salary, without following the usual selection process and without having either an open position or the available budget. The person in question didn't even have the academic qualifications and experience necessary to be employed at that level. I told my superior that, according to the internal rules approved by him, we couldn't proceed. He urged me, in a stern irritated tone, to think again. That night I woke up suddenly remembering Pedro's story and, at 3am, I sent an email listing the reasons why we shouldn't proceed: two pages full of notes. I thought, mistakenly, that the problem was solved.

I went on holiday and when I returned to the office I found among the various documents to be signed the letter of employment *for that person*. I called my superior so that I could talk to him, but he didn't answer and his very faithful assistant hastily told me to sign the letter, which wouldn't make any difference to me, 'just a quick signature, five seconds of work'. I didn't sign it, I left the letter directly on my boss's desk, adding firmly that he could sign it on his own. I later found out that he hadn't asked any another manager to do it.

After a year, this hiring was discussed in several newspapers and, rest assured, not positively, I was summoned by my boss to provide explanations at a meeting that I would call surreal, during which he asked me to resign immediately because of this unfortunate event, offering me a generous severance package to leave quickly and silently. I showed him the photocopies of both the email that I sent and the letter that I hadn't signed and I didn't say a single word. I felt like I was in a thriller movie, in a kind of duel. I walked out of my boss's office like a punch-drunk boxer; I needed to sit on the floor, my head was spinning. My superior gave me the cold-shoulder treatment for weeks. If he happened to be in the lift with me he pretended not to see me; his silence and his indifference hurt me. I realized that I had to leave as soon as possible. After so many years, *how that was done still wounds me.*[22]

The world's best chef. The pilot who landed his plane on a river. The magician who made history. The computer scientist who changed animated films forever. What do they have in common? They are all Rebels, as proved by the engaging book by Francesca Gino, *Rebel Talent.*[23] Rebels do break the rules but they also earn status and respect. History and progress is not made by docile followers but by Rebels who challenge the status quo. If you still don't believe the concept of Rebels as engines for meaningful change, take Winston Churchill and George Orwell:[24] they were also true Rebels. George Orwell wrote that one of the rules he learned in school was 'Break the rules or perish', inspiring a lifelong scepticism for authority. In fact both he and Churchill had the courage to see that a society and government that denies people basic rights and freedom is a totalitarian regime and as such needs to be resisted. They did so in a moment where authoritarian rulers were en vogue, when in 1938 German dictator Hitler got the cover page of *Time* as man of the year. Many years have passed; we need more rebels in organizations, not *Snakes, Parrots* or *Foxes*. I personally learned in my own career that it is better to ask for forgiveness after breaking the rules than to ask for permission before daring to break them. The same applies to Rebel companies. If you believe that Apple was the first, please visit the newly open Design Museum in London:[25] you will find an entire room dedicated to Olivetti and you will see typewriters made in the 70s – called Valentina – in sparkling blue, red, yellow, green and products with amazing designs and innovative technology. Adriano Olivetti put human beings, and their creativity at the centre of Olivetti, not himself or profit: and profit, by the way, came.

What would we have done?

Now I'm going to describe some brief situations, with the aim of presenting us with dilemmas linked with opportunities, and the ethics behind making certain choices.

- We're auditors at a prestigious company. We're in charge of carrying out a review for a pharmaceutical company, a very important client. When conducting our analysis, we realize that EUR 2 million has been recorded on the balance sheet for medicines that expired many years ago; eliminating this value from the balance sheet would mean the company would end the year making a loss. We tell our boss who, in no uncertain terms, tells us to let it go *because we can't afford to lose a client like them.* In the evening the client takes us out to dinner, orders expensive food and wine and gives us solid gold pens, counting on our *discreet collaboration.*

- We work in the legal department and we realize that the contract for a very important job was won by a company whose owner is a close relative of the CEO.

- We organize a training course in a foreign country, with about 120 participants coming from all over the world. The educational material we sent is stopped at the border without any reason. They inform us that the customs procedures can only be resolved with a payment of USD 5,000 in cash, otherwise we'll be obliged to cancel the course.

- We are doctors. A well-known pharmaceutical company invites us on a Caribbean cruise with our family, as long as our prescriptions only indicate their medicines.

- We have to do an executive search for a high number of senior roles. A consulting company contacts us offering us an amount equal to six months of our salary if we entrust the task to them.

- An employee sends in a medical certificate for three months, from June to September. We happen to bump into him at the end of July at the resort where we go to spend the holidays: healthy and tanned, he works there as a musician. The employee, a relative of the manager of the resort, offers us the holiday for free, provided we remain silent about seeing him.

- We're the representatives of our company for an important contract. A person from a competing company who is participating in the same tender offers us a nice new car. The condition: we have to submit a tender bid which is so high that it'll be certain that our company won't be awarded the contract.

- (And now my favourite story, which really happened.) Together with other colleagues, we have to negotiate debt restructuring for a medium-sized company. After a long journey, I arrive at a hotel owned by our client's company. I'm sleeping, when around midnight there's a knock at the door. I open it, annoyed: it's a prostitute who offers to spend the night with me, a gift from the hotel management. I laugh, thank her, decline the offer and return to sleep. Two hours later, there's another knock at the door: it is the same lady and she offers me the same service. Really annoyed I close the door in her face. At 4am, another knock on the door; this time I'm furious. But when I open the door there's a man standing in front of me, who tells me that since I *obviously* don't like women, the hotel management has decided to diversify the offer.

Reflections to remain free

All true stories, many of them have happened to me or to dear friends. What lessons can we draw from them? The first observation is related to our total lack of preparation to manage these situations: there are no university courses that cover this; *we just have our values and the choices we make.*

The second observation: we are talking about corruption, but can the devil take on different forms or even something deeper? I'm convinced that it's not only a matter of choosing between corruption and honesty but above all of deciding **whether or not to be free**. By accepting a recommendation, we'll become debtors; anyone who has debts is not free; accepting a holiday, an expensive gift, a treat of any kind, we will be blackmailed, automatically no longer free to act, think, write in whatever way we want. We'll become prisoners, we'll sell our integrity, our freedom. Will we let Mephistopheles win and take our soul or can we make the right choice? Viktor Frankl, author of the seminal book *Man's Search for Meaning*[26] said that in any situation we still have the freedom to choose and the possibility of finding meaning, even and especially in suffering. Freedom isn't therefore doing whatever we want. Freedom becomes making conscious choices that don't leave us open to blackmail. Victor Frankl said that *there is an external stimulus and our internal response. The space between stimulus and response is called choice and this choice is our freedom.* Please read it again.

There is an external stimulus and our internal response. The space between stimulus and response is called choice and this choice is our freedom.

We therefore need to use two tools wisely: our moral Compass and our Radar.

We started with two questions. What price do we pay – and do we make others pay – to advance our career? What price do we pay to reach an agreement with the devil? There are so many true stories, but some are perhaps extreme examples to explain what a pact with the devil is. The stories at companies are similar: driven by a figure of authority or in the name of a false god, many sell their soul without evaluating the consequences: company executives who falsify the balance sheets to pocket money; politicians who pocket bribes or steal votes; contests rigged to the detriment of serious qualified people; jobs given in exchange for favours of various kinds; recommendations for a relative to be hired at the expense of a well-qualified candidate; rigged contracts and illegal sexual favours. The list goes on.

The pact with the devil really exists, potentially within all of us. The experiments by Milgram and Zimbardo were shocking and devastating because they forced us to observe ourselves in front of a mirror and admit that we could have been the ones giving those electric shocks or much worse. The distance from Auschwitz was not so far. By being fully aware of it, by evaluating the consequences, we'll avoid the 'fatal embrace' of the diabolical pact, preserving our soul while remaining true to ourself. I've never worried about technical mistakes, I've made thousands of them, but when something smells rotten I keep my distance.

We make a pact with the devil when, letting others decide for us, we blindly obey and *follow orders* thus abdicating our free will, the ability to make choices – the greatest gift we have – in exchange for rewards of any kind. It's not a question of becoming obstinate, a pain in the neck, or behaving like a spanner in the works. It's a matter of always being on our guard with our ethical and moral values, avoiding unacceptable compromises that may arise under various seductive and dangerous forms. Never engage the autopilot when driving on dangerous roads.

We can agree that it's not easy to *resist* but do we really have any other valid choice? We're talking about our soul, our freedom as human beings. Under no circumstances does freedom mean doing whatever you want when you want to the detriment of others, but rather making thoughtful choices that allow you to remain autonomous and independent, respecting the rules and, above all, others: because we are the others. We are the others.

Believe me, I've seen and worked with too many people who have signed a pact with the devil, ending up forgotten and buried in the attic like the portrait of Dorian Gray or, worse, swallowed up by the underworld, without hope, like Mozart's Don Giovanni.

Part Three

Freedom

7

Success inside the Village. How to build a career and remain a decent person

'Success is the ability to go from failure to failure
without losing your enthusiasm.'
WINSTON CHURCHILL

Steps to building a career

It's not difficult to build a career. On the other hand, it can be complicated to build a career while remaining true to yourself.

There are only two ways to build a career: as decent people or not. This chapter only describes the first way, but teaches us how to protect ourselves from those acting according to other criteria since, as we have learned, we will find many like that on our journey. We need to learn not only to recognize them but also to manage them or at least limit the damage they cause.

To understand how to build a career we must, in the following order:

- stop believing that Santa Claus exists;
- understand who holds power;
- manage the relationship with our boss;
- invest in our relational capital and our presence.

I'm going to tell you a series of true stories. Brace yourself, this chapter has some highly emotional content.

Do we still believe in Santa Claus?

Ignac Semmelweis was born in 1818 near Budapest. He graduated in medicine at 26, specializing in obstetrics and in 1846 began working in one of the two maternity wards at the Vienna General Hospital. But during his first month of work he was left traumatized: out of 208 hospitalized women, 36 died, a mortality rate of 17 per cent. Although the hospital was free, built for people in need, many women preferred to give birth to their children on the street, because of the poor reputation of the health facility. Furthermore, Semmelweis noted that in the other maternity ward the mortality rate was much lower. Not content with official explanations without any scientific basis, Semmelweis sought rigorous and ascertainable causes that clarified the phenomenon: he noticed that near the maternity ward there was a morgue and that many doctors had got into the habit of both performing autopsies and assisting births. When a colleague cut himself with a scalpel used for an autopsy and died within a few days, Semmelweis noted that the wounds and the infection were the same as those of the women who had died in the delivery room and finally sensed the source of the problem. He immediately ordered all the doctors and nurses to wash their hands numerous times a day with chlorinated water and, as a result, the mortality rate was drastically reduced, reaching zero after two years.

His discovery (which seems obvious to us, but wasn't at that time) saved thousands of lives. Ignac shared the results of his discovery with the medical elite of Vienna, stating that the simple act of disinfecting his hands has defeated the scourge of maternal mortality. If the Nobel Prize for Medicine had existed at the time, don't you think he would have deserved it?

But Semmelweis soon realizes that his teachings are not well accepted by the medical community in Vienna, who attack and mock him. He leaves the General Hospital which, a year later, returns to its previous mortality rate. The Viennese medical community becomes openly hostile, and his book *Die Ätiologie, der Begriff und die Prophylaxe des Kindbettfiebers*[1] is ridiculed and deemed absolutely worthless. Semmelweis fights back, writing fiery letters in which he accuses doctors of being murderers; even his wife begins to doubt his mental health. In 1865, as a trap, he was invited to visit an asylum, where he was locked up against his will; put in a straitjacket, beaten by sadistic nurses. Forgotten by everyone, Semmelweis died after two weeks. He had the merit of making an exceptional scientific discovery but was wrong to antagonize his colleagues: a fatal mistake, in the true sense of the term.

Let's think about Winston Churchill, one of the greatest statesmen who ever lived. He was the most beloved Prime Minister in Britain, he defeated the Nazis, won the war, and yet he lost the 1945 elections.

Many people in the world of sport, politics, business or education are *removed* after having achieved brilliant results or remain in their place after sensational failures. Why? For the rational mind this does not make sense which is exactly my point: some decisions have nothing to do with rational thinking.

I'm just 24 years old; it's my first job and my first company crisis. The only way to save the Italian branch is to reduce costs by making

50 per cent of the staff redundant, in almost impossible times. I'm clearly unprepared to handle such a dramatic situation. My superior, who should take the reins, given his thirty years of experience and with a salary twenty times mine, leaves the company within a week and disappears without saying goodbye. I can't sleep at night; I'm scared. It would be a miracle to be able to keep the branch open and save 300 jobs out of about 600. I work 14–16 hours a day, six days a week, and every morning I expect to be fired. After eight months of negotiations, discussions, fierce struggles with colleagues, unions and with the American head office, they inform us that the branch, which has been heavily restructured, can remain open: a miracle. Qualified people lose their jobs and are sent home; others, who are more sly and clever, find a way to stay.

That day I lost my innocence: my utopian ideas had crumbled, thinking that to build a career – or keep your post – only happens to those who deserve it and work hard. I felt like a child who discovers not only that Santa Claus doesn't exist, but that he was a real fool to believe it. A German proverb says: '*A great war leaves the country with three armies – an army of cripples, an army of mourners, and an army of thieves*'; in my opinion, fierce corporate restructuring has almost the same devastating effects.

I've been working as a HR director for many years. Whichever company I worked in, I was always struck by the low correlation between results, talent and career progression. Having talent and achieving results are necessary but not sufficient conditions to *reach the top*. If we believe, then, that to build a career you just have to be good and work hard, it's time to understand that it's not always like this: Santa Claus doesn't exist.

It is difficult to keep faith when one loses his innocence. We're grown up enough to know that life is not necessarily *fair*, right. This awareness should not drive us into depression or turn us into cynical pessimists.

On the contrary, we must never talk about surrendering: we have to take it up a notch, aware of the difficulties that lie before us, but also aware of our abilities, talent, passions, heart, competence, merit, integrity: the things that move us. And the sweat, so much sweat, which is required. Believe it or not, but this is part of the fun in our job: the joy to prove them wrong and *the happiness of pursuit*, which is, to me, more meaningful than the pursuit of happiness.

Understanding who holds the power

At one of the companies where I was hired, I spent the first few weeks meeting the most important people. Every day I would listen to five to six directors and vice presidents, all with large offices and clear symbols of power. I notice that everyone tells me about a person *I should definitely meet*: her name is Mel, a tiny woman, her office is in a corner, hidden behind a plant. After meeting her I realize that she maintains a very low profile, presents herself in a simple way, doesn't wear make-up, comes to work by bike, speaks softly and doesn't say much, but always with a great deal of intelligence and depth. Although Mel is not at the top of the hierarchy, she is respected, consulted and welcomed by her colleagues and also by former employees who continue to trust in her judgement. Mel is certainly the most influential person in the whole organization; she knows it and manages this influence with grace, humility and a pinch of humour and a lot of love for her work and for her peers.

The mistake which many beginners make is to think that the hierarchical level is the only factor that establishes the power of a person within an organization. As demonstrated by the example just mentioned, another important element is the degree of personal influence. Based on these considerations, we can *visualize* a simple

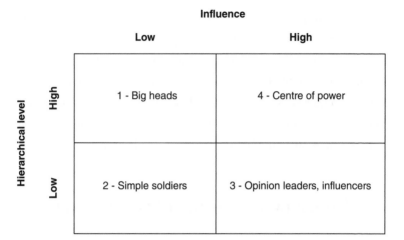

Figure 7.1 *The power matrix.*

power matrix[2] with one axis that indicates the hierarchical level of the position held in the organization and with the other the degree of influence.

In this matrix, in quadrant 1 we have the big heads, similar to the *Peacocks* in Chapter 5, people who have lofty-sounding titles (which say little, like 'Vice-President of Global and Strategic Projects'), without however having any specific weight or influence. Usually these people are in a difficult phase in their careers; other times they are on the way out.

In quadrant 2, similar to the faithful *Dogs*, we meet the simple soldiers, people with a degree of influence limited to their own backyard.

Moving to the right in the direction of power, we find people like Mel, with a great deal of influence but not necessarily at a high hierarchical level in the organization. We can compare this category to the *Owls*, wisemen, influencers, opinion leaders.

Undoubtedly the centre of power of an organization is located in quadrant 4: people who have both a high hierarchical level and the influence to manage power. And what do these people do besides deciding and commanding? Their *real job is to create or maintain the culture of the organization.* This element becomes evident when working at a family-owned company, where there is constant indoctrination to continuously inculcate and reiterate the teachings and the *modus operandi* of the founder.

To understand the power of a person in an organization we must also take into account other factors: years ago I couldn't explain why a young secretary was able to exercise power that was so disproportionate to her role; I underestimated her influence until I saw her passionately kissing the President at a classical music concert.

In summary, we have ascertained that Santa Claus doesn't exist and we have acquired an instrument to decipher who holds power according to hierarchical level and degree of influence. Who will be the most influential in our career? We'll be the most influential people, followed by our bosses.

Managing the relationship with our boss

When we become part of an organization, we always find ourselves with a 'boss'. In my career, I've had 18 different bosses, from 14 different countries, two of them perfect psychopaths, most of them just great people. I myself have been many people's boss, and it's a word I don't truly like. When we think of this figure, in general, we feel vulnerable, at the mercy of another person's whims, sometimes victims, sometimes more fortunate.

In fact we must *learn how to manage the relationship with our boss,* knowing that we are bound by a common purpose: our positive results will also be good for him/her. We must therefore start from a different perspective: our superior should not be understood in principle as an enemy or as a person to be avoided, but as someone with whom we must interact positively, knowing that we must adapt ourselves to them and not vice versa; it's a relationship to be experienced as an interdependence between two people with all their weaknesses, failings, defects, aspirations and different cultures.[3]

First of all, and I say this from experience, we should not expect too much from our boss, I don't in bad faith but because their time and energy is not infinite. When I started working at the World Bank I made a huge mistake: I promised that I would meet all the people on my team. The problem was that there were about 120 and it took me almost a year to keep my promise. When I finally got to know all the teammates, I realized that many people were irritated because they had waited so long for the first meeting, others because afterwards I neglected them for months. By trying the best I could, I disappointed several people.

What should we do to establish a good relationship with our superior? We begin by observing their management style and their personality.

Peter Drucker divides leaders into two categories, those who prefer to read and those who prefer to speak and listen.[4] It becomes fundamental to understand their habits: some love to have frequent and informal conversations, others only want to talk to us by appointment.

We need to learn their language. To understand our boss, it is important to observe who he is, what he does, what his management style is. You need to ask those who have been close to him for years: how does he work? What time does he arrive? What does he like to do? In what way does he prefer to delegate? What does he consider to be important and what does he see as secondary? Is he a formal or informal person? Where does he come from? What did he study? How old is he, does he have a family? How and when do you speak?

Do you communicate by email, text message, voice, telephone, intermediary? Does he like to draw out the conversation or does he prefer concise language? What does he not tolerate? What makes him angry? What are the topics that excite him and which ones are not to be mentioned?

I had a superior from Texas who looked like a cowboy caricature. Crocodile boots, cigar, swear words, he came into my office without knocking, telling dirty jokes out loud. He was replaced by the spoiled and genuinely unpleasant son of a diplomat, who spoke elegantly and would only receive me on Wednesday at 9 in the morning for quarter of an hour, not a minute longer; if there was an urgent problem to solve on Thursday, I had to wait for a week to talk to him. I was going crazy, then I realized that it was me who had to adapt to his rules, not the other way round.

Furthermore, it's necessary to take into account the development of the individual and how well-rounded they are: some leaders are mature and reasonable people, others are not at all.

A theory that is extraordinarily useful in this sense, to decipher and understand our boss and to evaluate ourselves too, is provided by Susanne R. Cook-Greuter, author of a powerful article[5] in which she demonstrates that the stages of psychological development of an adult are sequential and multiple. In the conventional phase of adult psychological development, we'll find many *opportunistic people or people who are exclusively interested in themselves and who see others only as tools for achieving results. This can apply to anyone, even more so to our superiors.* Continuing along this path, we adults enter a second phase, the *diplomatic* phase, in which we realize that we are not alone and must interact with our fellow man. In general, everyone then aspires to become good at something and to build a precise professional identity, before moving on to the *expert* stage. In the last conventional phase of adult development, we become *conquerors*, people who push the accelerator at full throttle to reach their goals. Some, about 15 per cent, manage to gain a deeper and more complete psychological development and become *alchemists*, capable of transforming not only themselves but also the people around them and the organizational systems they are part of. I've had only two out of 18 bosses who were able to operate and *be* at this level: these people helped to transform me with their method of management. Others have been opportunists or diplomats, terrified of any form of conflict or unable to make an important decision.

In the relationship established with our boss, it is important to understand and clarify the mutual expectations, especially regarding the results to be achieved. Here's a story to explain this.

The sales director, Silvio, calls me to his office urgently and I understand from his irritated tone that it won't be a pleasant conversation. 'We have to fire Roy! That slacker arrives in the office at lunch time, when all the others have arrived well before 9: it's outrageous! Get rid of him, today!' He was furious and didn't seem to want to discuss it any further. I walk out, concerned, and head to Roy's office: it is 10am and my colleagues confirm that he never arrives before noon. I leave various messages but he doesn't get back to me until early afternoon. His fate seems inevitable; Silvio's accusations seem well founded. I fix a meeting at the bar outside the office and Roy orders a triple espresso. In fact, he seems really tired. I'm thinking to myself: 'Not only does he arrive at 2pm, but he also needs a triple espresso to stay awake. What the hell is he doing?' Soon, however, I find that there's a rational explanation for all this: in fact, for about eight months Luca has been dealing with Asian customers. 'I'm happy to do it', he tells me, 'but I have to work according to their time zone. Last night, for example, I spoke to two clients, one in China, one in Japan, and I finished at 6 in the morning. I slept for a few hours and here I am. For months I have been working from noon till dawn. I can't take it anymore. I drink ten coffees a day, but it's not enough: can you help me?'

Roy has found it very difficult to talk to his boss Silvio, who obviously is not aware of the situation: 'I have tried many times, but he has always cancelled at the last minute; last week he made me wait for two hours without seeing me'. Two hours later I'm in Silvio's office. When I walk in he asks me if I have dismissed *that good for nothing*. However, Silvio is forced to listen to me while I explain the reasons why Luca deserves a bonus rather than a dismissal. Silvio almost falls off his chair, but then authorizes the bonus and agrees to have lunch with me and Roy. It's the first time that they've spoken in the space of 15 months.

I've helped organizations and teams with a very simple exercise. Working, for example, with a medium-sized team of about 30 people, I start by physically separating the manager (or group of managers) from the rest of the team. I ask the manager what the three most important things are to be done by the members of the group. Then I ask the team what they think are the three most important things to be done, based on what they consider to be the expectations of the boss. I've been doing this exercise for years and you can imagine the surprise when it turns out that the objectives set by the boss are always, and I mean *always*, different from what the team members are attempting, in good faith, to achieve. This doesn't happen because people are obtuse or acting in bad faith, but simply because of various reasons: poor communication, cultural barriers, lack of time are some of the continuous obstacles to the correct interpretation of the objectives to be achieved. It's a concept that's easy to understand, but remains at the root of most of the problems between managers and employees: the lack of clarity on the objectives and mutual expectations.

I spent the first six years of my career at a bank where my mandate was, always and above all, to save the organization money. Then I took a job that couldn't have been more different, with a boss whose greatest aspiration from his employees was to receive long and impeccable documents. Nobody talked about cutting costs; in fact, if I mentioned this, I received hostile glances, as if I'd said something out of place, vulgar. I advise you to have a conversation with your supervisor regarding objectives on at least a monthly basis, and more often if the professional relationship is only just beginning. It's important to clarify the mutual expectations, to clarify what 'success' means. Establishing mutual expectations means gaining the trust of your boss who, as we saw in the fourth chapter, is the key ingredient of a constructive professional relationship.

Sometimes your relationship with the boss gets worse and becomes a source of frustration and anxiety and can end with your dismissal. I've seen hundreds of cases like this, painful *divorces* for both employees and organizations, and expensive in economic and emotional terms. What should we do? An approach that usually works is to sit down at a table not immediately after a dispute, but as soon as the waters have calmed down and try to figure out what went wrong. The question to ask is not 'Whose fault is it?' But rather 'What can we do to improve the current situation?', aware that *we too* will be offering solutions and suggestions. Usually the relationship with the boss starts on the right foot; after all he's the one who selected us or, even if he didn't do it himself, he'll still be interested in seeing us succeed because he will benefit from it. Nobody likes to have a person in the team who doesn't get results: we must recognize the shared goal and work together to overcome common obstacles.

These considerations presuppose a normal professional relationship. Sometimes it is not so simple, the dynamics of power give rise to real harassment and moral violence.[6] Bullying, pranks, discrimination, sarcasm, humiliation, contempt, derision, exclusion, ostracism, racism, vulgarity, sexual harassment, mobbing, these are things that exist in the workplace. You may end up with a psychopath as a boss, a person who fully belongs to the category of *Snakes* in Chapter 5; I myself had two in my career who really made me suffer, before I learned how to cope with them. Be aware that psychopaths choose their victims with cunning and malice: they are real monsters from whom we must free ourselves, to take back our life, by asking for help from professionals, using the law, seeking support from those close to us. I've seen so much suffering, lives that have been damaged, in some cases destroyed. We always have the option of choosing not to be the victim. In extreme cases, it's advisable to request a transfer or even to give up your job – but only after putting up a fight – rather than sacrificing our health, self-esteem, love of life. We must fight, not be victims.

How to survive the new boss

When a new boss arrives, the risk of not being part of his team increases exponentially, as illustrated in an article by Kevin and Edward Coyne in the *Harvard Business Review* of May 2007.[7] According to a study conducted at American companies, if the new manager is a person promoted internally, turnover[8] goes from about 8 per cent to 12 per cent, reaching 26 per cent if the new boss arrives from outside the company. Generally the new boss decides who to keep and who to get rid of within the first two months, so making an excellent first impression becomes fundamental. When the new boss arrives, the indications in the previous paragraphs are valid: *study their management style and understand their agenda; the important thing is to show that we are useful, that we'll be part of the solution, not the problem*; listen, ask questions, be active, propose ideas. Having a new boss can bring new energy, especially if their predecessor was in a pre-retirement phase and/or mentally lazy. That said, sometimes the plans of the new boss are different from what we expected and we just can't work with them.

Never outshine the master

Nicolas Fouquet was the powerful French Minister of Finance between 1653 and 1661, under the reign of Louis XIV, also known as the Sun King, who was not known for his humility; a shining example of absolute monarchy who pontificated: 'I am the State'. On 17 August 1661 Fouquet, a very rich man thanks to two fortunate marriages, organized an extraordinary feast in honour of the Sun King at his castle on the outskirts of Paris, considered to be among the most sumptuous receptions of all time, with 3,000 guests, during which Molière debuted his new work, *The Bores*. Fouquet received compliments from the guests, the French aristocratic elite, who were delighted by the refined foods and wines and the theatrical, pyrotechnic and musical performances.

Louis XIV was deeply offended, feeling overshadowed by such grandeur. Jean-Baptiste Colbert, the King's adviser, a greedy and miserable character, took advantage of the situation and made the Sun King believe that Fouquet stole taxes that belonged to the Kingdom. Louis XIV had the Minister of Finance arrested, and he would later die in a royal prison, after 20 years of imprisonment. Voltaire wrote 'on 17 August at 6 in the evening, Fouquet was King of France; at 2 in the morning, he was nobody'.

Robert Greene, in his book *The 48 Laws of Power*,[9] states that the first law is: never outshine the master. The second law, I would add, is remember the first law very well. The third law says that if you forget the first two rules, soldiers are sent to detain you, put you in a cell and forget about you (obviously figuratively): the courts composed of dwarfs, dancers, buffoons, ruffians, courtesans and old fogies didn't disappear entirely after the reign of Louis XIV; they still exist, believe me. The business model of the Sun King remains an organizational model which is very much, as the French say, *en vogue*. An almost infallible method to understand if we've ended up in a 'court' is to see if the people who are part of it try and express *schadenfreude*, a German word that means feeling pleasure at witnessing the misfortune of others, a mixture of sadism and malice.

Summary of types of leaders

In any organization we work for, we'll always have a boss. We must learn to work with him, not go on holiday together. We can end up with wonderful bosses, proper coaches that will help us grow. Michael Jordan, the legendary basketball player, recalled his first coach as someone who was 'always available when I needed him'.[10] I'm still in touch with a superior I had 15 years ago, a person who is extraordinarily generous with his time and his wisdom, to whom I often turn for advice; I'm not ashamed to write that I am fond of him.

In extreme cases, there are also psychopathic bosses, the worst possible scenario. A recent study by the University of St Gallen in Switzerland[11] explains that some stockbrokers are more interested in harming their colleagues than doing their jobs well. We'll come across indifferent or lazy bosses or even superiors like Steve Jobs, who was famous for asking collaborators and employees to achieve impossible goals with crazy deadlines; for Jobs, those who managed to handle the pressure could become a part of his inner circle, but many threw in the towel, swallowed up by an absolute genius who didn't hesitate to destroy without regard those who he believed were not at his level.[12]

Then there are bosses who want to control everything and will never trust anyone; others who will behave like poker players without giving us any kind of feedback; individuals without emotions or distracted; superiors who are tormented or have massive personal problems; managers who are narcissists, naive (but they never last long), generous and reliable.

Now we're going to spend a few minutes analysing two particular categories of boss who we may end up working under: the *Assholes* and the *Idiots*.

Regarding the first category, the *Assholes*, Aaron James has dedicated a fun book to them.[13] The main characteristic of these people is that they are deeply convinced that they're at a higher level than ordinary mortals, assuming privileges with a sense of impunity because they consider themselves 'anointed by the Lord', immune to the complaints of others and possibly from any sanctions. *The law applies to others as they sincerely believe that THEY ARE the law.* They are distinguished by their smooth language and are stuffed full of hot air, or in another word, *bullshit*. In fact there is a quasi-scientific methodology to detect the quantity of bullshit: take a document – email – paper written by them and use the blablameter.com[14] that will tell you how much their thinking is affected by BS. It's a lot of fun, I guarantee. The book *On Bullshit* by Harry Frankfurt discusses the genesis, theory and scope of this topic.[15]

The human category of *Assholes* is so widespread and universal that in the United States they had the idea of dedicating a dictionary to them; it would be really quite hilarious if it wasn't for the fact that sometimes we personally have to put up with a, more or less massive, dose of bullshit.[16] The danger is that, after having swallowed so much, we can no longer distinguish it and therefore, like the radiation from nuclear power plants, we no longer see it but it has an ominous effect: we become 'healthy carriers' or, in more serious cases, we begin even thinking and dressing like the unhealthy 'producers' of bullshit. In extreme and terminal cases the poor victims even start to like it; we work for them or, even if this seems impossible, we end up voting for them. The ring, or maybe I should write *the noose*, closes.

I was able to read a letter sent by the former CEO of Gucci to his employees, written in the third person, in which he compared what he did during his reign to a wonderful but unfinished architectural work and labelled as *dwarfs* anyone who didn't share his, undoubtedly wonderful, extraordinary ideas.[17] When I read the letter, at first I laughed, then I was forced to admit that these characters exist, and how difficult it is to work with them.

To understand the category of *Idiots*, the book by Carlo Cipolla *Happy But Not Too Much*[18] is an absolute masterpiece, a work worthy of a genius. Some of the behaviour mentioned above can make us doubt that we are part of this group and lead us to think about some of the mistakes that are made. The 'golden law' of stupidity claims that a stupid person is a person who caused losses to another person or to a group of persons while himself deriving no gain and even possibly incurring losses. As a result, the *Idiot* can be very dangerous, much more than the bandit or the delinquent.

To understand if our boss falls into this category, just observe their actions. If they have the capacity to wear everyone out, to pit people against each other, to create a climate of war, a sort of 'all against all', to fight battles without quarter against other departments, there are high chances that the boss is an *Idiot*.

Saying what is strictly necessary

'Silence is a true friend who never betrays', said Confucius. Remember: *we are the masters of our silence, we are slaves of our words*. Or, as Oscar Wilde said, sometimes it is better to keep your mouth shut and appear stupid than to open your mouth and remove all doubt. If I think back to my career, how many times have I regretted having said, or written, something? Thousands of times. How many times have I regretted not having spoken? I think two or three times. Saying the bare necessities, or as we said at school, speak only when spoken to, will avoid headaches, misunderstandings and gossip. Furthermore, we should also avoid being too open for several other reasons: the first is that by revealing too much of ourselves and our intentions, for example by confessing how important a promotion may be, we will become vulnerable. Again Oscar Wilde claimed that a little sincerity is a dangerous thing, and a great deal of it is absolutely fatal.

The beautiful 1994 film, *The Shawshank Redemption*, tells a story of hope and redemption of two prisoners sentenced to life imprisonment, played by Morgan Freeman and Tim Robbins. I won't tell you how it ends, in case you haven't seen it yet. In short, the story describes how every five years the prisoners are questioned by a commission that assesses whether they have sincerely repented and can be released. Of course, the prisoners do their best to show that they are repentant but invariably the commission denies them their freedom. Until Morgan Freeman, instead of telling the same old story, says he no longer has any interest in freedom, that he's happy to be in prison and that, frankly, he doesn't give a damn about the opinion of the commission. He becomes the only one to be released. It's just a film but it contains a great truth: if we push too hard for that coveted promotion, for example, they could make us agonize over it for years. Let's not talk about it and, when it arrives, we can also pretend to be surprised.

Reputation

What do Gioacchino Rossini[19] and *The Barber of Seville* have to do with our journey? We read, perhaps humming, the words of the aria 'Calumny is a little breeze'.

Calumny is a little breeze,
a gentle zephyr
which insensibly, subtly,
lightly and sweetly,
commences to whisper.
Softly, softly, here and there,
sottovoce, sibilant,
it goes gliding, it goes rambling.
In the ears of the people,
it penetrates slyly
and the head and the brains
it stuns and it swells.
From the mouth re-emerging
the noise grows *crescendo*,
gathers force little by little,
runs its course from place to place,
seems like the thunder of the tempest
which from the depths of the forest
comes whistling, muttering,
freezing everyone in horror.
Finally with crack and crash,
it spreads afield, its force redoubled,
and produces an explosion
like the outburst of a cannon,
an earthquake, a whirlwind,
which makes the air resound.
And the poor slandered wretch,
vilified, trampled down,
sunk beneath the public lash,
by good fortune, falls to death.

Do you remember the *ladder effect*[20] described in Chapter 4? We need to be aware that one piece of distorted information is enough to ruin our reputation, so we must never give rise to possible criticism or slander and we must avoid potentially dangerous situations. Before taking any step, we must ask ourselves: 'If my boss, my colleagues, my family, my best friend ever found out, what would happen?' If the answer is *absolutely nothing*, then we have a green light. However, if the answer is different, better think twice; without becoming paranoid, of course, but in my work I have noticed that many careers have been damaged, sometimes irreparably, by slander or actions taken lightly without first assessing the consequences. We need to make sure that what we post online passes the reputation test. We also need to carefully monitor our own behaviour: I gave a colleague a lift home for three weeks as she broke her leg a few weeks earlier and could not yet walk properly; I had to stop when a colleague told me that everyone thought she was my secret lover. *Calumny is a little breeze.*

In January 1998 everyone was talking about the relationship between President Bill Clinton and the intern Monica Lewinsky. I was in the United States at the time and I still remember the cruel jokes and wisecracks that were circulating in industrial quantities. It was the first digital scandal, broadcast all over the world at the speed of light. Before that, there were only newspapers, radio and television; the arrival of the internet, and social media helped create this famous scandal. Lewinsky recounted this experience, sharing devastating moments in a moving talk on TED:[21] her guilt, falling in love with the wrong man at 22, the public humiliation and derision, the broken reputation, the mortification, the annihilation; the miracle to be still alive. I'm convinced that defending one's reputation is without a doubt a principle of life, not just a professional principle. It struck me like the famous book for children *Oh, the Places You'll Go* by Dr Seuss,[22] which starts from this point: *the choice not to go* to places populated by monsters that can destroy us, avoid situations that can get us into trouble.

Investing in our relational capital

In Chapter 1 we talked about the Johari window; we all have some blind spots, areas unknown to ourselves, aspects of our behaviour that we're not aware of but that are clear to others. It is therefore essential to become aware of them and the best method is to work with a coach or collect feedback from the people we trust. Especially when you start working in an organization, it's important to learn both how things work and how we're perceived.

Good news: over many years I have always – and I mean always – found people available to give feedback, 'direct' advice. Generally they're people who have been working in the same place for years and will be happy to take on the role of adviser. Just ask a question with humility: 'You've been here for so many years, you've seen so many people who have failed, others who have survived, others who have been successful. What's the difference between them?' We ask openly, we actively listen and we'll quickly learn what it means to succeed. The book *Never Eat Alone* by Keith Ferrazzi[23] illustrates the importance of building lasting relationships, urging us to never miss an opportunity to interact positively with people. Many people only think about networking when they need something, but we must always invest at least 10 per cent of our time building relationships, asking for feedback, making ourselves available. Each of us has relational capital that can have immense value if cultivated with intelligence, respect, generosity. Are we investing to increase this important relational capital?

Affiliation but with caution

What's the first thing we do when we meet a new person? We look for things in common: did we study at the same university? Do we come from the same city? Do we go on holiday to the same place? Looking for things in common will make it easier to gain approval from the new group and will simplify our life. That said, we must be careful not to be absorbed, assimilated to the point that we forget our values just to be accepted. Henry Fairlie, a British journalist, in the 1950s coined the word *establishment* to describe the connection between tradition, institutions and power.[24] Being accepted by the establishment, by the ruling class, will never be easy. The real difficulty will arise with the need to find a balance between being accepted and at the same time remaining oneself.

Presence

Presence is a concept that refers to a person's communication, gravitas, image and credibility. An interesting analysis was put forward by Sylvia Ann Hewlett,[25] who considers the presence of the link between merit and success in a successful career. Presence turns out to be a combination of different elements: how a person behaves, how they communicate and their image. I believe we can add emotional intelligence and *contextual intelligence,* that is the ability to *read* the situation, to make connections between different concepts, to understand those close to us. Here is a classic example: when making presentations, the starting point is to understand who is listening to us, not just what we want to say and achieve. Know how to listen, really listen. Furthermore, even if our image doesn't have to be to formal attire, be aware that we will be judged in a fraction of a second.

In this chapter we learned that Santa Claus doesn't exist, that we need to know who commands, manage our boss, be cautious, safeguard our reputation, build relationships and be accepted while remaining anchored to our values. If this chapter has clarified what we need to do, the next chapter will focus on a question: *Should I stay or should I go?*, the decision to either stay or leave the organization we are part of.

8

Should I stay or should I go? Deciding whether to stay in the organization or leave

'*A good decision is based on knowledge and not on numbers.*'
PLATO

Go towards or run away

The titles of the songs that I'll mention in this chapter offer us a chance to reflect on where we are and where we want to go. The song by the British punk band, the Clash, *Should I Stay or Should I Go*, was recorded back in 1982: many years have passed but the indecision when it comes to deciding whether to stay in a job or change remains the same. As with the affairs of the heart, also in the employment relationship both parties can decide to end the relationship. When deciding whether it's better to *stay or go*, we must first consider whether we're in a risky situation, whether there's a real chance we might be fired, if we're at a dead end, if we're going to miss the boat, if we have actual opportunities to grow. An assessment will never be realistic if it doesn't take into account how companies *really* judge us. I want to reveal some tricks of the trade and methodologies used *by all organizations* to evaluate employees. To get through this moment unscathed, a brief introspective examination will be useful to determine, critically and with intellectual honesty if we have become *Comfortably Numb* – like the title of a legendary Pink Floyd song – or if we're making a *Roar* – as the song by Katy Perry suggests – that is, growing without arrogance, with full conviction of our means.

We're also going to evaluate a different scenario, the conditions that make us decide to leave. A difficult choice, to be taken when we're fully aware of our internal motivations, which in turn could be purely negative, like escaping from an unsustainable situation, feeling like a fish out of water in our working environment, being attracted by the bright lights elsewhere or, even worse, clashing against an organizational culture that we consider morally unacceptable.

Once we're aware that we're positively motivated by the desire to *go towards* something new, rather than *escape from* a routine that is no longer good for us, we can confirm the decision to resign without hesitation, proceeding towards the realization of the project we have for ourselves and for the people around us. Even then, there are times and ways to separate ourselves from the company without making waves, keeping our reputation intact.

Superstar with a gun

Gilbert Arenas started playing basketball at college in Arizona, rising quickly because of his talent and speed. In 2001, he realized his dream of playing in the American professional championship, the NBA. He played for Golden State Warriors, in California for two years, then for the basketball team in Washington, at that time called Washington Bullets. For a few years he was a legend in the making, one triumph after another of victories, records, prizes, awards and a life lived to the full in every sense, often gaining the attention of the press off the court, as when, for his birthday, he organised a USD 1 million party. Suddenly, a knee injury forced him to slow down and he played very little during the rest of the season; despite all of this his team offered him a staggering new contract for an astronomical sum, the fans loved him and the press were always on his side.

Arenas alternated good performances with poor games, with only flashes of his talent on display. Moreover, some of his outrageous behaviour off the court began to leak out, to the point that the media started changing their tune and began to openly criticize his conduct. The situation reached a climax when it was discovered that Arenas had brought firearms into the locker room during training, according to him to 'settle' some gambling debts with his team mates. The news got out, the police investigated and the basketball player was convicted of carrying firearms in a public place.

When his suspension from the team and the NBA ended, he was ignored or whistled at by the fans and the decline began: he was sold to other teams, always playing badly, until he uselessly emigrated to China to play for Shanghai. His career was over, he was a professional destroyed and his reputation was broken. Currently nobody knows where he lives or what he's doing: Arenas has literally disappeared.

What mistakes did Arenas make? In the first place, his behaviour was insane; he was surrounded by bad advisers. The most serious mistake he made was to become complacent about his past successes and very high popularity, believing that they were necessary and sufficient conditions to remain safe. At the time when the newspapers documented his excesses, such as the famous million-dollar birthday party, they did it in a jovial tone, like: 'They're kids, let him have fun, he deserves it'. Once his descent had begun from hero to zero, the same birthday party was pulled out as an example of a lack of judgement, a scandal, an insult to poverty: an event analysed with two completely different lenses.

When people fall into disgrace, nothing is forgiven, including attitudes which were considered tolerable before. Arenas grew strong with a sort of impunity, but he was wrong; he didn't understand that in any organization it's not just about what we do – our results – but above all how we do it, our behaviour, our ability to adapt to the rules of the game. When we're in Rome, we do as the Romans do, right? We must therefore understand what the socially acceptable behaviours are in a given place, be it a city, a basketball team or an organization. Performance and results are certainly essential but our behaviour is more important.

What did I learn at Davos?

I have worked for four years at the World Economic Forum, world-famous for the annual meeting held in Davos, Switzerland, in accordance with a 48-year-old tradition, in the last week of January. During the event the international elite meet, discuss, work, exchange ideas and projects: this includes presidents, ministers, CEOs of the most important companies in the world, Nobel Prize laureates, academics, trade union representatives, religious leaders and artists. There's a unique feeling in the air, not surprisingly defined as *the spirit of Davos*, a positive atmosphere, full of energy, where about 3,000 people in key roles come from all over the world for four extraordinarily intense days.

The 2015 Davos meeting was my first. Naturally I have noticed what happens *behind the scenes*, by observing the behaviour of my colleagues. What struck me about this unique organization, was the immense collective effort of all the employees at the Forum both on a conceptual and organizational level. No detail is left to chance. The annual meeting begins: all the employees are summoned at 8am; there are about 500 of us, each with our own well-defined role.

Klaus Schwab, founder and President of the World Economic Forum, reminds us in simple and direct words that we are the hosts and as such we must make sure that our guests have an unforgettable experience, that we must be at their service with kindness, professionalism and warmth. Over the next few days we won't be performing our usual daily duties in Geneva, but we'll be working from the crack of dawn until late at night to make sure it's the best Davos ever. Hierarchies and roles disappear; we become a close-knit team with a single objective. With the imminent arrival of the participants, I feel the adrenaline flowing, the excitement is growing, our concentration is at its maximum.

What did I observe in terms of the behaviour of my colleagues? Everyone works *at least* 15–16 hours a day, they always smile and there is great solidarity. If a participant has a particular request, everyone bends over backwards to satisfy it, no matter what they need. Banal but indicative examples: a minister tells a colleague that his doctor has ordered him to drink a glass of orange juice three times a day and my colleague brings him the juice for the duration of the meeting; the president of an organization realizes he has lost a precious pen, and it was found by our staff after an extensive search and returned the following day; a large delegation realizes that they haven't got the bag containing the programme and conference material. It's 8pm, pitch dark and the temperature has dropped by a few degrees below zero. 'Paolo, would you be so kind as to take these bags for the delegation directly to their hotel?', and this is how I find myself together with other colleagues walking in the cold for about twenty minutes; we arrive freezing cold but with a smile and stop to drink a hot chocolate offered by the delegation. One of them tells me that he's a university professor; we speak for about 10 minutes. The next day I find out that he's the winner of a Nobel Prize; he hadn't told me.

The behaviour that everyone must have as employees of the Forum is – quite simply – that of being at the service of the guests, at all times and under any circumstances. After a week we all go back to Geneva, overwhelmed by fatigue but satisfied because everyone gave 100 per cent. We're convinced it was the best Davos ever, but we also know that the next one will be, and will have to be, even better. Happy but not completely satisfied, there's always something to be improved, new ideas. I understand and have learned that a person is hired because of their qualifications and experience, but to advance your career at the World Economic Forum you have to leave your ego at the door. I've decided to stay at the World Economic Forum after understanding what kind of behaviour is rewarded: that of showing a certain amount of humility, including bringing someone orange juice, if necessary. With a smile.

At Davos you feel and see power up close. Every person who attends Davos is a person *in charge of something*: it could be a multi-billion company, a university, a country, a monarchy. What most ignore is that if a person is not in charge anymore – with very few exceptions – they no longer go to Davos. So, while in Davos you also understand the limited 'longevity of power' of most people. A lesson to learn is that power is given but can be taken away by unhappy voters, dissatisfied board members, by fate, by your own mistakes or reputational issues that bring people from hero to zero in a few days.

How are we *really* evaluated?

What are the winning behaviours in our organization? The smartest thing to do is to observe the *old wise men*, the people who have a successful career and are respected, but not feared, as a result of the reputation they have built up. How do they behave? How did they gain trust? How do they move? We'll better understand the organizational culture by carefully studying those who have made a career and the many winning behaviours that are easily recognizable. We arrive on tiptoe, trying not to make a noise, and ask questions; in other words, it's important to spend the first few months listening and learning, without drawing hasty conclusions. We respect the hierarchy, we do things in full respect of our position. It works in the same way as a bank account, *first we have to make a deposit then we can make a withdrawal*: at the beginning we still don't have a line of credit nor have we acquired a sufficient reputation.

I made a big mistake when I started working at the World Bank. I'd just turned 30 and within a few weeks I thought I understood everything. I sent a message to my colleagues saying what they were doing wrong. From a purely technical point of view I was also right, but in doing so, I antagonized almost all my colleagues. It took time to mend these personal relationships that were jeopardized. Nobody likes being criticized by the last one through the door, especially if they're right.

Do you want to know how most companies evaluate their employees? Let's look at the following matrix. On the horizontal axis

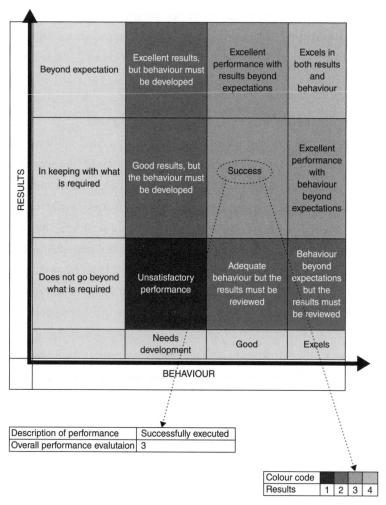

Figure 8.1 *Results vs behaviour matrix.*

we find Behaviour, on the vertical axis Results. Even in the absence of codification or the explicit use of this tool, people are always evaluated on the basis of these two dimensions. This matrix is also used for the famous *performance appraisal*, the annual assessment of employees. What does this mean? It's not only important how much we do, *the results*, but also how we do it, behaviours that – I'll never stop emphasizing this – have to be in line with the organization's culture. I've moderated, conducted and facilitated at least a hundred meetings where high-level managers had to decide who to promote and who instead to 'hold back' until next time, who to offer a future or who to show the door. Invariably these meetings, which are always very difficult and tense, focus on the behavioural aspect and emotional intelligence of the people. I have seen careers fast-tracked, destroyed, put on hold, because of the person's real or perceived behaviour, rather than on the basis of results. The key question is always the same: 'Can we trust this person?'

Comfortably numb or roaring lions?

Manuela and Silvano have been working at the same company for 20 years, the Italian branch of a large German company, with 600 employees, which has recorded substantial losses over the last two years. The parent company has settled the debts, making it clear that it'll be the last time. Silvano has had the same boss for ten years, someone he always sees eye to eye with, but who is going to retire in a few months. He's always received reasonable pay rises, his salary is about 20 per cent higher than the market average and has always had positive, but not exceptional, appraisals. He arrives at the office at 8:30am on the dot and always leaves at 5pm. He was hired because he spoke German well, which he's forgotten as he almost never uses it. His work is the administration of wages and salaries, control of absences and illnesses. A few years ago he'd been offered the opportunity to spend a few months at the company's head office but he'd politely refused because the idea of moving to Germany in the winter didn't excite him. A university graduate, he did some refresher courses on new technological systems but after discussing it with his boss he'd decided to keep the old system. Silvano gets on with everyone but doesn't have any special connection with anyone, except one colleague with whom he often goes to see football matches.

Manuela started at the age of eighteen as a secretary, she loves to speak English and she does evening classes to gain a good level of German and French. Passionate about technology, with the help of her boyfriend she became a self-taught web designer. Becoming aware of the opportunity to spend a few months in Germany, she persuaded her boss to let her go instead of Silvano and the six months she was supposed to spend at the head office became a year. When Manuela came back, she could speak excellent German. A year later, she helped the new division head to redesign the department's website, demonstrating her versatility. She managed to get one of the scholarships made available by the company, then enrolled on an evening university course and graduated. Although her salary is quite low, Manuela is curious and every day goes to lunch with her colleagues to keep up-to-date on what's happening. Due to the crisis, the company starts a cost-reduction plan: not only are promotions and pay rises cut, but also training courses, trips and projects, including the one related to the new website that Manuela was working on. Her boss warns her that she must limit herself to being a secretary and that there are difficult times ahead.

Julie and Chris have been working in a start-up for two years. The pace of work is crazy but there are plenty of opportunities to do new things, projects that sprout like mushrooms, sometimes a bit of confusion, a dynamic environment that is stressful but fun. Julie doesn't seem very happy, because the new boss has started lots of new projects and Julie often complains about the enormous amount of work. She's right, but even though everyone's in the same boat, Julie doesn't accept responsibility without a clear agreement on the benefits that will be obtained: if she's asked to work on extra projects, she politely declines, often repeating that she's underpaid in terms of her duties. One day Julie learns that a newly-hired colleague earns more than her and, outraged, takes two weeks' sick leave.

Chris works in finance but, when he's finished his duties, he spends a lot of time lending a hand on three projects that are not related to his department, but manages to make a significant contribution. He leaves the office very late, but doesn't seem as tired as Julie. He's also started a master's degree and is preparing his thesis on a topic of great importance to the company, in anticipation of the presentation of the results to the managers.

Let's observe this matrix carefully: on the horizontal axis we have the behaviour of the person. On the one hand we can see the *Comfortably Numb* attitude: in other words mentally lazy, addicted

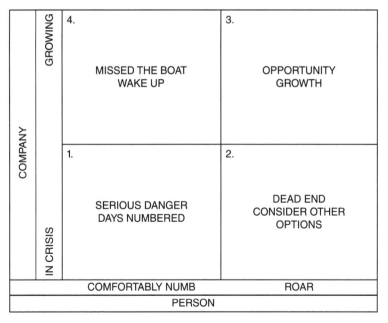

Figure 8.2 *Company view vs individual behaviour matrix.*

to an unvarying routine, year after year; on the other hand a *Roar* attitude, a person who is always ready to pounce like a tiger onto learning opportunities, who invests, with effort and pleasure, in their continuous improvement even in areas not strictly related to their job.

We see the company's point of view on the vertical axis: is it growing, dynamic, ready to invest in its talents or is it a company that is slowly shutting down, cutting costs indiscriminately, only seeing people as costs instead of talents to be developed? In which quadrant of this matrix would we place Silvano, Manuela, Julie and Chris? Let's reflect for a moment before continuing to read.

- **Silvano, quadrant 1.** I'm sorry to be blunt, but Silvano's days are numbered. He has a higher than average salary; not only has he not learned anything new, but he's even forgotten what he did know; the protection provided by his boss will come to an end soon and, following a serious cost review, he'll most likely be fired. Unfortunately Silvano doesn't even notice what's happening; he is isolated from everyone, more of his own choosing than for other reasons. Silvano will also have serious problems finding a new job with the same conditions. He'll be gone soon, without any valid alternatives. He's become *comfortably numb,* unaware that, without investing in one's professional growth, one ends up in the attic like an old radio that no longer has any use.

- **Manuela, quadrant 2**. Curious, enterprising, a great worker. Despite the crisis, the company will try to keep Manuela. But she'll have to ask herself whether it's worth staying: without prospects for growth, or even a career, what new things will she learn if she continues to work as a secretary after taking giant steps forward? She'll end up in a dead end, with no possibilities to move up the ladder, relegated to a limited role.

Perhaps she would be better off leaving and capitalizing on the opportunities offered at another company. After all, she speaks three languages, is a graduate, an expert in web design, still has a low salary and won't have difficulty finding another job where she can further develop her talent and her natural intellectual curiosity.

- **Chris, quadrant 3**. Chris is in the right place: he's making use of plenty of opportunities for growth, he's learning, he's investing a lot of energy. He works in a healthy company and will soon have the opportunity to grow further, not just economically, but also in terms of responsibility, trust, prospects.

- **Julie, quadrant 4**. Julie has missed the boat. Perennially dissatisfied, she doesn't seem to understand the opportunities around her; she survives instead of taking the initiative. While understanding concerns related to her workload, she seems to have a mechanical and in some ways mercenary approach. Isolated, she doesn't miss an opportunity to complain; if she continues on this path she'll probably be forgotten by everyone else while they are busy working and having fun.

Are we able to analyse our situation in the light of this matrix? What kind of organization are we working for? How do we behave? If we look inside ourselves, honestly, are we more like Silvano, Manuela, Julie or Chris?

Allow me to give you some advice. Think of yourself as a beautiful house with a garden full of wonderful flowers. To keep both the home and garden beautiful and functional, you must continually invest time, energy and resources, understanding what needs to be done according to the seasons. After a certain number of years, have we improved or worsened the house? If we sold it, what would be the asking price? Not investing today, nothing happens; never investing, the house will fall apart, it'll be worth less. I'm sure that we all want to invest in ourselves and above all grow as people. It would be a shame if we didn't let the flowers that we hold inside blossom.

Why do we leave?

Turnover, the rotation of staff, is a significant cost for companies, quantified by various studies as between one and two years of annual salary. It's calculated, as already described in Chapter 7, by dividing the number of people leaving an organization by the total number of employees: to give an example, a company with 1,000 employees of which 150 leave every year will have a turnover of 15 per cent.

But be careful: companies also evaluate the quality of turnover. This means that companies try to 'retain' those that they consider to be good, who get results and behave in line with the culture of the organization. Leigh Branham, in the book *The 7 Hidden Reasons Employees Leave*,[1] shares some significant statistics of the US labour market: 4 per cent of people leave their jobs during the first day and 50 per cent during the first six months. Of course something is wrong, if so many people change their minds so quickly. Gallup,[2] the market research company, has calculated that about 30 per cent of people are *engaged*, understood as interested or involved in their work, meanwhile 15 per cent are one step away from becoming genuine saboteurs, almost at the point that they hate their job. According to a study carried out by the University of Phoenix, in Arizona,[3] only 14 per cent of people believe they have a dream job, 73 per cent believe they're not doing the job they thought they would be doing. All this turns into huge financial costs for organizations, but also with regard to personal costs that are devastating for us all in terms of the tired and weary professional relationships that are created.

For about 20 years I've been dealing with what's commonly called the exit interview. It shouldn't be a therapy session – I'm not a psychologist – but it often turns into an intense, long conversation in which I ask only one thing: 'What would have made you stay?' Instead of the classic and repetitive question: 'Why are you leaving?'

During a study conducted by the Saratoga Institute in California,[4] managers were asked: 'What do you think is the main reason that causes people to resign?'; then the employees were asked: 'Why have you decided to leave?' Most managers (89 per cent) think that people are leaving for economic reasons, while 88 per cent of people leave for reasons *that have nothing to do with money*. Interesting, isn't it?

I'm sure you're curious to find out, in light of all these studies, and taking into account my personal experience, what I would do in your place, what I would do if I was asking myself the question: 'Should I stay or should I go?'

There's another factor that can influence your response. I've listened to and observed lots of children. Why have I done this? Because they know things that we adults have forgotten.

In your opinion, why do parents go to the plays at the end of the school year? Do we remember the excitement when we were children before the play?

My daughter has asked me a thousand times: 'Dad, have I improved? Dad, are you proud of me? Dad, do you love me?' I'm convinced that people are not *mercenaries*, but rather *missionaries* who have a real need for a deeper purpose together with emotional recognition, respect and dignity. We need our leaders and colleagues to tell us 'I'm proud of you' or just say *thank you*. Getting a 'Like' on Facebook is not the same thing but sometimes it becomes a substitute. People continue in their jobs for reasons that are related to the deeper sides of our humanity, regardless of the position: the need to feel trusted, to be respected, to value something as individuals, to have hope and opportunities for growth. If

I learned anything at the World Bank I'd have to say that the poorest people in the world – and I've seen so many – don't want charity and handouts; they want opportunities and dignity, with respect.

My first promotion was one of the most negative experiences of my professional life. I found the letter on my chair which informed me about it – my boss hadn't thought it appropriate to talk about it before – and I had to chase him for two months to get an interview. I would've paid a fortune to get a handshake, but instead they gave me some money and I had to shut up. One of the most positive experiences I've had is when *I didn't get the promotion* and my boss invited me to lunch to explain what I needed to improve next year to be promoted. I felt respected and, honestly, he was right. I improved and I then was promoted one year later.

But what are the reasons that make us decide to change jobs?

- **The job is not as expected.** In the second and third chapters we learned some ways to understand when the organization is somehow presenting its proposals in an untrustworthy way, if not actually false and misleading. The problem is often created by companies: let's see how.

- We've been selected as judges for the X-Factor television programme. We spend a few days together with our colleagues on the jury to evaluate the artistic skill of soloists and groups of singers. After a lot of discussions and debate, we reach a verdict: the winner is an opera singer, who we think is the new Pavarotti. At the end of the awards ceremony they tell us that the winner will be part of the Olympic clay shooting team. Obviously, the situation described is crazy, but often this is exactly what happens: companies and human resources selection committees spend days, if not months, assessing who the best candidate is in absolute terms and not in relation to the position they are applying for. Typical example: organizations that require someone with a doctorate in economics then send the selected candidates to manage a country that has just come out of a civil war.

- **The boss.** It's commonly said that people choose to go to work in a company but choose to leave because of their superior. In the previous chapter we analysed various types of boss. Beyond the character and psychological aspect, the real problem often lies in the lack of feedback, coaching, support, encouragement and, when needed, even constructive criticism.

- **We're not growing.** We all want to grow and I don't just mean in monetary terms. Growing means learning, becoming better at what we do, acquiring skills in new fields, working with smart people we can learn from. We don't just want a job, but a career, the prospect that there is a plan, a path for training and development. If we feel the lack of a project, after a certain period of time we get bored, a bit like in those semi-serious engagements that drag on for years by inertia but that don't lead to a project for a shared life.

- **Stress from too much work.** There are many causes: we feel overwhelmed, unable to manage expectations that are sometimes simply impossible, sometimes unwitting victims of bad company plans, unreasonable bosses or unrealistic goals. The price we pay sometimes becomes too high. Often people talk of corporate restructuring and people who lose their jobs just because they're innocent victims of an economic crisis or bad choices. However, there's no mention of the 'survivors' and the very high price they have to pay to keep their jobs, bearing the workload of those who have been fired.

- **Lack of trust in the people who run the organization.** To illustrate this, I'll use two short stories.

During managerial training courses I ask the participants to summarize in one word the best leader they've ever had; the terms used are always the same: integrity, humility, trust, availability, generosity. Many participants, then, cite the usual names, giants who have made history, such as Nelson Mandela, Mahatma Gandhi, Martin Luther King. Next, I ask if the CEO and the highest ranking people in their organization reflect these values: I almost always get a deafening, absolute silence. I've done this short exercise dozens of times, in different countries, and I always get the same results.

I recently interviewed a candidate who was currently working for the International Football Federation (FIFA) which, as we all know, has been in the eye of the storm: executives accused of corruption and the president, Sepp Blatter, hit by the scandals, tendered his resignation, then retired. The candidate admitted with candour that he was ashamed to work in such an organization and that he had lost all trust in the senior management. He had tears in his eyes when he showed me the statement of FIFA's ethical principles on the home page of the Federation website.[5]

What motivates us?

To celebrate their 65th anniversary, *Harvard Business Review* has republished an article with sales that have exceeded one million copies: it's a classic, 'One more time: how do you motivate employees?', written in 1968 by Frederick Herzberg.[6] The author explains how there are motivating factors which he refers to as 'hygiene' factors, that is to say, factors that do NOT motivate us but the absence of which demotivates us, such as conditions of work, salary, rules. The motivating factors are of a different calibre: the sense of achievement and improvement, the intrinsic pleasure of doing the job, the sense of responsibility, the human and professional growth of those who perform their work passionately, the pride of being part of the organization. Daniel Pink, in the book *Drive*,[7] explains that the motivating factors are to have a strong sense of purpose, autonomy, the possibility of improvement. If we think about it, the reasons why we decide to leave an organization and those that encourage us to stay are two sides of the same coin, they tell us the same story. Often the decision to leave is mulled over for a long time but explodes following a trauma, an unpleasant event, such as orders received by the boss in a despotic tone of voice, a quarrel with a colleague, a promotion not obtained, a wrong suffered. While deciding to leave is a long process, most people can remember a specific episode, the tipping point, the watershed moment when they finally decide to leave.

I want to share four true stories that will help us understand how different motivations can make us decide to leave or stay: some will produce short-lived effects while others can lead us on the right path. Provided we know where we really want to go.

- Carlo is really disappointed: about six months ago, his company changed his office, moving him to a less spacious room, and he hasn't had a pay rise in about two years. In addition, his boss has hired a younger candidate who has been given a better salary. Then the last straw: Carlo had the right to a parking space but, after a year on the waiting list, they assigned the space to the new colleague. Carlo decided to resign.

- Umberto tells me, four times in less than an hour, that *he expects a promotion* to manager. A few weeks later his boss decides not to promote him and, after a few months, Umberto asks me for an appointment. He hands me a letter with his resignation claiming to have received an offer as a D-I-R-E-C-T-O-R and emphasizing his new title and level with almost exasperating slowness. Umberto then adds that he's going to earn double and that he's also received a company car. I congratulate him and I don't hear from him again. For six months.

- Giovanna realizes that she's been doing exactly the same job for about ten years, she doesn't have much fun and, jokingly, tells her colleagues that when she gets to the office she goes into autopilot. The company doesn't offer exciting projects, they sell poor-quality food produced in China; she has a cordial but cold relationship with her boss and generally she has lunch alone because she hasn't connected much with her colleagues, who have very different interests to hers. Giovanna feels like a fish out of water.

- Roberta, recently graduated, received lots of offers but decided to work, despite the low salary, for the company ABC mainly because of the training courses that they offer. She has a huge amount of work to do, but also has the opportunity to travel and work on different interesting projects and, after an initial training phase of about three years, there will be a two-year stint abroad, where she can also learn a new language.

Let's think about these stories, putting them into a four-dimensional matrix. In the lower part of the matrix, we'll find negative factors that cause us *to escape, to get away from the existing situation*, while at the top we find positive factors, which drive us to *go towards something new*. On the left we think of the *external* motivating factors, understood as ephemeral, of short duration, for example a lofty-sounding title (manager, director), while on the right are long-

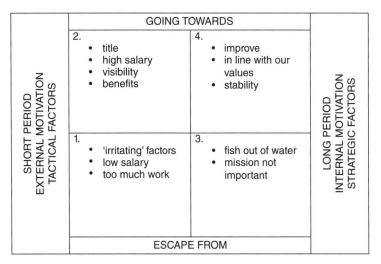

Figure 8.3 *Motivations matrix.*

term motivating factors, such as the possibility for growth, the purpose of our work, the alignment of our ethical values with those of the company we are part of.

Which of these motivations compel us to stay or leave an organization?

Carlo's situation is in box number 1. He's definitely frustrated by certain events but, in all honesty, do we really believe it's worth leaving an organization because of a small office or an unassigned parking space? Did Carlo ask the right questions?

Umberto, box 2, also visibly angry by the lack of a promotion, has been hypnotized by the 'bright lights', a lofty-sounding title and the mirage of a better salary. I met him after six months, disillusioned and disappointed by a company where there was more smoke than fire.

Giovanna, box 3, hasn't grown for years and she realizes that she's ended up in the wrong place: in her case, leaving would be a wise decision.

Roberta, box 4, made the right choice: she's learning on a daily basis, sacrificing some short-term goals in favour of a long-term work project. By deciding to stay, Roberta is investing in her professional growth and the opportunities that she'll be able to grasp in the future by following this path will repay her for the sacrifice.

We must also understand when the conditions have been created in which it is no longer appropriate to stay; making a comparison, it's as if we were guests who have outstayed our welcome, becoming *persona non grata*. You become a *persona non grata* when you don't understand that it would be better to leave. I have witnessed dozens of similar stories, a mixture of stubbornness to understand the situation and not wanting to go, with organizations that tend to become vindictive with a vortex of negativity both for the person and for the company.

Konstantinos Kavafis was modern Greece's most famous poet. He lived in Alexandria in Egypt, only sharing his works with the people closest to him and became known and appreciated only after his death in 1933. He wrote extraordinary poems[8] and in one of his first, *Mura*, he expresses the suffering of feeling isolated and excluded.[9] The last verses of his poetry read: 'But I never heard the noise or the sound of the builders. / Imperceptibly they shut me out of the world'.

Sometimes something similar can happen in our work, as shown by the example of Kathryn Bolkovac. A policewoman in the State of Nebraska, she was hired by DynCorp International, a company that has a turnover of USD 3 billion as a military contractor for the defence sector in the United States. In 1999, she was sent to Bosnia for a peacekeeping operation to support the UN blue helmets and realized that some of her colleagues were taking part in prostitution rings. Kathryn tries to put a stop to this horrendous situation and decides to denounce the scandal to her superiors. She then becomes a *whistleblower*, denouncing the corrupt practices in the organization where she works.

From that moment Kathryn's life becomes hell: initially she is excluded from every decision and from her team by her bosses and colleagues, then she is made to think her life is in danger and finally she's sacked with another colleague, also guilty of having spoken out against the trafficking in human beings. Bolkovac's experience is told in a film and, later, she also tells her story in a book;[10] she manages to win a legal battle against DynCorp, thanks to the overwhelming evidence in her favour.

Luckily we don't often find ourselves in such extreme situations that lead to a definitive break with the organization for reasons that are not strictly work-related but much more serious, as in the case of Bolkovac. The reflections, which we shared in Chapter 6 regarding the price to pay to make a career and the significance of making a pact with the devil, also remain valid in these situations, as does the importance of choosing a job in an organization that reflects our values.

Protecting our work identity and leaving gracefully

Andre Agassi was one of the greatest tennis players of all time. His autobiography,[11] told in a lucid and honest manner, begins with the story of his retirement: he is 36 years old and has now played more than 1,000 professional games; he has always suffered from an acute form of scoliosis with excruciating sciatic nerve pains and sleeps on the floor, the only way to relieve his back pain; when he wakes up he doesn't know where he is and he feels like a worn-out tennis racquet. He thinks to himself: 'Please let this be over', but then he realizes that he's not ready for it to be over.

To leave, as a tennis champion as well as a professional of any other trade, is a psychologically very difficult moment. We find ourselves divided between two opposite tendencies: the desire and at the same time the fear of staying and leaving, an emotional vortex. A job is not just a job, but over time it becomes our identity, our second skin. Leaving is a complex transformation process, as Herminia Ibarra explains in her book *Working Identity*.[12]

I understood what the concept of professional identity really means and the difficulty of leaving when I worked on a project to reform the pension system. In 1998 the World Bank had to solve two internal problems, which unfortunately became common to many public and private organizations: to change the pension system, which had become too expensive, and to reduce staff. The squaring of the circle was achieved with the proposal to offer an un-reduced pension to employees of at least 50 years of age and with a minimum of 10 years of service. In short, the rule was abolished by which generally speaking if you retire before the natural retirement age, say 65 years, the pension is reduced by about 4 per cent for each year that the retirement is brought forward.

Simultaneously, the pension system was changed, for the worse, for all the people who had started working for the Bank from May 1998 onwards. At that time the World Bank had about 11,000 employees, of which more than 2,000 had the right to take early retirement, and we feared a mass exodus. When the fateful day arrived, we expected *queues at the gates* that not even a concert given by U2 or Coldplay would attract. The offer of an unreduced pension represented an opportunity which would be far too attractive, especially for people who know how to do the maths. How many people accepted this plan? Less than 10 per cent of those entitled. I would never have believed that, given the chance, almost everyone would have decided to continue in their job, choosing to work for a slightly higher income than a comfortable pension. Intrigued, I listened to some of these people: why did they make this choice? After a few conversations

I realized that they weren't doing a job but they were the job they did, they'd never considered leaving and never would, regardless of the economic conditions. Complete identity between work and individual.

What did I learn from this story? Choosing to leave a job is not limited to the financial aspect but a decision anchored in the deepest part of our soul, in our identity. The moment of choice, *Should I stay or should I go*, is sometimes lacerating, a moment of great uncertainty and of conflicting emotions. We remain anchored to our identity, without having understood what our new one will be, as sailors who sail optimistically towards unknown lands and at the same time fearful of seeing the port they know moving away in the darkness of the night. As a coach I have helped many people with this transition. I found my own transition difficult until I utilized a coach to help.

The moment to leave comes for everyone sooner or later. There are a number of key questions: if we were to resign, would it be worth changing our minds if we had a counter-offer from our employer? Is it worth returning after a certain period of time? When are the right times? How and when to leave? We'll address these questions one at a time.

- **If we were to resign, would it be worth changing our minds if we had a counter-offer from our employer?**

  I believe that the decision to leave, to resign *should not be the result of a reaction but rather a reflection.* If, after careful consideration, we decide to go, we mustn't put a price on this decision. In my opinion the best way is to take out the yellow card, before the red one. Let me explain: if we're dissatisfied because we see that we are not growing, that we have no opportunities and/or that we won't be promoted, let's talk honestly with our boss and, in an intelligent and constructive way, we can propose plausible alternatives. Very often these conversations take a natural course and you can find a solution, coming out of a potentially negative situation.

Conversely, if nothing happens or, worse, our expectations are immediately ruled out, then we must move to the red card. Delivering a letter of resignation means reaching the point of no-return, a definitive alteration of the fiduciary relationship between employee and organization. Based on my experience, people who have been persuaded to stay then leave within a year because, for example, a salary increase alone is not enough to change an overall assessment.

- **Is it worth returning after a certain period of time?**

It depends. Companies tend to hire people who have previously worked in the company itself, provided there has not been a stormy divorce. It's worth getting recognition for the skills acquired, but I think it's not the case if we had to go back to doing exactly the same tasks we did before: a kind of reheated soup, not particularly exciting. Warning: our relationship with old colleagues will be altered and different if we return to a position with greater responsibility, fomenting possible internal jealousy. The idea therefore to return must not be excluded a priori but rather weighed up carefully and with attention paid to group dynamics. When I returned to the World Bank after seven years in London, I became my colleagues' boss: some still haven't forgiven me.

- **When are the right times?**

We can't provide a mathematical formula that can define a perfect time, but there are common conventions and perceptions. Let's look at them together.

Realistically, we can analyse the problem by 'areas'. Red area: if we're at a company for less than 18 months, we'll have difficulty explaining why we want to leave so soon. We must have a valid reason, like 'The company has transferred all production activities overseas', so that we have a valid argument to use. If this valid reason is not there, we'll have not there, we may have greater difficulty getting a new job. Yellow area: between 18 months and three years, we're in an area which is easier to manage, because within this time it's considered socially acceptable to look for a new job. But be careful: this timing is best suited to juniors, new diploma holders or university graduates, not so much for managers or executives. Green area: between three and five years, the timing is almost perfect because it's possible to demonstrate how we've learned and contributed positively in the organization.

If we stayed in the same workplace between five and seven years, we return to the yellow area: why did we stay that long? It therefore becomes important to explain how we've grown and we've obtained greater responsibility. If however we have done the same job for more than seven years without having progressed in our role, we are back to the red area again. Think about this problem from the point of view of a company that is trying to hire a professional with 15 years of experience. There are three candidates: the first has only worked in one company, the second has worked in three different companies for about five years in each role, the third in 10 different companies. All three candidates therefore have the 15 years of experience required, but acquired differently. Who would you choose?

- **How to leave?**

Three words: with grace, respect and gratitude. And good manners, always. Even if we haven't been treated well, we must never ever burn down bridges, even if we are strongly tempted to slam the door and send those who hurt us where they belong. Some, however, decide to do things differently.

Greg Smith decided to resign in an original way: he writes a letter to the *New York Times*, entitled 'Why I left Goldman Sachs', published on 14 March 2012, his last day of work.[13] Goldman Sachs is the most powerful and famous investment bank in the world. In his letter Greg Smith denounces the destructive and toxic organizational culture. According to Greg, the only concern of this company where he had worked for a decade is to make money at the expense of its clients who were insultingly labelled *muppets*, like the puppets of a famous television programme. Read by 3 million people, the letter goes viral and Greg writes a book with the same title.[14]

Do you think Greg was right or wrong? What we know is that, by choosing such a belligerent and visible method, it burns all bridges irrevocably, not only with the company but also with the whole environment which it belongs to.

Knowing how to choose the right moment and leave gracefully remains an extraordinary quality. David Heenan, in the book *Leaving on Top*,[15] tells various stories about top managers who have chosen to resign, differentiating various categories. In the first there are people who, despite their age and decades of experience behind them, are still extraordinary professionals. I am reminded of the director and actor Clint Eastwood, now in his 80s or the singer and musician Bruce Springsteen now close to his 70s, who can still put on extraordinary concerts lasting at least three hours.

In the second category we find the aged despots; examples include the former President of Zimbabwe, Robert Mugabe, forced to resign after 37 years that have brought his country to utmost ruin, and other politicians, as well as sportsmen, businessmen or artists who don't realize the fact that it's time to leave the stage. Pope Francis, in my opinion the last true revolutionary on Earth, spoke precisely about this theme in St. Peter's Square on 3 July 2015: 'There is great temptation for leaders to believe they are indispensable [...] step by step, they slip into authoritarianism, into personalism. Power leads to vanity and then one feels one can do anything, leaders must also step aside if necessary'. Some businessmen or politicians who 'see their retreat as a middle ground between euthanasia and castration' constitute a category apart.[16]

Finally, let's remember the people that Heenan calls those who 'step out of the scene gracefully', leaving the reins of command to others with wisdom, respect and class. In the masterpiece *Memoirs of Hadrian*, Marguerite Yourcenar[17] decribes the inner thoughts of the Roman emperor Hadrian, creating at the same time a work of poetry, a historical novel and a psychological analysis. I was impressed by the consideration of Hadrian: he understands that he was a good emperor because Rome *no longer needs him*. As a professional coach, I can say that he has developed the people around him without creating dependencies. He is ready to leave. The exact opposite of the fake leaders, who won't leave even with a gun pointed at their head; they remain nailed down to their seats, unable even to conceive that they are not indispensable. Some reminded us of the Greek god Kronos who, according to a myth, was destined to be replaced by his own sons, just as he had overthrown his own father. As a result, living in constant fear of losing his power, Kronos devoured each one as soon as they were born to prevent the prophecy occuring.

On 4 November 2008, Barack Obama is elected president of the United States. The defeated Republican candidate is Arizona Senator John McCain who, up until a few hours earlier, had understandably led a fierce campaign against him. At 9pm, in his general headquarters, McCain stands before the cameras and in front of his most loyal supporters: he must give what is called the *concession speech*,[18] the speech given by the defeated candidate, a bitter pill to swallow. In just a few minutes he demonstrates a grace and a sense of duty which is out of the ordinary. He displays no resentment; on the contrary, he offers sincere congratulations to the newly elected President, firmly silences some of his supporters who whistled at Obama and commits himself to working without reservations with the new head of government for the common good of the United States, referring to the values they have in common. A departure by a real gentleman and statesman.

Here, then, we return to the key words: gratitude, wisdom, class, respect, courtesy. Good manners. The final acts of our tenure will be remembered and will be part of our reputation and legacy, of the memories that people will have when we leave. By following these rules we will help build our reputation as free and decent people.

9

Taking stock of the journey. What really matters?

'Try not to become a man of success, but rather try to become a man of value.'

ALBERT EINSTEIN

The broken toy

During the journey we have taken together, we've tried to understand, especially on the basis of who we are, what organizational culture and job suits us. We've discovered who to turn to, in order to establish alliances and to avoid misunderstandings and problems. We know how to gain trust, how to progress a career by assessing the price to pay and avoiding a pact with the devil. We know when the right time to leave is and how to do it. The last fundamental question remains: *what really matters?* How is personal and professional success measured and, above all, who measures it?

When I started working, a person introduced me to someone who didn't tell me his name but his hierarchical rank: 'I'm a Managing Director'. He argued that I *absolutely* had to become vice-president in three years, stating that, according to him and according to the organization, only a rapid career progression could be defined as successful: I had to rise quickly through the ranks, get a promotion every year, increase my salary. After some time, I realized I had made two mistakes: not only did I believe what the *Managing Director* had told me, but I hadn't even asked if there were other ways to define a career? I was prisoner of this dysfunctional mindset for at least 15 years.

When we enter an organization, we are told and we believe that career advancement is the only criterion for measuring whether and how we are progressing; I believe, on the other hand, this is just *one way* to measure success in our working life and, frankly, not the most important. The current reference model doesn't work; the toy is broken for at least three reasons:

1 By referring exclusively to the hierarchical aspect – *anyone who reaches the top has won, those who don't get there have lost* – we immediately create a negative result. 99.99 per cent of people will lose by definition, leaving an army of frustrated and unhappy people, believing – often wrongly – that only those who get to the top have triumphed.

2 By defining your career as if it were a race, in which only one chosen person arrives first and all the others lose, we enter a state of continuous struggle, no holds barred. I think stress is related not so much to the amount of work, but rather to the quality of the relationships we develop with our colleagues. The 'everyone for themselves' climate leads to a barbarization, to the debasement of relationships that become only

transactional, utilitarian, losing any connection between human beings. The consequence of this way of life is that *we stop existing and we only worry about appearing,* leaving a trace in form, but not in substance; we only care about our prestige, our social status, to gain the approval of others and, without even realizing it, we lose our soul.

3   As I've already explained, we end up being involved in the so-called rat race. We're so busy trying to win this race that we forget that even if we win it, we'll always be rats. I have worked in a company where the mantra was 'faster, faster!!!' As I was working there I felt many times that the answer should have been 'Deeper, not always faster!' Not only that: all the economic crises, corporate restructuring or simple events that we don't control, such as a change at the top in organizations, can overturn corporate hierarchies. So all of a sudden we're out of the game, expelled without even understanding the reasons, convinced that our identity is forgotten, destroyed with all the resulting emotional and social consequences. The toy is really broken, can we invent a new one? Yes, we can.

I have watched and followed hundreds of people and their careers and I have reflected on this for years. I want to share with you not only what it means to have a successful career[1] but also how to monitor and measure it according to our own personal criteria, not those defined by others. I will provide you with a practical tool, the result of 30 years of experience in observing people who, in different organizations, have tried to quickly climb the hierarchical ladder, a reference model that, as we have seen, doesn't work. We're missing out on what really matters; we risk wasting our working life, a mortal sin, unforgivable, without appeal. What counts is the journey and the meaning we attribute to it, not getting to the finishing line, elbowing our way through anxiously to become the king of the rats. David Brooks in his book *The Road to Character*[2] talks about two distinct career types. The first type, called Resume Virtues is focused on creating a CV highlighting earnings, visibility, power, status, promotions. The second type of career called Eulogy Virtues, is where we relate to who we really are: authenticity, honesty, substance, in which others are 'competitors' but allies and not enemies. So, what really matters in our career?

What really matters?

There are 10 ingredients that define a successful career, but I would like to replace 'success' with a very different word, linked to the meaning: 'value'. A career thus becomes a concept connected to human and professional growth, more about the verb **to be** than the verb to have. I think it is preferable to be a person of value rather than a successful person; it's the same difference between Nelson Mandela and any person who is perhaps rich or famous, but without great substance.

Positive relationships

What do we want more than anything else, believing that it can make us happy? Most believe that the obvious answer to this question is: *'money and fame'*, that is, being rich and famous. This combination is considered even more important than enjoying good health, love or more general success. Really? A powerful Harvard Medical School study,[3] started in 1938 and which lasted more than 75 years, tried to explain what made a heterogeneous group of 724 people happy, healthy and long-lived, observing them over the course of their lives. In this survey, several generations of researchers have analysed and followed, year after year, the lives of these people born and raised in Boston – 60 of whom are still living today – asking them questions about work, health, habits, relationships with the family, the community and the outside world. The conclusion of this study provides a surprising and banal response at the same time: what makes us happy *are the positive and lasting relationships with the people around us, whom we love and respect*.[4] Living with negative relationships has toxic, detrimental effects on our health, on our personal happiness and, consequently, on our life expectancy. On the other hand, positive relationships with others, based on trust, respect and love, not only lengthen our lives, making us happier, but also protect us from disease. Knowing that we can count on those who love us – which doesn't always mean agreeing on everything – gives us that inner confidence and that feeling of not being alone that makes us happy.

There are five regions in the World where the number of centenarians is much higher than the rest of the planet. Barbagia in Sardinia, Italy, Okinawa in Japan, Loma Linda in California, Costa Rica and the Greek island of Ikaria. Dan Butter calls these cases of longevity 'The Blue Zones'[5] and has spent many years studying these unique places and their inhabitants. So, what do these places and their habitants have in common? They become centenarians thanks to good diet e.g. many vegetables and fruits, little or no meat, physical activity, limited pressure and – you should know where I am going by now – elderly people are a vital part of their communities and their families. People are not left behind or forgotten in some dark places as if they do not exist anymore. Other people around us and our families therefore make us live longer, with the exceptions of the *Snakes* and *Foxes* we met in Chapter 5.

Have I convinced you yet? Let's move on to evaluate aspects related to the professional sphere. Others, the people around us, help us make better decisions. Let's say, for example, we're lost at the North Pole, we have 20 objects with us, but we have to choose to keep only a few to survive. Which will we choose? This exercise, which I have tried many times with the teams I've worked with, always emphasizes that individual decisions are never as positive and effective as group ones. What does this mean? It means that others will always help us to make better decisions; others are very important for giving us the feedback we need to grow; others can mention our name for a job or tell us about a position.

When we work, we spend at least 40 hours a week with other people. Of course, colleagues are not our life partners but they represent those positive relationships – of respect, collaboration and trust – that become essential for our happiness. People who have lost this serenity are well aware they work in toxic working environments, thick with negative energy. Knowing that what really matters is the quality of the relationships we have with those around us, both in our personal and professional life, will allow us to see others not as enemies or as instruments to be used but as precious allies on our journey. When you evaluate the quality of relationships in the place where you work, would you say that they are based on power, manipulation and control or trust, transparency and Respect?

Cura personalis

Cura personalis[6] is a Latin phrase used by the Jesuit order; it indicates the *care for the entire person*: health and wellbeing understood in a human and profound sense, not economic. Are we in good shape? Do we sleep deeply at least 7 hours a night, or better 8? Do we exercise, do we walk enough? What and how much do we eat; what do we include in our diet? Our physical state greatly affects our cognitive abilities. To get immediate feedback, we could do a trial on www.lumosity.com:

this will show us how cognitive and emotional abilities are closely related to our physical wellbeing and mental state. Speed, flexibility, the ability to solve problems, to remember, to pay attention are skills that must be protected and developed: like muscles, they weaken if they're not used. A sleepless night reduces our cognitive abilities dramatically: scientific studies[7] have shown that the best strategy before making an important decision is to sleep on it, without rushing to decide.[8] A bad diet, based on sugars or fats, causes the same effects as insufficient sleep; a sedentary life causes irreversible damage.

When do we really disconnect from our working life? Can we remain in absolute silence, enjoying the moment, reflecting? Those who exercise, especially in the morning, benefit from a good mood – a positive predisposition for life – even 12 hours after training. Do we observe the rule of doing at least 10,000 steps a day? Let's try, for example, to turn off our phone from 8pm to 8am, to do sports or maybe just a long walk at least three times a week, to drink at least two litres of water a day, to remove sugars and carbohydrates from our diet, to reduce or, better, eliminate alcohol and coffee, to immediately stop smoking, to go on holiday to a place without an internet connection, a true digital detox; these are small tricks that we can put into practice easily.

We are perpetually occupied, I would say lost, by a thousand messages, meetings, interruptions, interference: do we have time to reflect, instead of reacting quickly as if we were in a constant fight against someone? I confess that, after a furious day spent at the office, I have the feeling I'm in a video game with special effects, ever faster, without interruption. Can we turn off the smartphone that is turning us into zombies,[9] can we control the anxiety of being connected 24 hours a day and that is making us almost chronic misfits?

Cura personalis has above all a profound human, spiritual value: do we have at least one person who loves us and whom we love in our life? Do we have space and energy for the people we love? Can we count on a support group – do you remember the Men's Club in Chapter 6 – or on a friend who we can talk to without being judged? Can we give space to our creativity, our artistic side, our spirituality? Do we remember how we felt the last time we got to gaze at the stars, watch a sunset by the sea, a snowfall in the mountains? Have we had the opportunity to dedicate time to being in contact with nature? It's here then that *cura personalis* doesn't become just a way of defining how fit we are, but also a condition for being authentic, to have full control of our lives, without being seduced by dangerous shortcuts that lead to forms of addiction and dependency. Very often in organizations we reward employees willing to 'run the extra mile' to do more than they have time to do. While these efforts are commendable, they are also 'expensive' for those who make them. In the long run 'the extra mile' leads to exhaustion and absolutely must not be the rule that is followed daily but the exception. [10]

Purpose

Sisyphus, a shrewd and cunning man, is a character in Greek mythology who dared to challenge the gods of Olympus: he lost the battle. How was he punished? Prison? Capital punishment? Torture? None of this: he was sentenced directly by Zeus to push a huge stone up a mountain only to see it roll down and start all over again, for eternity. *The Rolling Stone* mythological version: real punishment becomes the awareness of not being able to give any meaning to what is being done: a purpose-less life.

Robben Island, South Africa, is the prison where Nelson Mandela spent 16 terrible years. When I visited this place, I was accompanied by a former prisoner who was my guide. He told me that the prisoners had to work every day in a small limestone quarry which was completely exhausted after a certain number of years. What did the ruthless head of the prison then decide to do? The prisoners had to move a certain amount of limestone into the quarry and then bring it back out on alternate weeks: some prisoners went mad. Sisyphus was recreated in a horrible South African prison.

I found the meaning for the work I was doing for the World Bank in a remote village in Cameroon. The driver, George, had to take me to visit an agricultural project; after many kilometres on dirt roads, he stopped in front of a well and told me that, before it was built, his mother had to walk 12 kilometres to go to the river to collect water. Then the World Bank had dug that well, only a few hundred metres away from the village where he lived and his life had changed. George wanted to thank me, even though I personally had nothing to do with that well, and he took me to visit his village. I met his mother, we hugged for a short while; she was a woman with tremendous dignity. When I got back into the car, my heart finally understood what I was doing in that forgotten village.

We're all purpose-seekers, meaning we seek the purpose to our existence, as Viktor Frankl taught us.[11]

Our purpose is not the title written on our business card, as the managing director in the previous section thought, nor is promotion to the next level; the purpose is not related to what we do but to *why we do it and how we do it.*

Also be careful not to confuse having a *goal* with having an impact with clear purpose. Goals are limited in time and don't fill life with meaning. Example? A goal can be 'I want to get a promotion', while a purpose is 'I want to become really good at what I do'. Let's look at the difference. We may not get the promotion, I speak from personal experience, but nobody can take away the pleasure of learning, of improving yourself. An example of a classic goal in a company is to increase sales by 20 per cent per year, while one purpose is to provide our customers with the best possible product or service; it is not the same, as we know.

Edgar Lee Masters, author of the *Spoon River Anthology*, wrote in George Gray's poetry-epitaph[12]: 'To put meaning in one's life may end in madness, but life without meaning is the torture of restlessness and vague desire. It is a boat longing for the sea and yet afraid'.

The question then becomes: what is our real purpose? What impact[13] do we have on others if we achieve our purpose?

Love

Yes, you read it correctly: Love.

It's a very simple question: *Do we love what we do?* As we saw at the beginning of this book, being able to maintain our passion and our talent remains one of the cornerstones for a career of value. If we love what we do, fatigue will become a pleasure. Being *in the zone,* an almost ecstatic state of mind in which our being is totally concentrated in what we are doing: we stop doing and begin to be what we are doing. If we look at children when they play, we can see that they're in the zone.

In June 2005, Steve Jobs, the founder of Apple who died in 2011, gave a year-end speech, now available on YouTube, to recent graduates of the prestigious Stanford University, California. In this speech, which is simply extraordinary, Jobs told his audience to look in the mirror every morning and ask yourselves: 'If today was the last day of my life, would I do what I'm going to do?'; the entrepreneur added that if the answer was no for too many consecutive days, it would be better to change jobs. So we must continually ask ourselves if we love our work.

Would we be able to do the same job with passion, love and creativity for 50 consecutive years? Charles M. Schultz, legendary creator of Charlie Brown and Snoopy, succeeded. He began publishing his cartoons in 1950 and on 3 January 2000, after half a century of extraordinary success, he decided to stop, stating that no other person could continue to draw the Peanuts comics. In his last cartoon, Schultz wrote that drawing Peanuts had been his life's dream. The last farewell sentence: 'Charlie Brown, Snoopy, Linus, Lucy ... how can I ever forget them?' He died the day before the publication of his last strip, 12 February 2000. In reading his tender and moving cartoon strip, we understand that it was a declaration of love for what he had done 17,897 times in 50 years.[14]

The Spanish explorer Juan Ponce de León first came to Florida in 1513 in search of the fountain of youth, whose miraculous waters, according to legend, stopped the ageing process. The fountain obviously doesn't exist, but there is a way to stay young inside: we just have to find out what we really love, the treasure is within us.

We observe the genius of Picasso, who created hundreds of works of art when he was over 80 years old; we think of the creativity of Gualtiero Marchesi, a true artist, certainly not a simple chef, a man able to integrate artistic beauty with the most refined taste, or so many entrepreneurs, artists, writers, in the fullness of their expressive abilities even at a very advanced age. What do their stories tell us? *To love what one does is the true discovery of the fountain of youth and happiness.* Confucius has 'revealed' a secret: if we choose a job we love we will never have to work for a lifetime. To love what one does is an infinite joy and to love one's work means to do it with devotion. We go from the emotional and abstract concept of 'love' to the specific activity and application of loving: let's put into practice the love we say we have!

The documentary film *Jiro Dreams of Sushi*[15] tells the story of Jiro Ono, who at 85 strives to achieve absolute perfection in the art of preparing sushi. Jiro has been preparing extraordinary dishes for 65 years and has no intention of quitting; he expresses a form of respectful devotion to making the perfect sushi.

In 2015 Flavia Pennetta won, against all the odds, the prestigious US Open tennis tournament, beating another Italian, Roberta Vinci in the final. At the end of the game, a journalist tells her that her forehand winner was a stroke of genius. Flavia replies: 'Stroke of genius? I've worked on *that* forehand for years'. Flavia expresses a form of total devotion to being a world-class tennis player.

Being devoted to your cause means having the conviction that we can improve if we have the will to do so. The American psychologist Carol Dweck talks about Growth Mindset,[16] a positive growth mentality that makes you think that you're not wrong but only learning, that everything can be learned with the right passion and determination. In my opinion, the word failure must be rethought: *failure is not the opposite of success but the process to get there.*

Success is 10 per cent inspiration, 90 per cent effort: it requires absolute devotion; there are no shortcuts. Continuous discipline, sweat, effort, total focus on what we first must learn and which then becomes automatic and seems easy. Beware of interference.[17] Let me explain with a formula: our Performance will be equal to the difference between our Potential and Interference.

$$P = (P - I)$$

What are the interferences? Anything that diverts us and distracts us from our purpose.

Let's try an exercise: we'll write down the five most important things in our life on a piece of paper. Then let's observe and evaluate how much time and effort we are actually investing in achieving these goals and objectives. We must constantly monitor the possible interferences, trying to minimize and manage them. The time we have is not an infinite resource: it is much better to waste money than time; money can be recovered, but no one will ever be able to give you back yesterday. The time available to us is an inestimable wealth. I've noticed that many people make an extraordinary effort in doing what they do, but they act in a disorderly way, without discipline and get themselves into trouble, experience anxiety, and are unable to stop and reflect; they don't value their time. If their system doesn't work, they try to speed up and go faster. It would be better to stop to understand what are the interferences, unnecessary distractions, including negative situations and people: it requires continuous effort and focus to avoid dangerous interferences. Speed is not the only thing that counts; the direction and the ability to minimize dangerous deviations from our life path, our original course are also important. Beware some interferences may only take away a few minutes, but others can cause us to lose whole years. We need to identify the latter and eliminate them or at least reduce them to a minimum and be mindful of the 'chronic takers' we are meeting on our journey and, with kindness, avoid them.

Learning

We should become true machines for continuous learning. Let me reword that: we **must** become true machines for continuous learning. We have no other choice. Why?

First, life expectancy is increasing.[18] This means that our careers will last 50 years not 30 or 35. We therefore need to recalibrate our mindset: we used to think that our life was divided into three parts. First education until our early 20s then 30 or so years of work and at the end, finally, retirement. The point is that our current skills will last 3–5 years at best, so we need to continuously learn new skills and adapt. There is no choice or we will be condidered obsolete workers.

I confess that for years I've started interviews with candidates regardless of the job with this question: 'What have you learned in the last six months?' The majority of candidates don't expect this question and can't answer, or reply with a banal statement: game over. If we have a degree, do we consider this to be the point of arrival or departure? If we consider it the point of arrival we are deceiving ourselves. If we think about our abilities, do we imagine them as immutable or something we can learn to develop over time? I'm convinced that we must have learning agility, the ability to remain open to new ways of reasoning, to learn continuously, to do it in an innovative way, to reflect, to enter unknown territories, thus coming out of our stupor. Think of the set of skills and competencies you currently have: do you believe that these skills will be sufficient to take you until the end of your career or that you need to keep learning? The good news is that we all are natural born learners[19] but we also must become learning machines.

To become machines of continuous learning we mustn't forget three important rules:

- **Rule no. 1.** Let's start with a question: if we think about Leonardo da Vinci what comes to mind? Painter? Scientist? Writer? Inventor? Architect? Leonardo was all these things: the term *Renaissance man* indicates the ability to switch between various disciplines avoiding excessive specialization that would reduce the capacity for systemic understanding. The first rule is not to limit one's learning to a single subject-discipline. Steve Jobs once explained why Apple products are so elegant, modern and perfectly designed: when he was a student he attended a calligraphy course and wanted to translate this artistic beauty into his company's products; the design of Apple products remains a hallmark.

  We return to Leonardo da Vinci, who said: 'Learning never tires the mind'; so let's not just learn one topic. Have you ever coached a kids team? Good, you have started learning how to manage a team. Have you ever helped a student study for an exam? Good, you have learned how to motivate a person. Have you ever sold any products or services? Good, you understand the psychology of buyers. Have you ever been involved in any political activity? Good, you understood the complexity and dynamics of the group. Have you ever been a tour guide when visiting museums or your city? Good, you understand how to get attention or speak in public. Have you ever been a bartender? Good, you've managed customers. Have you ever been a bouncer at a nightclub? Good, you have learned how to handle conflicts and difficult customers. Have you ever been a babysitter? Good, you have shown a sense of responsibility. Did you sit comfortably waiting for your parents to give you pocket money? Wake up! In other words, many of the jobs you do, perhaps just to save up a bit of money for the holidays, will become key elements in your work experience.

- **Rule no. 2.** *We collect many failures but those which help us learn not to repeat the same mistake are successes.* You learn by trial and error, not by just following a lesson. Confucius wrote: 'If I listen, I forget. If I see, I remember. If I do, I understand'; if I make a mistake, I don't forget, I learn and I can explain it to others. I don't believe much in traditional learning systems, those in which one person speaks, the others listen or at the most take note; one learns a lot more by doing and considering failure not as a disease to be avoided, but rather as an essential step in our learning process. Henry Ford wrote that failure is simply the opportunity to begin again, this time more intelligently. If we've never made a mistake, we haven't learned anything significant. Learning really means getting out of our comfort zone; in some ways, it can mean suffering at first and then taking flight.

- **Rule no. 3.** *Never stop learning.* In 1938 Ingeborg Syllm-Rapoport had just finished writing her thesis in medicine and was about to become a doctor but, due to the hateful racial laws approved by the Nazi regime, she was denied the title. Syllm-Rapoport emigrated to the United States, where she continued her medical studies, working in many hospitals as a paediatrician and neonatologist; in the 50s she returned to East Germany where she founded the first neonatal clinic in East Berlin. In 2015, the University of Hamburg decided to remedy the injustice suffered by the woman and, after 77 years, Syllm-Rapoport was allowed to discuss her thesis from 1938, successfully passing the exam and obtaining a new doctorate at the age of 102 years: in every respect, she's one of my heroes.

Awareness

'*Why do you look at the splinter in your brother's eye but don't notice the beam of wood in your own eye?*' This famous phrase from the Gospel of Luke forces us to reflect: what we see in others we don't see in ourselves. We talked about it at the beginning of the book: the Johari window, that's to say the blind spot we're not aware of, implies the need to improve our self-awareness. I clearly remember an innocent April Fool's Day joke: I was at primary school and some of my classmates stuck a little paper fish to my back; everyone saw it – and laughed – except me. I wasn't aware of it and I didn't understand why the other children were laughing at me. Understanding that others know something about us that we're unaware of is a powerful feeling; it destabilizes us, makes us insecure. Self-awareness, don't forget, is one of the characteristics that define our emotional intelligence;

full awareness is, in fact, a fundamental ingredient for acting with confidence and working with intellectual honesty to improve our weak points. Some organizations use a very effective tool to evaluate their managers: it's called '360-degree feedback',[20] an anonymous survey system in which several people assign scores to the manager's behaviour. This is generally a very accurate assessment: the opinion of lots of people provides a very clear and plausible narrative about the leadership style of a manager, who also has to conduct a self-evaluation.

I have always found it very interesting to observe – and evaluate – the difference between what people think of themselves and what others think about them. The greater the difference, the lower the self-awareness. In these cases the role of the coach becomes essential. They must help us to discover our blind spots. If we have the opportunity to be monitored by a coach or be evaluated with tools such as 360-degree feedback, I recommend continually listening carefully to what we are told. After university I had a job interview with a company; the interviews went well, I was sure they were going to give me the job. But they didn't. So I called the company to find out why: I wanted some feedback. They told me that I seemed more interested in being perceived as a friend than in getting results. This sentence struck me like an arrow to the heart. I couldn't change their mind, but since then, I've changed my behavioural strategy at interviews. If I hadn't asked, I would never have known. Asking for sincere feedback with a pinch of humility will increase our awareness exponentially.

Zengility

We live in times of VUCRA: a perennial state of Volatility, Uncertainty, Complexity, Risk and Ambiguity. The problem is that we believe that we cannot control most of the variables that cause this incessant, constant change. What is the best way to prepare ourselves mentally for VUCRA times? I propose a neologism: *Zengility*,[21] a combination of Zen Buddhist philosophy and the mental agility to understand and make sense of our surroundings. Let's take as an example the ability to have both an overview, strategic and general, and a timely and analytical knowledge. I recently met two colleagues. The first, Bill, spoke with me at length about the great political and social issues that are changing the world; when, after an hour of interesting conversation, we talked about his team, Bill barely knew the names of the people around him. He was unaware that one person had resigned and another had been ill for two months. Bill 'flies' at ten thousand metres: he has a fantastic strategic vision, but does not know what happens in his team. Elena is the exact opposite: she knew everything about everyone down to the last detail, but was not able to explain her strategy, or the vision for her team. She flies at a height of ten metres, unable to see and articulate a strategic overview.

Agility, in this case, means acting like the famous Google Earth application, which is able to show us both the building where we live and the whole Earth as observed from the Moon. Each of us has a tendency to *fly* at a certain height, to see reality with a particular perspective. We must be able to adjust our flying altitude at all times.

But it's hard to stay calm and cool when we are under pressure: the brain, when under stress, emits a substance called cortisol, which reduces our cognitive abilities. Stress-management techniques will allow us not only to fly at different altitudes, but also to have full control of ourselves and of the situation around us. Adopting a Zen approach will help us stay calm enough to be aware of what is happening around us enabling us to use our emotional and intellectual intelligence. Try meditation, or, if you don't have time, try to breathe deeply, from the diaphragm, for three minutes: you will calm down gradually.

Trust

'Build bridges, not walls'.[22] We can easily understand the meaningful phrase delivered by Pope Francis in a speech to the Scouts, in June 2015 but how can we put it into practice? Let's take a piece of paper and a pen and write down the names of the 20 or 30 people we work with the most. Then, using a simple monthly table, write down how many times we have had positive encounters, in which we have given something – usually our time and our experience – to each of these people. Try to keep the table updated: it'll show you if we're building bridges and trust or if we've forgotten someone. Let's Do the same thing with people who don't work at your company but with whom it's appropriate to maintain an open dialogue. At least two or three times a year get in contact with them without asking for anything, for example by sending an interesting article that we think may be useful or simply meeting up for a coffee. If they call you respond and make yourselves available, as far as possible.

We don't work alone; we always need others. We must constantly show that we're working honestly with our colleagues, including those who may not be very nice. I confess that one of the criteria I use for assessing whether my day has been positive or not is based precisely on this: by maintaining relationships of trust, investing generously to help others. Ask yourself every day: 'Have I laid at least one brick to build the bridge?' Bridges are built little by little but endure for a long time and open up roads and possibilities. Let's remember that the majority of the work is based on the knowledge and trust we have built, as we saw in the fourth chapter.

But be mindful of people who are only interested in taking energy from us. I advise you to apply the rule of three: if we've had three encounters in which we've been the ones giving and have never received anything, we should challenge that person; if they play innocent, maybe it's not worth thinking about continuing to invest in them. Building trust but also giving trust. An extraordinary act of trust is to ask for help, to demonstrate that not only are we not infallible, but that we also have the courage to show that we are weak and vulnerable.

Impact

What do we know how to do? Have we been able to put our purpose into practice? Have we managed to make an impact, one that goes deeper than just results? Can we explain in 10 seconds what we can do and what impact we have had in doing so?

I'm going to tell you about how a conversation has saved millions of lives. In January 2000, the founder of Microsoft, the Director General of the World Health Organization and the founder of the World Economic Forum met and asked themselves a simple question: which investment in health would have the greatest impact? The answer: vaccinate children, with mortality rates that read like a cry for help. Bill Gates, with his foundation, decides to invest USD 750 million over five years and a new organization is born, the Global Alliance for Vaccine and Immunization, GAVI. Since 2000, GAVI has vaccinated 500 million children, saving 7 million. GAVI aims to vaccinate another 300 million children by 2020, protecting another 5 or 6 million lives. I can't think of a greater impact than this.

Impact is a broader concept than result[23]: it means creating lasting and meaningful change. We can all make an impact: think of the teacher who has the ability to make his students interested in a subject, the professional who manages to help a young person grow with advice and examples, the nurse who helps a sick patient. Doing your work well, with integrity and authority, means you're making an impact.

I'll let you in on a secret. At interviews everyone is able to describe what they do, some can measure the results, but few are able to convincingly explain the impact they've had in their work. We must be able to quantify what we have done and create a narrative, a story, convincing, honest, measurable. In each interview we'll be asked what we can do and we should demonstrate it by explaining what impact we've made.

Reputation

I am convinced that we have left the Information Era and entered into the Reputation Era. I am not referring solely to companies that have damaged their reputation by treating their staff or their clients badly, such as Starbucks[24] or United Airlines.[25] I am referring to, for example, Facebook and the misuse of private information for hidden purposes such as selling data of 87 million users to Cambridge Analytica[26] for political purposes and manipulation.

The same applies to us, individually and as candidates for jobs. Everything becomes irrelevant if we have a negative reputation or even if the perception people have of us is not positive. As discussed in the sixth chapter, maintaining one's integrity and a sparkling reputation is not just a question of not doing anything illegal: it's about autonomously making daily choices that won't leave us exposed to blackmail and will allow us to remain free. It takes years to build a reputation, and just a few minutes to destroy it. Everyone will forget the results we've achieved, but no one will forget our reputation, what they say about us when we're not here. Our reputation, our integrity is all we have; we won't take anything else with us when we leave.

Organizations decide whether to hire, promote or remove us from our role based primarily on the reputation we have built. As reported by several newspapers, one out of three candidates is excluded due to an improper use of Facebook and other social media; we must also keep our web reputation intact and unobjectionable.

Conclusions

During the journey we have taken together, we've learned many things. In this last chapter we have understood that we define what it means to be a person of value, not just successful, based on human criteria which is significant, relevant and above all defined by us and not imposed by someone else.

Let's review together:

- Pay attention to the other people around us.

- Look after ourselves, *cura personalis*

- Have a profound purpose, not ephemeral goals

- Love what we do, with devotion

- Keep learning, from failures, from others, from different points of view

- Be aware of ourselves and how others see us

- Develop Zengility, the ability to manage change with lightness and agility

- Build and give trust, be optimistic

- Make a lasting, measurable, profound impact

- Establish and maintain a sparkling reputation, as a decent person, at all times.

There'll be many joyful and difficult moments in our careers, and sometimes we'll feel like a kite lost in the middle of the storm. We must constantly use our Compass and our Radar. We must always keep in mind what really matters. In doing so we'll have full control of ourselves, our career and our lives. To have a meaningful and successful career and to be valuable people, we must both understand the environment and those around us and be anchored to who we are, our values, our authenticity.

The ten ingredients, the essential components described in this chapter will serve as a compass on our journey; our radar will prevent us from walking into an ambush or crashing into a wall. Success, real success, is therefore not a privilege reserved for others, the lucky chosen few, but is within everyone's reach, if we undertake our journey as people of value, and remain respectful of the impact we'll have on the people we love and that are around us.

When we observe what's happening in the world and assess the difficulties of finding a job, we can sometimes feel lost, discouraged and frightened. I know this only too well. So let's try to think about what we would be able to do if we were not afraid, if we didn't put limits on ourselves every time we wanted to take a certain path, start a project, chase an idea or a dream. **Let's ask ourselves: What could we do if we weren't afraid?** The answer lies in our courage to dare, to invest in ourselves, in our abilities and to value our dreams that are the purpose of our existence, what we really live for and which make life worth living. *There's a moment in life which comes to all of us, where we finally stop being afraid of failing and we come to a realization in our heart that the real failure would be in not trying to become what – potentially – we already are.*

10

The Future of Jobs and the Jobs of the Future

Understanding who we really are: the journey within ourselves. Understanding the true colours – the culture – of the organization, how to build trust, who can we trust 'in the jungle', which price are we really willing to pay to build our career. We have re-defined the concept of a successful career based on criteria that we choose rather than those imposed on us by someone else. So is it enough to use our internal Compass and Radar? I believe that we also need to have a sound understanding of 'what is coming next', a glimpse into the future to further calibrate and adjust our Compass and Radar. No one has a crystal ball, but we can all have an idea of the big picture unfolding right now in front of us in order to find a meaningful role in the disruptive changes we are witnessing.

So, what are the main mega-trends in the jobs market? Are technological changes (e.g. digital and artificial intelligence) to be feared or embraced? Ignoring what is happening now with the fourth Industrial Revolution is not an option unless we aim to become obsolete and irrelevant.

Mega-trends in the job market

We've become accustomed to thinking that technological advances are eliminating jobs and tasks that require low-level professional qualifications. From automated toll booths to supermarket tills, we're used to the erosion of low-paid–low-skills jobs.

Yet new forms of technology and automation are also making more highly qualified professionals obsolete, like financial analysts, lawyers and tax experts. In 2000, Goldman Sachs employed more than 600 traders. In 2017 only two equity traders were left because algorithms handled by computer engineers could perform the same work. The same thing is happening in all the traditional investment banks on Wall Street. At the same time, everything from self-completing online tax returns to machine learning approaches to accountancy are disrupting jobs in financial services.

So what are the 'megatrends' in this evolving job market?

1 **Impermanence.** Most of the jobs created in advanced
   economies don't offer permanent contracts, but involve
   self-employed or freelance consultants. This means that
   these people have no social 'safety nets' like insurance,
   medical coverage, social security, or paid holidays. In the
   US, 94 per cent of the new jobs created from 2005 to 2015
   fell into this category, giving these workers no protection
   at all. This gives rise to growing employee vulnerability on the
   one hand and a challenge to the relevance of trade unions
   on the other.

2 **Life expectancy.** The good news is that this rises by about two
   years for every decade that passes. In Japan, Italy and
   Germany, life expectancy for women is nearer 90 than 80,
   while men have now topped 80. But let's think about two

consequences of this. First, can we reasonably expect to enjoy a nice pension for nearly 20 years of our lives? Recently, newspapers reported that in Italy there are more than 700,000 people who have been collecting a pension since 1982. In other words, they've been retired for at least 35 years; in most cases longer than they were employed. The book *The 100-Year Life*[1] is a wonderful analysis of the different ramifications of the challenges.

Second, we've always thought of our lives as divided into three parts: formal education until we are in the mid-20s, then work for about 35–40 years, then retirement from age 62–65 onwards. But we have to rethink this mindset and realise we have a life of continuous learning ahead of us. In previous articles I've written that to 'beat' machine-learning, it's up to us to become learning machines. The set of skills and competence we have right now will become obsolete in three to five years' time. By not investing in our learning we will make ourself redundant.

3 **New professions**. Technology creates more jobs than it destroys, but change is painful. A recent McKinsey study reveals that 56 per cent of new jobs are in brand-new professions. If you take a look at the World Economic Forum's career page, you'll see the kinds of professionals we're looking for: experts in artificial intelligence, the Internet of things, cyber-security, Internet governance, social media, start-ups, machine-learning, robotics, 3D printing, autonomous vehicles, Blockchain and so on. Across the job market, salaries are skyrocketing for new professions and slowly shrinking for traditional ones. The skills that will be needed for jobs in the fourth Industrial Revolution are . . . what makes us human:

critical thinking, cooperation, creativity, the capacity to motivate people with compassion and 'soul' not with carrots and sticks, contextual intelligence, the capacity to connect the dots, and to see how different elements in the systems are closely correlated to each other, empathy, system thinking. These are the kind of skills that AI will not provide. We lose the game with AI if we compete in speed and accuracy, but we win the game if we compete in depth and human connections.

4 **Women.** They make up 52 per cent of the population, but are more likely to remain underpaid and employed in roles that are below their level of skill and expertise. But I'm convinced that the future belongs to women. Why? Because they tend to possess the human characteristics that will give them the advantage in the new jobs of the fourth Industrial Revolution: the capacity for collaboration (instead of competition), empathy, creativity, listening and learning.

Given the changes in the job market, we have to redesign organizations as well. We can no longer build and utilize 'mechanical' companies, offspring of the first Industrial Revolution, where the worker was simply considered a replaceable 'spare part'. We can't assume that the bureaucratic models of the public sector will still work either. We have to reconfigure both state and private enterprises, keeping in mind that people have to be empowered, not controlled or forced to live with the recurring nightmare of losing their job and giving up a life of dignity.

We can't pay new university graduates USD 500 a month, or worse, expect them to work for free. Science and psychology provide hundreds of studies and research showing that knowledge-workers are motivated by purpose, autonomy, their capacity for self-improvement, and a sense of fairness and transparency in the system.

As long as we keep motivating people using the carrot and the stick method, it won't work.

We have moved from the age of deference and blind obedience to the age of inclusion, autonomy, respect and dignity – even if some political or corporate dictators seems oblivious to these changes. They all have the season ticket for the wrong side of history and will soon be forgotten as many of this cursed breed before them. Martin Luther King Jr once said 'Let us realise that the arc of the moral universe is long, but it bends towards justice'. Point is – as Bruce Springsteen recently wrote – that the arc of justice doesn't bend on its own. It needs all of us leaning on it, nudging it in the right direction day after day. We need to keep on working on our dreams. Because if you don't work, someone will – maybe – recruit you to make their dreams come true. Theirs, not yours.

The new reality of the fourth Industrial Revolution forces us to think and act in a new way: we can't solve new problems by applying old methodologies or outdated mindsets. To truly adapt to the future of work, we will need to be guided by a 'Compass' and 'Radar' that helps us avoid dangers and allows us to create opportunities for everybody.

Questions from *Frankenstein*[2]

Exactly 200 years ago, in 1818, Mary Shelley wrote *Frankenstein*, during a cold and rainy summer spent in Cologny, close to Geneva. Not everyone knows that this book has a subtitle, *The Modern Prometheus*, referring to the Titan who, according to Greek mythology, had donated the discovery of fire to men and was therefore punished by Zeus. 'Frankenstein has now become the real creation-myth of modern times … it's no longer Adam and Eve in the Garden of Eden', as noted by

Christopher Frayling.[3] Perhaps we have forgotten that Frankenstein is not the 'monster' but the doctor, Victor Frankenstein who created it. In fact, Mary Shelley doesn't give a name to the main character of the book; she calls it (or him?) the 'monster', the 'ugly thing', or the 'creature'. Why? *Frankenstein* was written at the peak of the first Industrial Revolution, a period of enormous change that provoked a wave of disruption in society: lives spent working on noisy and dangerous assembly lines, child labour, high pollution, low wages, changes that brought Karl Marx to write *Das Kapital* fifty years later. *Frankenstein* asked powerful, searching questions about man's relationship with rapid technological changes. Are we creating a monster we cannot control, are we losing our humanity, our compassion, our ability to feel empathy and emotions? What are we learning? Which choices are we making? What is our moral compass?

These powerful questions have become, 200 years later, even more relevant. Are we – yet again – creating a monster? The World Economic Forum is located just a few steps away from the villa where Mary Shelley wrote *Frankenstein* and its messages still resonate: 'it' is still alive. The theme of the 2016 annual meeting in Davos was the fourth Industrial Revolution[4] which, in the words of the founder and executive chairman, Professor Klaus Schwab, has the potential to 'not only change what we do, but change us *from within*.' The latest breakthroughs in technology and medicine make the gap between man and machine ever narrower. Even the concept of privacy now has a different meaning. Privacy is disappearing: if privacy is outlawed does it mean that only outlaws will have privacy?

The question for today is therefore: in the age of stem cells, digital transformation, 3D-printing, nano technologies, robotics, virtual reality, genetic engineering, cybersecurity threats, Blockchain and cryptocurrencies, are we, humanity, transforming into who we aspire to become or into something else: a new monster? Are we losing our identities and – like the Blade Runner – unable to distinguish who is a human being and who is a machine?

I believe that we should keep our focus on two components. The first relates to our abilities and behaviour to manage the complexity of these changes: so we need a radar. The second is related to ethics, so we need our moral compass.

Starting with the first, our 'capacity', I don't refer to the technical skills but to a broader and deeper concept. Some believe that AI is indeed the end of the Human Era, such as James Barrat explores in his book entitled *Our Final Invention*.[5] AI will furthermore destroy millions of jobs with explosive social and political consequences. Reading Martin Ford's book *Rise of the Robots* will give you nightmares of a jobless future.[6] For years, experts have warned against the unanticipated effects of general artificial intelligence on society. Ray Kurzweil predicts that by 2029 intelligent machines will be able to outsmart human beings. Stephen Hawking argues 'once humans develop full AI, it will take off on its own and redesign itself at an ever-increasing rate'.[7] Elon Musk warns that AI may constitute a 'fundamental risk to the existence of human civilization' and that AI will become an 'Immoral Dictator'.[8] Alarmist views on the terrifying potential of general AI abound in the media.[9] They have solid arguments to support their ideas.

For sure AI needs to be regulated by lawmakers. Public risks require public oversight like those we have for food, drugs, aircrafts and cars. Elon Musk tweeted: 'In a few years robots will move so fast you will need a strobe light to see them'.[10] Let's not forget the words pronounced by Mary Shelley's monster to Doctor Frankenstein: '**You are my creator but I will be your Master**'.

Fortunately, not all intelligence is artificial. Some believe that AI and the changes of the fourth Industrial Revolution will create incredible amazing opportunities for a better future in every discipline.

Mark Zuckerberg, the founder of Facebook, agrees with the mantra of the Singularity University and their enthusiastic adepts.

Who is right then?

I believe that both sides have many valid points. Still, I would like to offer another possible interpretation, which is neither pessimistic nor optimistic: it's simply human-centred; it's about you and me and our responsibilities and our freedom. Jobs with a high degree of automatism will disappear faster than ever, and are already being replaced. We notice it every day as we do our check-in at the airport and buy everything online, go to our local bank with no employees and communicate via our smartphones. We are always connected and yet frequently isolated. This issue brings us to the second point, the ethical.

There are still jobs that cannot and will not be replaced by artificial intelligence, jobs where human qualities are essential components. Perhaps we should ask about the jobs of the future rather than the future of jobs. Jobs and functions where main elements are exclusively human, such as judgement, empathy, critical thinking, a positive attitude, entrepreneurial spirit, cooperation, creativity and compassion will continue to exist and will develop further. We need contextual intelligence defined not only as the capacity to connect the dots but also the capacity to connect people, us, the human kind. This can only be done with reciprocal trust and is based on our judgement and character: our moral compass.

You maybe don't know it, but if you are over 35 years old, you are alive today probably because of a decision taken by an unknown Soviet military officer. On 26 September 1983,[12] duty officer Stanislaw Petrov was in charge of an early warning radar system in a bunker near Moscow when computer readouts suggested several missiles had been launched from the US towards the USSR. The protocol for the Soviet military would have been to immediately launch a retaliatory nuclear counter-attack, but Petrov decided not to alert his superiors.

Data available to Stanislaw strongly suggested that it was a missile attack from the US. In 1983 the world was still in the middle of the Cold War. A few days earlier an aeroplane travelling from Alaska to Seoul in South Korea was obliterated by the Soviets, with 269 innocent people on board, as the aeroplane erroneously deviated from its usual route to fly over a military Soviet zone: a very costly mistake. The President of the United States, Ronald Reagan, was furious and went on national TV the same day to condemn this act. The world expected the United States to react.

In this tense geopolitical context Petrov had to take, within minutes, the most important decision of his life. Human survival depended on him: he suspected a computer error and he decided not to start a counter-attack that would wipe out half of the planet. He was right: it was a system error. He trusted his gut instinct and moral compass more than a radar system that was not reliable. He was neither punished nor rewarded for his decision as rewarding him would have been interpreted as meaning that the system was 'wrong'; the amazing beauty of bureaucracy and hypocrisy, I suppose. This is the difference between systems and human decision: having doubts, asking more questions, asking for help, connecting as human beings not via technologically advanced devices. Stanislaw understood what the external radar told him but listened to his inner compass. In a way, he behaved like a Rebel and decided not to follow orders. He also understood that technology could be a useful servant but cannot become our – dangerous – master. It is better to keep our Moral Compass and our Radar handy for the challenging times ahead and for the Journey we all need to take.

The book, our journey, begins with the story of my father who came to pick me up after the first day of school.[13] In a flight of fantasy, I now imagine that the last day of school has arrived and that my father has come to pick me up again. He then asks me three questions: 'Do you love what you do? Did you learn something? Did you help others?' Nothing else matters. Today I can answer that I've been lucky enough to have a job I love and I've learned a lot, also by writing this book. But I can't answer the last question, whether I've managed to help others.

If I succeed with this book, let me know so I can finally give an answer to all the questions from Renzo Gallo, my father.

www.paologallo.net
www.linkedin.com/in/paologallo
twitter @pgallobussola1

Notes

Introduction

1 The story of my father's questions is told in this TEDx talk: https://www.youtube.com/watch?v=CpapPfVuq0I

2 Viktor Frankl, *Man's Search for Meaning*, Beacon Press, 1959.

3 From Leonardo Sciascia last interview from *Le Monde*, 6 October 1989.

1 The hidden treasure

1 This story was written by the author for his daughter.

2 Roger von Oech, *A Kick in the Seat of the Pants*, Harper Perennial, 1986.

3 Roger Von Oech *A Whack on The Side of the Head*, Warner Books, 1990, p. 23.

4 Roger Von Oech *A Whack on The Side of the Head*, Warner Books, 1990, p. 44.

5 http://lancemackey.com/lance-mackey/

6 Pablo Neruda *The Complete Works, Love Poems*, Edizioni Nuova Academia, 1963.

7 Tom Rath, *StrengthsFinder 2.0*, Gallup Press, 2007, p. 20.

8 http://thisibelieve.org

9 http://thisibelieve.org/essay/170985/

10 *Flow: The Psychology of Optimal Experience*, by Mihaly Csikszentmihalyi, Harper Perennial Modern Classics, 2008.

11 How to increase self-awareness: https://www.weforum.org/agenda/2016/05/ why-you-need-to-listen-to-your-360-feedback

12 Source Wikipedia: https://en.wikipedia.org/wiki/Johari_window

2 Before setting off. Understanding which is the right Village for us

1 Andrew Pettigrew: 'Organizational Culture: A Family of Concepts', in *Companies as Cultures*, edited by Pasquale Gagliardi, Turin, Petrino Editions, 1986, p. 480.

2 Gary Chapman, *The Five Love Languages*, Northfield Publishing, Chicago, 2010.

3 David Kantor, *Reading the Room: Group Dynamics for Coaches and Leaders*, Jossey-Bass, 2012.

4 Daniel Pink, *Drive*, Riverheads Books, 2009, p. 166.

5 Adam Grant, *Give and Take*, Penguin Books, 2014.

3 Destination identified. Arriving at the Village that's right for us

1 Rosamund Stone Zander and Benjamin Zander, *The Art of Possibility: Transforming Professional and Personal Life*, Penguin Books, 2002.

2 https://www.bookdepository.com/What-Color-Is-Your-Parachute-2018-Richard-N.-Bolles/9780399579639?redirected=true&utm_medium= Google&utm_campaign=Base1&utm_source=CH&utm_content=What-Color-Is-Your-Parachute-2018&selectCurrency=CHF&w=AF72AU9SCZ FUL6A80RHK&pdg=pla-73702222419:kwd-73702222419:cmp-710481580:adg-35519416965:crv-163866623710:pid-9780399579639:dev-c&gclid=EAIaIQobChMIyNv8w6Xa2wIVE5AYCh2inwk6EAQYASABE gJwnfD_BwE

3 Permission for the reproduction of this matrix was granted by Accipiter, a consulting firm in London; author: Anthony McAlister.

4   See, for example, as told by Regina Hartley, Director of Human Resources at UPS Information Services, in her TED talk entitled 'Why the best hire might not have the perfect resume', i.e. why the best people to hire might not have a perfect CV (you can listen to it online via the following link http://www.ted.com/talks/regina_hartley_why_the_best_hire_might_not_have_the_perfect_resume#t-331629).

5   Malcolm Gladwell, *The Tipping Point*, Little, Brown and Company, 2000, p. 38.

6   Adam Grant, *Give and Take*, Penguin Books, 2014.

7   Claudia Goldin and Cecilia Rouse, 'Orchestrating Impartiality: the Impact of "Blind" Auditions on Female Musicians', Working paper 5903, National Bureau of Research, Harvard University, 1997.

8   W. Timothy Gallwey, *The Inner Game of Tennis*, Random House, 1974, p. 17.

9   Daniel Goleman, *Focus: The Inner Driver of Excellence*, Harper Collins, 2013.

10 http://www.ted.com/talks/amy_cuddy_your_body_language_shapes_who_you_are

11 Quote from Allan & Barbara Pease, *Why do we lie with our eyes and feel ashamed with our feet?*, Sonzogno, 2007, p. 9.

12 Ben & Jerry's is a well-known brand of ice cream in the United States: employees are dressed up like hippies from the 1960s and the ice cream flavours are inspired by the music of the Grateful Dead.

13 Daniel H. Pink, *To Sell is Human*, Riverheads Books, 2012.

14 'The one question you should ask about every new job' by Adam Grant, *The New York Times*, 19 December 2015.

15 Daniel Goleman, *Emotional Intelligence*, Rizzoli, 1995.

16 Daniel Goleman, *Working with Emotional Intelligence*, Rizzoli, 1998.

17 For a more in-depth discussion about body language, see Allan & Barbara Pease, *Why do we Lie with our Eyes and Feel Ashamed with Our Feet?*, Sonzogno, 2005.

18 The bibliography dedicated to interviews is endless: for a candidate it may be useful to understand the questions from the point of view of a company. See, for example, the book by Paul Falcone, *96 Great Interview Questions to Ask Before You Hire*, Amacom, 1997.

19   Richard Fear & Robert Chiron, *The Evaluation Interview*, McGraw-Hill, 1990, 4th edition.

4 Entering the Village. How to gain trust

1   *All's Well That Ends Well*, Act I, Scene I.

2   The issue of trust from the point of view of the company is dealt with in the study coordinated by the World Economic Forum: www3.weforum.org/docs/WEF_EvolutionTrustBusinessDeliveryValues_report_2015.pdf

3   https://www.researchgate.net/publication/303379730_A_large-scale_study_of_executive_and_workplace_coaching_The_relative_contributions_of_relationship_personality_match_and_self-efficacy

4   Vaclav Havel, President of the Czech Republic from 1989 to 1993, passed away in 2011.

5   Nelson Mandela, *Long Walk to Freedom: the Autobiography of Nelson Mandela*, Little, Brown and Company, 1994, pp. 449–450.

6   www.un.org/Depts/OHRM/salaries_allowances/salary.htm. If you are interested in working at the UN, add yourself to Sebastian Rottmair's job list at http://unjoblist.org/

7   Daniel Kahneman, Nobel Prize winner for Economics in 2002, was among the first to study the *anchoring* effect in our decisions.

8   http://www.dailymail.co.uk/femail/article-4412440/Average-salary-145-UK-jobs-revealed.html

9   Invented by the *Economist* in 1986 and certainly not considered seriously in an academic environment, the Big Mac index is a useful guide to assess purchasing power and the exchange rate. For example, if in the United States a Big Mac costs 4 dollars and in China 2.50, the exchange rate tells us that the Chinese currency (yuan) is undervalued by 37.5 per cent.

10   www.mercer.com/newsroom/cost-of-living-survey.html

11   Phil Rosenzweig, *The Halo Effect*, Free Press, 2007.

12   The *ladder of inference* was invented by Chris Argyris (1923–2013), a professor of management at Harvard.

13   https://en.wikipedia.org/wiki/The_Sixth_Sense

14 Companies typically tend to give perks that reflect their business. A bank could grant subsidized loans, a hotel chain discounts for stays and so on.

15 How to become learning machines? https://www.weforum.org/agenda/2016/05/why-should-we-become-machines-of-continuous-learning

16 Eric Schmidt and Jonathan Rosenberg, *How Google Works*, Rizzoli Etas, 2014.

17 Think of the famous 'prisoner's dilemma' created by the American mathematician A. W. Tucker (1905–1995). See https://en.wikipedia.org/wiki/Prisoner%27s_dilemma

18 Stephen R. Covey, *The 7 Habits of Highly Effective People*, Free Press, 1989.

19 https://www.youtube.com/watch?v=6_5XnKvlL5E

20 Michael Watkins, *The First 90 Days: Critical Success Strategies for New Leaders at All Levels*, Harvard Business School Press, 2003.

21 David H. Maister, Charles H. Green, Robert M. Galford, *The Trusted Advisor*, Touchstone Books, 2000.

22 Giulio Gili, *La credibilità*, Rubbettino Editore, 2005.

23 www.motherteresa.org

24 https://www.theguardian.com/world/2017/oct/02/donald-trump-puerto-rico-presidents-cup-golf-trophy-hurricane-victims

25 http://it.wikipedia.org/wiki/Conflitto_di_interessi

26 http://en.wikipedia.org/wiki/Paul_Wolfowitz

27 The words used were 'Blood, toil, tears and sweat'.

28 *Never Give In! The Best of Winston Churchill's Speeches*, Hyperion, 2003, p. 204.

5 Meeting the locals. Understanding the rules of the game

1 'Seek first to understand, then to be understood', Stephen R. Covey, *The 7 Habits of Highly Effective People*, Free Press, 1989, p. 235.

2 In the mid 1800s Murderers Bay was renamed Golden Bay and is now a surfer's paradise.

3   *Springboks* are small, very fast antelopes found in the savannahs of southern and south-western Africa.

4   *Invictus*, the Latin word meaning 'invincible' is the title of a poem written in the Victorian era, in 1875, by the British poet William Ernest Henley.

5   Henry Kimsey-House, Karen Kimsey-House, Phillip Sandahl, Laura Whitworth, *Co-Active Coaching: Changing Business, Transforming Lives*, Nicholas Brealey, 2011, pp. 31–47.

6   Thesis supported in the book by Rebecca Shafir, *The Zen of Listening: Mindful Communication in the Age of Distraction*, Quest Books, 2000.

7   Leonard and Natalie Zunin, *Contact: The First Four Minutes*, Ballantine Books, 1979.

8   Wilson Mizner, American writer and entrepreneur, 1876–1933.

9   See the previously mentioned book by Michael Watkins, *The First 90 Days*, Harvard Business School Press, 2003.

10 Marilee Adams, *Change Your Questions, Change Your Life*, Berrett-Koehler Publishers, 2009.

11 Roger Fisher and Daniel Shapiro, *Beyond Reason: Using Emotions as You Negotiate*, Penguin Books, 2003.

12 Study cited by Karen Dillon, *HBR Guide to Office Politics*, 2014, introduction p. 9.

13 Nicholas DiFonzo and Prashant Bordia, *Rumor Psychology: Social and Organizational Approaches*, American Psychological Association, 2007.

14 Peter M. Senge, *The Fifth Discipline: The Art & Practice of the Learning Organization*, Currency, 1990.

15 *The Swiss Confederation: A Brief Guide*, 2014, p. 1.

16 Harry Truman, 1884–1972, US President 1945–1953.

17 Dino Buzzati, *The Tartar Steppe*, first edition Rizzoli, 1940.

18 https://en.wikipedia.org/wiki/Molotov-Ribbentrop_Pact

19 Sandy Hotchkiss, *Why Is It Always About You? The Seven Deadly Sins of Narcissism*, Free Press, 2002.

20 Michael Maccoby, 'Narcissistic Leaders: The Incredible Pros, the Inevitable Cons', *Harvard Business Review*, January–February 2000.

21 Sandy Hotchkiss, *Why Is It Always About You? The Seven Deadly Sins of Narcissism*, Free Press, 2002, p. 155.

22 Psychopathy is a personality disorder.

23 'Executive psychopaths' by Gardiner Morse, *Harvard Business Review*, October 2004.

24 *Snakes in Suits: When Psychopaths Go to Work*, by Paul Babiak & Robert Hare, Harper Publishing, 2006.

25 Hervey Cleckley, *The Mask of Sanity: An Attempt to Clarify Some Issues about the So-Called Psychopathic Personality*, Lightning Source, 2011.

26 Robert D. Hare, *Without Conscience: The Disturbing World of the Psychopaths Among Us*, 2009, second edition.

27 To find out the details of these experiments, see *Snakes in Suits: When Psychopaths Go to Work*, Paul Babiak & Robert D. Hare, Happer edizioni, 2006, pp. 52–55.

28 Truman Capote, *In Cold Blood*, 1965, first edition.

29 *The Psychopath Test: A Journey Through the Madness Industry*. Jon Ronson, Penguin Books, 2011 first edition.

30 *The Psychopath Test*, by Jon Ronson, 2011 Picardor, p. 11.

31 Guido Piovene, writer born in Vicenza in 1907, died in London in 1974. *Confession of a Novice* was his first novel, written in 1941.

32 Guido Piovene, *Confession of a Novice*, Bompiani, 1991, p. V, Introduction.

33 Latin word that means weight, dignity, and connotes depth of character.

34 www.treccani.it/scuola/lezioni/in_aula/lingua_e_letteratura/intertestualita/carnero.html

35 http://en.wikipedia.org/wiki/Rosa_Parks

36 http://www.giorgioperlasca.it

37 The story of Giorgio Perlasca is contained in the book by Enrico Deaglio, *The Banality of Goodness*, Feltrinelli, 2002.

38 *The Hero Journey* by Joseph Campbell, New World Library publishing edition 2003.

39 Bruce Springsteen, 'Walk tall or don't walk at all', from the song *New York City Serenade*, CBS Records, 1973.

6 The pact with the devil. The price you pay for your career

1   https://www.goodreads.com/quotes/27409-the-awful-thing-is-that-beauty-is-mysterious-as-well

2   Robert and Edward Skidelsky, *How Much is Enough? Money and the Good Life*, Other Press, 2012.

3   *Badlands* is featured on Bruce Springsteen's album *Darkness on the Edge of Town*, 1978.

4   Roberto Petrini, 'It was better when it was worse: happiness and growth don't go hand in hand', *la Repubblica*, 17 July 2015.

5   Leo Tolstoy (1828–1910), Russian writer, thinker and philosopher, author of some of the masterpieces of literature such as *War and Peace, Anna Karenina, The Kreutzer Sonata*.

6   Giovanni Verga (1894–1922), Sicilian writer, considered the greatest exponent of realism, author of works such as *The House by the Medlar Tree* and *Mastro don Gesualdo* and numerous novels. *Property* belongs to the collection of short stories *Little Novels of Sicily*, published in 1883.

7   Enrico Franceschini, 'Stress slaughters bankers: excessive pace even for the "wolves"', *la Repubblica*, 29 January 2014.

8   Marco Letizia, 'Goldman Sachs puts an end to backbreaking shifts for interns: they can't work more than 17 hours a day', *Corriere della Sera*, 17 June 2015.

9   This story is told in Robert Reich's book, *The Future of Success*, Vintage, 2000, p. 7.

10 Eugene O'Kelly, *Chasing Daylight: How My Forthcoming Death Transformed My Life*, McGraw-Hill, 2008.

11 Paul Kalanithi, *When Breath Becomes Air*, Random House, 2016.

12 Randy Pausch, *The Last Lecture*, Hachette Books, 2008.

13 Jeffrey Pfeffer, *Power: Why Some People Have It and Others Don't*, Harper Business, 2010.

14 Jerry B. Harvey, 'Organizations as Phrog Farms', *Organizational Dynamics*, Spring 1977.

15 The group is called Young Global Leaders, a community of young entrepreneurs coordinated by the World Economic Forum.

16 Stanley Milgram (1933–1982), American psychologist, taught Social Psychology at Yale, Harvard and New York.

17 https://en.wikipedia.org/wiki/Stanford_prison_experiment

18 Daniel Jonah Goldhagen, *Hitler's Willing Executioners*, Mondadori, 1997.

19 The complete story of Eric Fair is told in the article by Riccardo Stagliano, 'I confess: this is how, in Abu Ghraib, I sold my soul to the God of torture', in *il venerdì di Repubblica*, 20 July 2012, p. 22–26.

20 www.washingtonpost.com/wp-dyn/content/article/2007/02/08/AR2007020801680.html

21 *The Lucifer Effect: How Good People Turn Evil*, Philip Zimbardo, Random House, USA, 2007.

22 Dante Alighieri, *Divine Comedy – Inferno* V, 102.

23 *Rebel Talent: Why it Pays to Break the Rules at Work and in Life* by Francesca Gino, Macmillan, 2018.

24 *Churchill and Orwell: The Fight for Freedom* by Thomas E. Ricks, Duckworth Overlook, 2018.

25 https://designmuseum.org

26 Viktor Frankl, *Man's Search for Meaning*, Beacon Press, 1959. This book by an Austrian psychiatrist of Jewish origins, survivor of imprisonment in the Nazi concentration camps, originally written in German *(Ein Psychologe erlebt das Konzentrationslager)* and published in 1946, has been translated into twenty-six languages.

7 Success inside the Village. How to build a career and remain a decent person

1 Ignaz Phillip Semmelweis, *Die Ätiologie, der Begriff und die Prophylaxe des Kindbettfiebers*, Hartleben, 1861.

2 Marie McIntyre, *Secrets to Winning at Office Politics*, St. Martin's Griffin, 2005, p. 147.

3 John J. Gabarro, John P. Kotter, 'Managing your Boss', *Harvard Business Review*, May–June 1993. A classic to be read carefully.

4   *The Essential Drucker: The Best of Sixty Years of Peter Drucker's Essential Writings on Management*, Harper Collins, 2001.

5   Susanne R. Cook-Greuter, 'Making the Case for a Developmental Perspective', *Industrial and Commercial Training*, Emerald Group Publishing, volume 36, n. 7, 2004.

6   Marie-France Hirigoyen, *Moral Harassment. The Perverse Violence in Everyday Life*, Einaudi, 2000.

7   Kevin and Edward Coyne, 'Surviving your new CEO', *Harvard Business Review*, May 2007.

8   Turnover is the percentage of employees who leave an organization during a certain period of time. For example, a company with 100 employees, in which 8 resign in one year, will have a turnover of 8 per cent.

9   Robert Greene (edited by Joost Elffers), *The 48 Laws of Power*, Baldini & Castoldi, 2014, p. 29, law number 1.

10   *USA Today*, 9 February 2015, front page.

11   'Going Rogue: Share Traders More Reckless Than Psychopath', *Der Speigel* online, 26 September 2011, www.spiegel.de/international/zeitgeist

12   To get a good understanding of the personality and genius of Steve Jobs, Walter Isaacson, *Steve Jobs*, Mondadori, 2011.

13   Aaron James, *Ass-holes: A Theory*, Anchor Books, 2014.

14   http://www.blablameter.com

15   Harry G. Frankfurt, *On Bullshit*, Princeton University Press, 2005.

16   www.goodreads.com/book/show/3491.The_Dictionary_of_Corporate_ Bullshit

17   https://www.nytimes.com/2015/02/26/fashion/at-gucci-a-messy-exit-for-one-designer-opens-an-unlikely-door-for-another.html

18   Carlo M. Cipolla, *Happy But Not Too Much. The Basic Laws of Human Stupidity*, Il Mulino, 1988, p. 58.

19   The Italian composer Gioachino Rossini (1792–1868) created *The Barber of Seville* at just 24 years of age, in 1816.

20   The aforementioned mental model of the 'ladder of inference', invented by Chris Argyris.

21   www.ted.com/talks/monica_lewinsky_the_price_of_shame

22 Dr. Seuss, *Oh, the Places You'll Go*, Random House, 1990.

23 Keith Ferrazzi with Tahal Raz, *Never Eat Alone: And Other Secrets to Success, One Relationship at a Time*, Currency-Random House, 2005.

24 Philip Stephens, 'The great fragmentation', *Financial Times*, 25 February 2015, p. 5.

25 Sylvia Ann Hewlett, *Executive Presence: The Missing Link Between Merit and Success*, Harper Business, 2014.

8 *Should I stay or should I go?*

1 Leigh Branham, *The 7 Hidden Reasons Employees Leave*, Amacom, 2005, p. 33.

2 www.gallup.com

3 'Dream job? Most U.S. workers want to change careers – pool', http://www.reuters.com/article/us-usa-work-idUSBRE96015Z20130701, accessed 1 July 2013.

4 The survey is cited by Leigh Branham, *The 7 Hidden Reasons Employees Leave*, Amacom, 2005, p. 3.

5 www.fifa.com/governance/how-fifa-works/index.html

6 https://hbr.org/2003/01/one-more-time-how-do-you-motivate-employees

7 Daniel Pink, *Drive*, Riverheads Books, 2009.

8 C. P. Cavafy, *Collected Poems*, Princeton University Press, 1998.

9 This video explains the same suffering often experienced in the workplace: www.youtube.com/watch?v=0iTTbSWt67Y

10 *The Whistleblower*, 2010 film, directed by Larysa Kondracki; Kathryn Bolkovac with Cari Lynn, *The Whistleblower: Sex Trafficking, Military Contractors, and One Woman's Fight for Justice*, St Martin's Press, 2011.

11 Andre Agassi, *Open. An Autobiography*, Einaudi, 2011.

12 Herminia Ibarra, *Working Identity*, Harvard Business School Press, 2004.

13 www.nytimes.com/2012/03/14/opinion/why-i-am-leaving-goldman-sachs.html?_r=0

14 Greg Smith, *Why I Left Goldman Sachs: A Wall Street Story*, Grand Central Publishing, 2012.

15 David Heenan, *Leaving on Top: Graceful Exits for Leaders*, Nicholas Brealey publishing, 2012.

16 Leon A. Danco, The Center for family business.

17 Marguerite Yourcenar, *Memoirs of Hadrian*, Einaudi, 1988.

18 www.youtube.com/watch?v=bss6lTP8BJ8

9 Taking stock of the journey. What really matters?

1 The wonderful book *The Art of Work: A Proven Path to Discovering What You Were Meant To Do* by Jeff Goings (edition Nelson Books, 2015) offers lots of interesting reflections.

2 *The Road to Character*, David Brooks, Random House, 2015.

3 Directed by Dr. Robert Waldinger who talks about it in more detail on TED https://www.ted.com/talks/robert_waldinger_what_makes_a_good_life_lessons_from_the_longest_study_on_happiness

4 https://www.forbes.com/sites/worldeconomicforum/2016/03/16/this-is-why-relationships-matter-at-work/#799ffce87f33

5 'The Blue Zones' Nine Lessons for Living Longer* by Dan Buettner, National Geographic 2008.

6 https://www.forbes.com/sites/worldeconomicforum/2016/03/23/cura-personalis-what-it-is-and-why-you-need-it-at-work/#28f30a524d4c

7 Read the wake up call for sleepy managers research written by Vicky Culpin and Angela Velan on the effects of lack of sleep on managers. http://viewswire.eiu.com/report_dl.asp?mode=fi&fi=1394495524.PDF

8 Frank Partnoy, *Wait: The Art and Science of Delay*, PublicAffairs, 2013.

9 The End of Absence: Reclaiming What We've Lost in a World of Constant Connection By Michael Harris, Penguin Group, 2014.

10 https://www.weforum.org/agenda/2017/10/the-danger-of-running-the-extra-mile

11 See note 133.

12 Edgar Lee Masters, *Spoon River Anthology*, edited by Fernanda Pivano, Einaudi, 1971, p. 67.

13 https://www.weforum.org/agenda/2016/06/want-to-improve-your-career-focus-on-impact-not-results-7803de89-1a66-4444-9d22-57a41bdf14a4

14 https://www.weforum.org/agenda/2016/04/do-you-need-to-love-what-you-do/

15 *Jiro Dreams of Sushi* is a 2011 documentary film, directed by David Gelb.

16 Carol Dweck, *Mindset: The New Psychology of Success,* Random House, 2006.

17 https://www.weforum.org/agenda/2016/04/how-to-de-clutter-your-career

18 https://www.weforum.org/agenda/2017/10/what-the-machine-age-means-for-the-way-you-learn

19 *Natural Born Learners* by Alex Beard, Weidenfeld & Nicolson, 2018.

20 https://www.weforum.org/agenda/2016/05/why-you-need-to-listen-to-your-360-feedback

21 https://www.forbes.com/sites/worldeconomicforum/2016/05/19/how-to-be-agile-and-zen-in-todays-working-world/#25116757589U

22 Bridges, not walls. https://www.weforum.org/agenda/2016/05/bridges-or-walls

23 https://www.weforum.org/agenda/2016/06/want-to-improve-your-career-focus-on-impact-not-results-7803de89-1a66-4444-9d22-57a41bdf14a4/

24 https://edition.cnn.com/2018/04/14/us/philadelphia-police-starbucks-arrests/index.html

25 https://en.wikipedia.org/wiki/United_Express_Flight_3411_incident

26 https://www.theguardian.com/us-news/2018/mar/22/steve-bannon-on-cambridge-analytica-facebook-data-is-for-sale-all-over-the-world

10 The Future of jobs and the Jobs of the Future

1 Please use the hyperlink https://www.bloomsbury.com/uk/the-100-year-life-9781472930170/ . . . this is an article I have written recently.

2 Refer to TEDx Rome, April 8, 2017. https://www.youtube.com/watch?v=dVMpEqfjk3c

3 https://www.nytimes.com/2017/10/23/books/review/christopher-frayling-frankenstein.html

4 The Fourth Industrial Revolution by Professor Klaus Schwab, 2016 @World Economic Forum.

5 *Our Final Invention: Artificial Intelligence and the End of Human Era* by James Barrat, Thomas Dunnes Books, 2013.

6 Martin Ford, *The Rise of the Robots: Technology and the Threat of a Jobless Future,* Basic Books, 2016.

7 See https://www.weforum.org/agenda/2016/12/stephen-hawking-this-will-be-the-impact-of-automation-and-ai-on-jobs

8 See https://www.livescience.com/62239-elon-musk-immortal-artificial-intelligence-dictator.html

9 Article from V. Plonsky and J. Zavalishina. https://www.weforum.org/agenda/2017/11/3-ways-to-build-more-moral-robots

10 https://www.cnbc.com/2017/11/27/elon-musk-robots-of-the-future-need-to-be-regulated.html

11 https://www.weforum.org/agenda/2018/05/the-4-emerging-truths-of-the-4IR-job-market

12 http://www.independent.co.uk/news/world/europe/stanislav-petrov-dead-soviet-officer-nuclear-war-1983-saved-world-dies-died-77-robert-de-niro-a7952361.html

13 https://www.youtube.com/watch?v=CpapPfVuq0I, TEDx, Paolo Gallo

Index